Read This First

The information in this book is as up to date and accurate as we can make it. But it's important to realize that the law changes frequently, as do fees, forms, and procedures. If you handle your own legal matters, it's up to you to be sure that all information you use—including the information in this book—is accurate. Here are some suggestions to help you:

First, make sure you've got the most recent edition of this book. To learn whether a later edition is available, check the edition number on the book's spine and then go to Nolo's online Law Store at www.nolo.com or call Nolo's Customer Service Department at 800-728-3555.

Next, even if you have a current edition, you need to be sure it's fully up to date. The law can change overnight. At www.nolo.com, we post notices of major legal and practical changes that affect the latest edition of a book. To check for updates, find your book in the Law Store on Nolo's website (you can use the "A to Z Product List" and click the book's title). If you see an "Updates" link on the left side of the page, click it. If you don't see a link, that means we haven't posted any updates. (But check back regularly.)

Finally, we believe accurate and current legal information should help you solve many of your own legal problems on a cost-efficient basis. But this text is not a substitute for personalized advice from a knowledgeable lawyer. If you want the help of a trained professional, consult an attorney licensed to practice in your state.

2nd edition

Becoming a U.S. Citizen

A Guide to the Law, Exam, and Interview

by Attorney Ilona M. Bray

SECOND EDITION	OCTOBER 2004
Book Design	TERRI HEARSH
Cover Design	MARY E. ALBANESE
Proofreading	EMILY K. WOLMAN
Index	ELLEN DAVENPORT
Printing	DELTA PRINTING SOLUTIONS, INC.

Bray, Ilona M., 1962-
 Becoming a U.S. Citizen : a guide to the law, exam, and interview / by Ilona Bray --
2nd ed.
  p. cm.
 Includes index.
 ISBN 0-4133-0093-6 (alk. paper)
  1. Natualization--United States--Popular works.   2. Citizenship--United
States--Examinations, questions, etc. I. Title: Becoming a U.S. Citizen. II. Title: Becoming
a United States citizen. III. Title.

KF4710.Z9B73 2004
342.73'083--dc222

2004055248

Acknowledgments

This book was inspired by the efforts of my clients, many of whom overcame huge obstacles in order to become U.S. citizens. A couple of memories stand out in particular. There was Eduardo, who in the last months before his death from cancer, madly studied the U.S. history and government exam questions so that he could become a citizen before he died—and succeeded. Then there was Jose, who, after failing the English writing requirement during his first interview, passed it during the second one with the sentence "the sky is blue," and happily proclaimed this phrase to the world during the whole trip home.

I couldn't have written this without the help of others, who generously shared their knowledge and experience. Particular thanks go to Barbara Horn, who continued to take my phone calls even when she knew it was going to be another obscure question. Lynette Parker and Carmen Reyes-Yossiff also contributed invaluable information and sample documents. Though this book helps you avoid certain types of attorneys, it's ones like Barbara, Lynette, and Carmen who show what it truly means to be in a service profession. Justin Kimball, a citizenship instructor, also made valuable contributions.

Thanks also go to the staff at Nolo: Mary Randolph and Janet Portman, who can organize anything into sensible shape; Amy DelPo and Rich Stim, unfailingly careful and encouraging editors even as my comma placement became increasingly erratic; and the magicians who turn stacks of paper into books, including Margaret Livingston, Susan Putney, Terri Hearsh, and Mary Albanese.

Table of Contents

11 After You Are Approved

Glossary

Appendixes

A USCIS District Office and Sub-Office Addresses

B 100 Sample U.S. History and Government Questions With Answers

C Tear-Out Immigration Forms

Index

Introduction

Getting the Most From This Book

This book will guide you through the process of applying for U.S. citizenship (through what's called "naturalization") and explain U.S. Citizenship and Immigration Service (USCIS) procedures and rules. We'll help you determine if you're eligible, fill out the right forms, prepare for the exams, present yourself at your citizenship interview, and enjoy your new rights as a U.S. citizen.

Note: USCIS is a new agency, a branch of the Department of Homeland Security (DHS), which was established in 2003. With the creation of DHS, the agency known as the Immigration and Naturalization Service (INS) was eliminated. USCIS took over most of the INS's service-related duties. However, you may continue to see the name INS on various USCIS forms and documents, until they've had a chance to update everything. (In fact, you'll see mostly the same faces behind the counter, too—very little has changed except the agency's name.) This book will mainly use the word "USCIS" when referring to the agency in charge of immigration, except when talking about something historical that happened under the old INS.

⚠ **If you are or have ever been in deportation proceedings—that is, Immigration Court proceedings in which the INS or USCIS tries to remove you from the United States—you must see a lawyer.** If the proceedings aren't over or are on appeal, you may not be allowed to apply for citizenship through naturalization at this time. Even if the proceedings are over, you should ask a lawyer whether the outcome affects your current application.

But let's not get ahead of ourselves. Not everyone who wants to become a U.S. citizen will qualify. To save you some time and heartache, let's make sure you're on the right track.

- **Are you already a U.S. citizen?** It's possible that you acquired citizenship automatically through your parents or, in rare cases, your grandparents if they were born or naturalized U.S. citizens. This could have occurred even though you were born outside the United States. In order to determine this, you'll need to do some research. Start with Nolo's online Legal Encyclopedia (www.nolo.com). Click "Legal Encyclopedia" on the home page, then click "Immigration and Green Cards." Look for the article entitled "U.S. Citizenship by Birth or Through Parents." If, after reading this information, you have unanswered questions, consult a lawyer.
- **Do you have a green card?** If you don't have a green card, you can't apply for citizenship. It doesn't matter if you've just married a U.S. citizen, won the visa lottery, or invested $1

million in the U.S. economy. Before applying for U.S. citizenship, you must first apply to be, and spend time as, a "lawful permanent resident" (also called a "permanent resident" or a "green card holder"). (The one exception is for certain people who have served in the U.S. military, as discussed in Chapter 2, Section A.)

- **Are you old enough to apply for citizenship?** The naturalization process is only open to immigrants older than age 18. If you're under 18, however, look again at whether you might have gained U.S. citizenship through your parents.

If you've answered these questions and still believe that U.S. citizenship is right for you, then this book can help. Since U.S. citizenship is the highest status you can receive under the immigration laws, the laws strictly limit who can become a U.S. citizen. However, once you have citizenship, it's very difficult for the government to take it away.

Here's how this book will guide you through the process of applying for U.S. citizenship:

- **Chapter 1** will explain the advantages and disadvantages of applying for citizenship. Keep in mind that applying for citizenship may uncover flaws in your green card approval that could lead to your being deported.
- **Chapter 2** will help you learn whether you're eligible for U.S. citizenship, covering such topics as whether you've had your green card for the appropriate length of time, whether you've spent enough of your time as a green card holder living in the United States, whether you have good moral character, whether you can pass the English language and U.S. history and government exams, and more.

You have the burden of proving that you are eligible for citizenship. That's why it's important that you start with these preliminary chapters of this book, rather than launching straight into filling out the application form. Filling out the paperwork and hoping for the best could lead not only to your being denied citizenship, but also, in certain circumstances, to your being deported.

Once you've analyzed your eligibility, you'll move into the procedural parts of this book. Your quest for citizenship will, if all goes normally, require you to:

- file a written application
- attend an interview at a local USCIS office about one year later, and
- after you're approved, attend a "swearing in" ceremony (usually a few months after your interview).

Here's how the later chapters will help you accomplish these steps:

- **Chapter 3** takes you through the written application, including how to fill out the forms and guard against losses and delays by USCIS.
- **Chapter 4** describes how to deal with the long wait for your interview, and explains how to inform USCIS if you've moved and how to question USCIS regarding delays.
- **Chapter 5** includes tips on learning English for the exam portion of your citizenship application.
- **Chapter 6** prepares you for the U.S. history and government portion of the citizenship exam, including USCIS's official list of 100 possible questions.
- **Chapter 7** advises you on procedures to follow if you are disabled and need extra accommodations or waivers in regard to your interview.
- **Chapter 8** guides you through the interview at the USCIS office.
- **Chapter 9** provides some preliminary advice on what to do if your case is denied at the interview—you may need to seek expert legal advice.
- **Chapter 10** explains you how to find a good lawyer and how to make the most out of your legal relationship.
- **Chapter 11** describes the swearing-in ceremony and gives you advice on enjoying your new rights as a citizen—including how to obtain proof of your new status, register to vote, and determine which family members you can now help immigrate.

References to the Immigration Laws in This Book

Throughout this book are references to the federal immigration laws that govern U.S. citizenship and to the USCIS regulations that describe how USCIS will apply those laws to you. (They look like this: "I.N.A. § 319(a), 8 U.S.C. § 1430(a)" or "8 C.F.R. § 316.5.") We include these references where we feel it is important to indicate our sources for information and to help you research the immigration laws on your own. See Chapter 10 for more detail on what these references mean and how you can look them up.

Golden Gate Bridge—San Francisco, California

Icons Used in This Book

To aid you in using this book, we use the following icons:

 The caution icon warns you of potential problems.

 This icon indicates that the information is a useful tip.

 This icon refers you to helpful books or other resources.

 This icon indicates when you should consider consulting an attorney or other expert.

 This icon refers you to a further discussion of the topic somewhere else in this book.

 This icon tells you when a form or other document is contained in an appendix of this book.

This icon reminds you to add a special document to your citizenship application— one that most applicants won't have to include, so that you'll need to keep track of it yourself; it won't be listed on our standard application checklist.

1

Deciding Whether to Apply for Citizenship

Many people spend their entire lives in the United States without ever trading in their green cards for citizenship—and their friends probably never know it. Their reasons vary: Some of these long-time permanent residents want to show their loyalty to their native country, some are worried that they'll fail the citizenship exam, and some just never get around to applying.

For many green-card holders, however, the advantages of U.S. citizenship—for example, security from deportation, freedom of travel, and eligibility for public benefits—far outweigh the drawbacks. And as we'll see, citizenship offers some refuge from political decisions that whittle away at green card rights.

In this chapter, we'll discuss the advantages and disadvantages of applying for and obtaining U.S. citizenship. By reading this, you'll come to better understand your rights as a permanent resident and how secure or insecure your current status is. We'll also try to dispel some myths about citizenship. In Section A, we detail potential disadvantages of applying for citizenship; in Section B, we discuss the advantages.

⚠️ **Read this chapter even if you are sure you want to apply for U.S. citizenship.** Focus in particular on Section A1, where we explain how applying for U.S. citizenship can lead to your deportation either if your original green card application should not have been approved or if you've committed acts since receiving your green card that make you deportable.

A. The Disadvantages of Applying for Citizenship

We'll start with the negative aspects of applying for and receiving U.S. citizenship—but not because they outweigh the positive aspects. We simply want you to fully appreciate the risks and possible pitfalls of applying for or receiving U.S. citizenship. These include:

- if you got your green card fraudulently or have since become deportable, applying for citizen-

ship may bring you to USCIS's attention and result in your deportation (see Section A1)
- your native country may not allow dual citizenship (see Section A2)
- carrying a U.S. passport may be a security risk in some countries (see Section A3), and
- you may not be allowed to serve your home country in times of conflict (see Section A4).

1. The Risk of Deportation

If something happened in your past that makes you deportable, you should not apply for U.S. citizenship—or, at the very least, you should talk to a lawyer before doing so. The citizenship process may uncover whatever it is you're hiding and send you directly into deportation proceedings. Perhaps your green card should never have been approved in the first place because you lied on the application, or maybe you've committed a crime that no one at USCIS seems to have noticed yet. Either way, applying for citizenship gives USCIS a chance to review your whole immigration history, from the time you entered the United States to the present. If something isn't quite right, you could find yourself fighting deportation in Immigration Court.

In this section, we look separately at the two most common types of problems:
- a green card that shouldn't have been approved in the first place, and
- a green card that USCIS can take away because you've done something that violates its terms.

a. If Your Green Card Application Shouldn't Have Been Approved

USCIS would be the first to admit that it makes mistakes, sometimes approving people for green cards who were not eligible for them. You probably already know if you committed outright fraud—that is, lied or deliberately omitted something—on your green card application. Common types of fraud include faking a marriage, hiding a criminal conviction in one's home country, and creating false documents to show a sponsor who doesn't exist.

However, you might also have unintentionally committed a lie—for example, gotten a green card through a relative whose own green card had already been revoked (cancelled or taken away), or turned 21 before you got a green card, not realizing that the category for "children" of permanent residents applied only while you remained younger than age 21.

EXAMPLE 1: Rodrigo got his green card through the farmworker amnesty program in the 1980s. In truth, he was a car mechanic, but he bought a letter from a farmer stating that he had picked strawberries during the required time period. During the citizenship interview, the USCIS officer asks Rodrigo how high he had to reach to pick the strawberries. Rodrigo answers, "Oh, no more than eight feet." The officer, knowing that strawberries don't grow on trees, takes a look at Rodrigo's old INS file. She notices that the employer who swore to Rodrigo's work was one whom USCIS believes to have made a lot of money selling fake letters. Rodrigo's citizenship application is denied, and he is placed in deportation proceedings.

EXAMPLE 2: Leonora applied for a green card as the unmarried child of a U.S. permanent resident. She was on the waiting list for a number of years, during which time she fell in love and married her sweetheart. Finally, her green card came through. She didn't say anything about her marriage, and the U.S. consulate forgot to ask. However, had the marriage been revealed, her green card would have been denied, because the category she applied in was meant only for unmarried children. When Leonora applies for citizenship, she lists the date of her marriage. The USCIS officer notices that the marriage occurred before Leonora's green card was approved—in other words, Leonora was ineligible for her green card. Leonora faces deportation proceedings.

If you are unsure about whether you really deserve your green card, see a lawyer. The lawyer can request a copy of your USCIS file and analyze it for problems.

Times Square—New York, New York

If You Divorce

People who receive their green card through marriage to a U.S. citizen or permanent resident but later divorce that person often worry about how this will affect their citizenship application. They wonder whether the divorce makes their green card invalid or will spur USCIS to deny their citizenship.

As long as your marriage was the real thing—that is, not a sham solely for purposes of acquiring your green card—and you got all the way to being approved for permanent (not merely conditional) residence, divorce will not invalidate your green card. Many people get divorced, and the immigration laws recognize that the United States may have become home to the divorced immigrant, with or without the ex-spouse.

The divorce may, however, raise certain questions in the mind of the USCIS officer interviewing you for citizenship. You'll need to be prepared for these questions.

The first question that may arise is whether your marriage was indeed real, or whether you faked it through the green card application process. USCIS officers won't automatically *assume* from your divorce that your marriage was a sham—but they may want some reassurance. Prepare for this by gathering documents that prove your marriage was genuine (and make sure they're more recent than

the documents already in the USCIS file from your green card application). Don't include these documents with your citizenship application. Instead, make copies and take these, with the originals, to your citizenship interview. The following documents may help:

- rent receipts or a home title in both your and your ex-spouse's names (showing that you lived together)
- birth certificates of children born to the two of you
- a letter from your spiritual or psychological counselor describing your meetings—particularly where your marriage was discussed. (If possible, the letter should emphasize that you worked hard to save your marriage and that the issues you discussed were the thorny ones faced by people truly trying to share their lives)
- evidence of joint bank accounts, credit cards and club memberships
- photographs of the two of you on vacations or sharing important occasions (preferably where the camera has automatically inserted the date), and
- subscriptions to magazines and newspapers at your shared address.

⚠ **When the cause of your divorce was that you had an affair, USCIS may conclude that your moral character is not good enough to qualify you for citizenship.** See Chapter 2, Section D, for details.

b. If You've Become Deportable After Getting Your Green Card

U.S. laws contain a list of activities that can cause a green card holder to lose the right to live in the United States. Commit one of these activities and you become deportable. If anything on the list below

looks like something you've done, do not file your citizenship application until you see an immigration attorney. (We can't give you extensive details on each of these activities, so don't rely on this list alone.)

- You were inadmissible when you last entered the United States (see "Actions and Conditions That Make You Inadmissible," below, for more about inadmissibility).
- You have violated a condition of your U.S. stay.
- You were unsuccessful in turning your conditional residence into permanent residence (primarily affecting people who married U.S. citizens).

- You have helped smuggle someone into the United States within five years of when you entered the country (with limited exceptions for close family).
- You have entered into a fake marriage to try to get a green card.
- You have committed a crime of moral turpitude within five years of becoming a resident (or ten years if you got your residency after living in the United States illegally, by paying a penalty fee under Section 245(i) of the I.N.A.). There is no USCIS-approved list of crimes of moral turpitude (see "What Constitutes Moral Turpitude?," below).
- You have committed a crime of moral turpitude for which the judge could have imposed a sentence of one year or more.
- You committed two or more separate crimes of moral turpitude.
- You committed an aggravated felony.
- You have committed a drug-related crime (except a single conviction for possession of 30 grams of marijuana or less).
- You use or are addicted to illegal drugs.
- You have committed a gun-related crime (such as selling, possessing, or using a gun illegally).
- You have violated federal laws regarding spying, treason, sedition (insurrection against the U.S. government or providing support to an enemy government), or assisting others to enter or leave the United States illegally.
- You have committed a domestic violence crime or violated anti-stalking, child abuse, neglect, or abandonment laws.
- You deliberately failed to notify the INS or USCIS of your new address within ten days of moving.
- You have fraudulently acquired a visa or other official document (that is, you got it by lying or deliberately omitting information).
- You have falsely claimed to be a U.S. citizen.
- You are a threat to public safety, national security, or U.S. foreign policy.
- You have tried to overthrow the U.S. government.
- You have assisted in Nazi persecution.
- You have engaged in genocide.

- You became a public charge (received welfare payments) within five years of your approval for U.S. residency.
- You have voted in a U.S. election. (Green card holders cannot vote in the United States.)

In most cases, whatever you did wrong will have come to the attention of the INS or USCIS right after it happened. For example, USCIS checks the names of people in jail and asks the police to turn over criminal immigrants for possible deportation. If you've been out of the country, the border officer checks whether you are admissible, looking in particular at whether you stayed away too long or resettled elsewhere. But sometimes violations go undetected by the U.S. government. For example, a person who pleads guilty to a crime but never goes to jail may escape USCIS's attention. Similarly, border patrol officers sometimes let in green card holders when they should have kept them out.

In short, if you've done something to make you deportable and USCIS hasn't yet caught up with you, applying for U.S. citizenship will give the agency the perfect opportunity.

EXAMPLE 1: Matilda got her green card as a result of marrying a U.S. citizen. She and her husband have fiery tempers, and their arguments sometimes become physical. After one violent encounter, Matilda's husband had her arrested for domestic violence. She tried to have him arrested too, but since he was bleeding a lot more than she was, the police checked him into a hospital instead. Matilda pled guilty to a domestic violence charge in order to avoid jail time. When Matilda applies for citizenship, the USCIS officer notices the conviction on her FBI record. Since domestic violence is a ground for deportation, the officer places Matilda in deportation proceedings.

EXAMPLE 2: Patrick's U.S. employer got him a green card. He lived and worked in the United States for two years and then went back to his native Britain for two years. After that, he returned to the United States using his British passport (British citizens can enter the United States without a visa). He then used his U.S.

green card to live and work in the United States for the next five years. Although his two-year stay in Britain meant that Patrick had given up his green card, his employer had no way of knowing this, because he still held the physical card that he could show to his boss. When Patrick applied for citizenship, the USCIS officer determined that Patrick had abandoned his U.S. residence during the two years in Britain and it was therefore inappropriate for Patrick to claim green card status after he reentered the United States. USCIS places Patrick in deportation proceedings.

EXAMPLE 3: Leticia applies for U.S. citizenship. She has one minor crime on her record—fraudulent use of an ex-friend's credit card. However, USCIS considers this a crime of moral turpitude (see "What Constitutes Moral Turpitude?"). However, even though a single crime of moral turpitude isn't grounds for deportation, it is grounds for denying Leticia readmission to the U.S. if she left and attempted to return. After being released from jail, Leticia took a trip to Canada. When she returned to the United States, the border patrol officer didn't ask about her criminal record. Since Leticia was inadmissible during that entry, she is deportable now. After Leticia applies for citizenship, the USCIS officer at her interview realizes that an error occurred at the U.S. border, denies citizenship, and places Leticia in deportation proceedings.

What Constitutes Moral Turpitude?

According to USCIS, a crime of moral turpitude is inherently base, vile, or depraved, contrary to social standards of morality and done with a reckless, malicious, or evil intent. In short, this is a subjective, catchall term that can be used for any crime that USCIS considers offensive. For example, USCIS has judged moral turpitude to be present in crimes involving great bodily injury, sexual offenses, kidnapping, stalking, fraud, theft, embezzlement, and bribery.

To read the deportability law, see I.N.A. § 237(a), 8 U.S.C. § 1227(a). You can find this at your local law library or on the Internet at Nolo's Legal Research Center (www.nolo.com). On the Nolo.com home page, click "U.S. Laws and Regulations." Then, under the section for the U.S. Code, enter "8" in the Title box and "1227" in the Section box. After reading the law, you will still need the help of an immigration lawyer to answer questions about whether or not you have done something that makes you deportable. Many of the terms used in the law, like "moral turpitude" and "aggravated felony," are unique to the immigration laws, and you won't be able to tell by looking at your court record whether you've committed one.

Every law has its exceptions. Deportability rules are not always as harsh as they first appear. Some come with exceptions and waivers (opportunities to apply to USCIS for legal forgiveness). So, even if you have done something that makes you deportable, you might be able to save yourself—and your chances of becoming a citizen—by qualifying for one of these exceptions or applying for a waiver. We're unable to cover the various exceptions and waivers in this book, but an immigration lawyer can alert you to the ones that apply.

You can access the law on inadmissibility (I.N.A. § 212(a); 8 U.S.C. § 1182) at your local law library or on the Internet at Nolo's Legal Research Center (www.nolo.com). On the home page, click "U.S. Laws and Regulations." Under the entry for the U.S. Code, type "8" in the Title box and "1182" in the Section box. Alternatively, this statute is available at the USCIS's Web page (www.uscis.gov); click "Immigration Laws, Regulations, and Guides," and follow the links from there. See an immigration lawyer for additional help.

2. Some Countries Won't Allow Dual Citizenship

If USCIS approves your citizenship application, you will attend a ceremony where you will have to swear to "absolutely and entirely renounce and abjure all

Actions and Conditions That Make You Inadmissible

No, you're not seeing double. The activities that make you inadmissible overlap in many ways with the activities that make you deportable. Inadmissibility affects whether you can enter the United States, regardless of whether it's for the first time or with a green card (although, if you had a green card and you reentered the U.S. after April 1, 1997, you're affected by these only if you were out of the U.S. for 180 days or more, or did something illegal during your trip). If you've committed any of the activities below, USCIS can keep you from entering. And if you were let into the United States when you shouldn't have been—that is, when you were inadmissible USCIS will deny you citizenship and can take away your green card.

You are (or were) inadmissible if, when entering the United States, you:

- had a communicable disease, such as tuberculosis or HIV
- had a physical or mental disorder that makes you harmful to others
- were likely to become a public charge (receive welfare benefits)—something USCIS determines based on your current income, ability to work, and family resources
- were a drug abuser (if you've tried illegal drugs more than once in the past three years, that's enough for USCIS)
- had committed or been convicted of a crime of moral turpitude
- had been convicted of two or more crimes (whether misdemeanors or felonies), where the total sentence you received was five years or more

- had been convicted of certain specified crimes, such as prostitution or drug trafficking
- are the immediate family member of a drug trafficker and have knowingly benefited from their illicit money within the last five years
- had committed espionage or sabotage against the United States
- were a member of the Communist Party or other totalitarian organization
- were a Nazi or had participated in genocide
- were seeking entry as a health care or other certified worker but had failed to meet licensing requirements
- had previously violated the immigration laws or lied or committed fraud during immigration procedures
- had falsely claimed to have U.S. citizenship
- had spent time in the United States unlawfully or hadn't obtained proper documentation to enter the United States (not an issue for immigrants who hold valid green cards)
- had previously been removed or deported from the United States
- believed that polygamy is valid (that is, believe in being married to more than one person at the same time), regardless of whether you were actually a polygamist
- had committed international child abduction (taking a child across international borders),
- were on a J-1 or J-2 exchange visitor visa and were subject to the two-year foreign residence requirement.

allegiance and fidelity to any foreign prince, potentate, state, or sovereignty of whom or which [you] have heretofore been a subject or citizen." Does this mean that you must give up the citizenship (and passport) of your country of origin? Not necessarily. It depends on both U.S. law and the law of your home country. Many people today successfully hold dual citizenship—that is, they are simultaneously U.S. citizens and citizens of another country.

Dual citizenship can be important for a number of reasons. You may feel a huge sense of loss in giving up the passport of the country you once called home. More practically, the laws of your home country may require that you give up other important rights along with your citizenship—such as your rights to a pension, to government-paid health care if you are elderly or disabled, to vote, or to own land.

U.S. law concerning dual citizenship is very vague. Nowhere does it say that you can be a dual citizen—but then, nowhere does it say that you can't. Historically, the U.S. government has used this vagueness as an opportunity to make people believe that choosing U.S. citizenship excludes all others.

The oath that people take at their swearing-in ceremony (quoted above) would make anyone think that they were agreeing to give up all other citizenships right then and there. However, it has become evident that the United States will not stop you from keeping your citizenship in your home country after becoming a U.S. citizen—if that is what you want, and provided your home country allows it.

Because the U.S. government does not formally sanction dual citizenship, there are no particular procedures to follow. No one will give you a certificate or other evidence that the U.S. government recognizes and approves your dual status. Your home country, however, may require more. First, find out whether your home country will cancel your citizenship if you are naturalized as a U.S. citizen. If cancellation isn't automatic, find out whether you have to take special steps to keep your home citizenship. Some countries allow it automatically, others allow it after an application process and still others offer something less than full citizenship, with or without an application.

This book is published in the United States, and we don't pretend to be experts on the complex laws of every other country in the world. But, take heart—the majority of countries around the globe do allow dual citizenship, at least in some form.

Below is a list of the countries that allowed some form of dual citizenship in 2004. (Keep in mind that this list may have changed by the time you read it.) Since we don't have space to provide all of the procedures for and limits on retaining your non-U.S. citizenship, you should look for further information on your own. A good starting point is the embassy of your home country in the United States. You can usually find it in the Washington, D.C., phone book. (If you can't locate a D.C. phone book at your local library, call D.C. directory assistance, 202-555-1212.) You can find Internet links to the various embassies, at www.embassy.org or www.embpage.org.

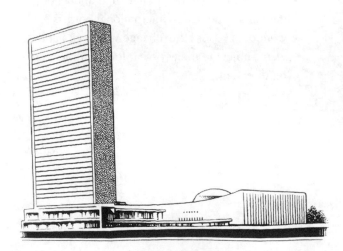

United Nations Building—New York, New York

Countries That Allowed Some Form of Dual Citizenship in 2004

Albania, Antigua & Barbuda, Argentina, Australia, Bahamas, Bangladesh, Barbados, Belarus, Belize, Benin, Bolivia, Brazil, Bulgaria, Burkina Faso, Cambodia, Canada, Cape Verde, Chile, Colombia, Costa Rica, Croatia, Cyprus, Cyprus (North), Dominica, Dominican Republic, Ecuador, Egypt, El Salvador, Federal Republic of Yugoslavia, Fiji, France, Germany, Ghana, Greece, Grenada, Guatemala, Guyana, Haiti, Hungary, India, Iran, Ireland, Israel, Italy, Jamaica, Jordan, Latvia, Lebanon, Lesotho, Liechtenstein, Lithuania, Macao, Macedonia, Madagascar, Malta, Mexico, Montenegro (Yugoslavia), Mongolia, Morocco, Netherlands, New Zealand, Nicaragua, Nigeria, Northern Ireland, Panama, Pakistan, Paraguay, Peru, Pitcairn, Philippines, Poland, Portugal, Romania, Russia, Saint Kitts (Saint Christopher) and Nevis, Saint Lucia, Saint Vincent, Serbia (Yugoslavia), Slovenia, South Africa, Spain, Sri Lanka, Sweden, Switzerland, Syria, Taiwan, Tonga, Trinidad/Tobago, Thailand, Tibet, Turkey, United Kingdom, United States, Ukraine, Uruguay, Vietnam, and Western Samoa.

3. Carrying a U.S. Passport in Unfriendly Territory

As a large and powerful country, the United States is a focus of public opinion and debate, both positive and negative. Unfortunately, anger against the U.S. government is sometimes directed against its citizens traveling overseas. There is no way to predict whether, where, or how a guerrilla or terrorist group might make you a scapegoat for U.S. foreign policy. You'll have to assess the risks yourself based on where you plan to travel and what you observe of world events.

Of course, if you have dual citizenship, you can always carry the passport of your home country on a trip—but you'll need to show your U.S. passport when you depart and return to the United States. You can use the other passport to travel with—that is, show it on entry to other countries. However, if you do so, the U.S. consulate there may refuse to help you if you get into a jam. Also, don't flaunt your non-U.S. passport when you return to the United States. U.S. border officials are suspicious of people who carry two passports, and they will probably question you to confirm that everything is aboveboard.

4. You May Not Be Allowed to Serve Your Native Country During War

The United States requires that its citizens demonstrate loyalty in any conflict. In fact, you'll be asked on the citizenship application if you're willing to serve in the U.S. military, either in a combat or a supporting role, if the need arises. (We'll discuss this more in Chapter 3, which covers how to fill out the citizenship application.) This also means that the United States may take action against you if you join your own country in a war that's against the United States or its allies or interests.

B. The Advantages of U.S. Citizenship

U.S. citizenship is definitely an improvement over permanent resident status. At the very least, you won't have to renew your green card every ten years—or even carry the card around. But wait, there's more! As a U.S. citizen you get:

- the right to vote and obtain certain federal jobs (see Section B1)
- security from anti-immigrant laws (see Section B2)
- security from deportation (see Section B3)
- the right to live or take long trips outside the United States (see Section B4)
- special rights and protections when traveling outside the United States (see Section B5)
- an unquestioned right to return to the United States (see Section B6)

- the ability to bring other family members to the United States or to pass citizenship to your children (see Section B7), and
- the right to apply for public benefits (see Section B8).

1. The Right to Vote and Hold Certain Federal Jobs

Green card holders cannot vote in any U.S. election, be it local, state, or federal. (If you *did* vote, see an immigration lawyer immediately—this could result in denial of your application for citizenship.) Once you receive U.S. citizenship, however, you can make your voice heard in local and national elections. Politicians are increasingly aware of the voting-bloc power of immigrants—and are offering meaningful choices and reforms to immigrant voters as a result.

In addition to voting, U.S. citizenship will open the door to many federal job opportunities. The federal government is a huge employer, offering good salaries and job stability. You may not realize how many U.S. government branch offices are in your community—the Social Security Administration, the Environmental Protection Agency, and more. Many U.S. Foreign Service jobs also require U.S. citizenship. If you've got political aspirations, you can run for elected office—although you'll never be able to run for U.S. president or vice president. (You must be born in the U.S.A. to qualify for either of these jobs.)

2. Security From Anti-Immigrant Laws

These days, you can't open the newspaper without seeing a proposed change toughening up the federal immigration laws. These new laws primarily affect people who are here illegally or don't have green cards—but even legal immigrants with green cards aren't immune. Congress—limited only by Constitutional guarantees like free speech and equal protection—can change the rights of green card holders at any time.

A dramatic example of this occurred in the late 1990s, when Congress decided to make green card holders ineligible for various federal benefits such as Supplemental Security Income (SSI). Thousands of elderly and disabled immigrants with low financial resources were suddenly cut off from their lifeline of cash support and medical or nursing home care. (The decision reportedly led to some suicides.) Congress subsequently softened this law, but tight restrictions remain. For example, immigrants who entered the United States after August 22, 1996, can qualify for SSI only if they've had a green card for five years and have worked 40 "quarters" (ten years) in the United States—or fall into one of a few similarly narrow categories.

More recently, Congress has responded to U.S. security concerns by requiring that all airport baggage and passenger screeners be U.S. citizens.

As a U.S. citizen, you can stop worrying about Congress's latest idea. You'll have the same basic rights as any other U.S. citizen.

3. Security From Deportation

Although most green card holders can live in the United States for years without problems, an unfortunate number become deportable and lose their green cards. (We provided reasons for deportation in Section A1, above.)

With U.S. citizenship, the specter of deportation is removed. The grounds of deportation do not apply to U.S. citizens. However, USCIS—although it rarely does so—can take away your citizenship if it finds you lied when seeking your green card or citizenship.

4. The Right to Live Outside the U.S. or to Take Long Trips

A green card holder who spends more than six months abroad, or shows signs of resettling elsewhere, can lose permanent residence rights. Ironically, becoming a U.S. citizen allows you to spend less time in the United States—even to make your home elsewhere if you wish. No one will take away your citizenship as a result. In addition, and unlike U.S. permanent residents, you will be allowed to continue receiving any retirement or other benefits you've earned from Social Security while you're living abroad.

Even if you want to retain your primary home inside the United States, gaining citizenship will be a huge help if you travel a great deal or have close family members or other obligations outside the United States. If family emergencies arise, you'll be able to attend to them, confident of your easy return to the United States.

5. Special Rights and Protections When Traveling Outside the U.S.

If you enjoy visiting other countries, you'll find your U.S. passport helpful. Many countries lighten their visa requirements and restrictions for citizens of the United States and other developed nations.

You'll also enjoy the protection of the U.S. State Department while you're traveling. The State Department takes very seriously its role in protecting U.S. citizens abroad. If you are injured, robbed, or run into other problems beyond your control, you'll find the local U.S. consulate invaluable in helping you arrange care and transportation home.

If you're arrested abroad, the State Department will help you find an attorney and see that you're treated humanely. (However, if you've actually committed a crime, don't count on the State Department to pressure the foreign state to stop your punishment. The degree of help you get depends on the seriousness of your crime and the relations between the United States and the foreign government.)

For a fuller picture of these services see the State Department website (www.state.gov).

6. Ease in Returning to the U.S.

Remember those long lines for green card holders that you stood in when you last entered the United States? The lines are much shorter for U.S. citizens. You'll still have to pass border patrol officials, but at least they won't be asking questions designed to see whether they should take away your green card. You will no longer be subject to inadmissibility rules every time you reenter the United States.

As we indicated in Section A1, above, green card holders must meet admissibility standards every time they enter the United States, and failing these standards can result in being barred from entry and from citizenship.

For more on inadmissibility, see the Immigration and Green Cards section of Nolo's online Legal Encyclopedia at www.nolo.com. Look for the article entitled "When the U.S. Can Keep You Out." Also see *U.S. Immigration Made Easy*, by Laurence A. Canter and Martha S. Siegel (Nolo).

7. Increased Ability to Help Family Members Immigrate

As a U.S. citizen, your existing children with green cards, any children you adopt, and any children born to you after you receive your citizenship automatically (well, almost automatically, depending on the circumstances) become U.S. citizens. For more on passing citizenship to your children, see Chapter 11.

In addition, you can submit a petition to sponsor certain other family members for U.S. green cards (but not citizenship—they'll have to wait a few years just like you did). You'll be able to submit petitions for your parents, your children, your spouse, and your brothers and sisters. Unfortunately, not all of these petitions result in your family member getting a green card right away. If your children are older than 21 or are married, they'll be put on a waiting list that usually lasts several years. Your brothers and sisters will also be put on a waiting list that averages at least ten years in length. Without your citizenship, however, the same family members would either wait much longer or have no rights to immigrate at all.

For more information on how your citizenship can help your family members to immigrate, see Chapter 11.

8. Eligibility for Public Benefits

If your life takes a difficult turn and you discover you can't pay for your own food or medical care, you'll have a much easier time qualifying for government help if you're a U.S. citizen. You will be permitted to apply for SSI (if you're disabled and low-income), federal food stamps, general assistance (cash support), nonemergency medical services, and a variety of state assistance programs—all of which are off limits or severely restricted while you're a permanent resident. Even if you never plan to rely on government help, knowing it's available in an emergency can be reassuring. ■

Are You Eligible for U.S. Citizenship?

No matter how eager you are to become a U.S. citizen, you should start with an honest assessment of whether you are eligible. If you're not entitled to citizenship, the application process could do you more harm than good—wasting your time and energy, or worse, sending you into deportation proceedings.

If, after reading this chapter, you conclude that you aren't eligible, consult with an attorney to confirm your conclusion. If your attorney agrees, you will have saved yourself a lot of aggravation and difficulty. If you conclude that you are eligible, congratulations! You can continue through the application process with confidence.

If you are in the United States illegally, you have a temporary visa or status, or you are in removal (deportation) proceedings, stop now—this book can't help you. No matter who you are or how you came to the United States, you have to start the citizenship process by getting a green card. You cannot jump from having no immigration status to U.S. citizenship. The only exceptions are for the children and, in rare cases, the grandchildren of U.S. citizens, and for service people who served honorably and on active-duty during certain military operations.

If you meet all of the following criteria, you are eligible for U.S. citizenship:

- You have had permanent residence (a "green card") for the required number of years—usually five, but fewer for certain categories of applicants (see Section A).
- You have been "physically present"—that is, lived in the United States, for at least half your required years of permanent residence (usually two and a half out of five years) (see Section B).
- You been "continuously present" in the United States—that is, have not spent long stretches of time (six months or more) overseas (see Section B).
- You have lived in the same U.S. state or USCIS district for three months before applying to the USCIS there (see Section B).
- You are at least 18 years old at the time of filing the application (see Section C).

- You have demonstrated good moral character in the years leading up to your application for citizenship—for example, by paying your taxes and child support and not committing any crimes (see Section D).
- You can speak, read, and write English (see Section E).
- You can pass a brief oral test covering U.S. history and government (see Section F).
- You are willing to affirm loyalty to the United States and serve in its military if necessary (see Section G).

In this chapter, we'll briefly explain how to prove that you meet each of these requirements.

Keep your eyes out for this icon, which alerts you to unique situations when you may have to submit extra documents (and explanations) with your citizenship application.

A. Confirming Your Permanent Resident Status

Before you can become a citizen, you must—with some exceptions (see Section A3, below)—have been a lawful permanent U.S. resident for at least five years. It's important to be accurate when determining your time as a lawful permanent resident, because if you turn in your application even one day before the date you're eligible, USCIS can disqualify it and make you submit it all over again. In the following sections, we'll help you analyze the length and status of your permanent residency.

1. Are You a Lawful Permanent Resident?

Your green card—not a work permit, visa, or other temporary right to live in the United States—is what demonstrates that you are a permanent resident. Your green card should look similar to the one shown in Section 2, below.

It's not enough to possess the card; you also have to "deserve" it. If you have been ordered deported or have violated the terms of your stay, you may have lost your legal right to permanent residence even though you still carry your card. Not only could you be ineligible for citizenship, but you risk deportation by applying for it.

However, if your green card expired (which it does every ten years)—you are still a permanent resident. Renew your card before applying for citizenship. Instructions for renewal are in Chapter 3.

2. How Long Have You Been a Permanent Resident?

To determine how many years you've been a permanent resident, calculate from the date that the INS or USCIS approved your permanent residence—it's shown on your green card, as seen in the picture below.

As you calculate the time, don't round it off to calendar years. In other words, four years, 11 months, and 20 days does not equal five years. When it comes to determining the date at which you can apply for citizenship, USCIS wants you to count full 365-day years.

> **EXAMPLE:** Loc was granted permanent residence on December 15, 2000. On January 15, 2005, he incorrectly decides that he has been a permanent resident for five years and files his citizenship application. (In actual years, he has been a permanent resident for only four years and one month.) His application will be returned, and Loc will not be eligible for citizenship until

December 15, 2005 (although, as we'll see in Section 3, below, a special provision allows him and other applicants to file applications three months before they're eligible).

What if your first two years of U.S. residence are "conditional" rather than "permanent"? Conditional residence is like permanent residence, but it gives USCIS a chance to reevaluate your case at the end of two years (when the conditional residence automatically expires). Often, people who marry U.S. citizens must go through these two years of conditional residence before applying for permanent residence. Similarly, immigrants who get their green cards as entrepreneurs (by investing at least $500,000 in a U.S. business) must spend two years as conditional residents before becoming permanent residents.

If you spent two years as a conditional resident, there's good news—when it comes to applying for citizenship, those two years count as permanent residence so long as you successfully became a permanent resident at the end of them. Count your years of residence starting at the date you were approved for conditional residence. You'll find that date on your green card.

> **EXAMPLE:** Tam invested $500,000 in NetMiser, a U.S. company, and was approved for conditional residence on April 7, 2001. USCIS approved Tam for permanent residence in July, 2003. Tam is eligible for citizenship on April 7, 2006—five years from the date he was approved for conditional residence.

Date of Residency

Old-Style Green Card (Front)

Old-Style Green Card (Back)

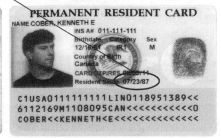

New-Style Green Card (Front)

Conditional residents who married U.S. citizens —more good news! Assuming your marriage to your U.S. citizen spouse hasn't broken up, you have to wait only three years as a permanent resident before applying for citizenship. That means you can apply one year after the end of your conditional residence.

3. How Many Years of Permanent Residence Are Required?

In this section, we'll help you determine the earliest possible date upon which you can turn in your citizenship application. For most people, that will be after five years of permanent residence, but for some—depending on their circumstances—that date may be sooner.

Don't count on USCIS to tell you've counted the days wrong. Although USCIS has recently started trying to advise people of errors in their application date soon after they submit it, some applications are bound to slip through the cracks. In other words, you could arrive at your interview only to be told you have to file again. For that reason, do your best to count your permanent residency time accurately.

a. The 90-Day Early Application Rule

You can turn in your citizenship application 90 days before your required years of permanent residence have passed. This 90-day period compensates for the fact that USCIS probably won't act on your application for at least a year. (This doesn't change the fact that you're eligible for citizenship only after the full number of years have passed, but in this rare instance, USCIS allows you to become eligible after you submit your application, not before).

> **EXAMPLE:** Loc (from the example above) became a permanent resident on December 15, 2000. He carelessly counts off five years on his fingers and decides that he can apply for citizenship in 2005. He turns in his citizenship application in August 2005. His application comes back in the mail—he is told he applied too early and must reapply. If he'd waited another month, he could have applied legally on September 15, 2005 (five years minus 90 days from December 15, 2000).

b. The Five-Year Requirement

Most immigrants must wait for a full five years of permanent residency before they are eligible for citizenship. In other words, if you were approved for permanent residency on December 15, 2000, you would not be eligible for citizenship until December 15, 2005. (Due to the 90-day period discussed in Subsection a, above, you could file your application on September 15, 2005.)

c. Exceptions to the Five-Year Requirement

You don't have to accumulate five years of permanent residence before applying for citizenship if you are:

- a spouse of a U.S. citizen (nonmilitary) who stays married for three years (see Subsection i, below)
- a battered spouse of a U.S. citizen, even if divorced or separated (see Subsection ii, below)
- a refugee or political asylee (see Subsection iii, below)
- in the U.S. military or a military widow or widower (see Subsection iv, below), or
- a spouse of a U.S. citizen in certain overseas jobs (see Subsection v, below).

Below, we'll give you the "fine print" on these exceptions and alert you to special documentation you'll need to provide to claim the exception. However, if you can't tell whether you fit into one of these exceptions, or if you have additional questions about how these exceptions apply to your case, consult with an immigration attorney.

i. Spouses of U.S. Citizens (Nonmilitary) Who Stay Married for Three Years

You can apply for citizenship after three years if, during that time, you have been a permanent resident and have been married to and living with a U.S. citizen. It doesn't matter whether you got your green card through this marriage. You will, however, need to stay married to your citizen spouse all the way through your citizenship interview. This exception won't apply and you will be required to wait five years if:

- you separate or divorce legally prior to your interview
- you choose to stop living with your spouse, or
- your spouse dies.

Also, your spouse must be a citizen during all of your three years of permanent residency. If, for example, your spouse had a green card when you got married and became a naturalized citizen one year later, you'll have to wait three years from the date he or she became a citizen—that is, for a total of four years.

One more bureaucratic hitch: Applicants claiming this three-year exception may not be able to use the 90-day rule (see Section A3) that allows you to file your application early. Some local USCIS offices insist on your having been married for three years—not one day less. So, if you got married at around the same time that you received your permanent residence, it's safest not to file your application 90 days early. If you were married to a U.S. citizen for more than three months prior to obtaining permanent residency, you can file early.

> **EXAMPLE 1:** Edna entered the United States on a fiancé visa, married Edric (a U.S. citizen), and applied for permanent residence the day after their marriage. By some miracle, her local USCIS office wasn't busy, and her application was approved the next day. Two years and 275 days later (three years minus 90 days), Edna applies for citizenship. Edna's local USCIS won't accept her application, insisting that she must wait until she's been married to Edric for a full three years.

> **EXAMPLE 2:** Bhagwan, a U.S. citizen, married Brinda while she was a foreign student in the United States. After her studies were nearly over, he petitioned for her to receive U.S. residence. By the time her residence was granted, they had already been married and living together for three years. Brinda can submit her citizenship application in another nine months—90 days before her three years of permanent residence are up. Although Brinda's situation seems very similar to Edna's, above, Brinda is lucky—her marriage began long before she became a permanent resident. Therefore she can show a full three years of marriage and apply 90 days before reaching three years of permanent residence.

Married with documentation. If you are married to a U.S. citizen and eligible to apply after three years, you'll need to prove it. Include with your application a copy of your marriage certificate, a copy of your spouse's U.S. passport, citizenship certificate, or other proof of citizenship, certificates showing that your and your spouse's previous marriages (if any) were legally ended by death, divorce, or annulment, and materials to show that the two of you are actually living as man and wife, such as your children's birth certificates, a home title, or rental receipts showing both your names, copies of joint credit card statements, and more.

ii. Battered Spouses or Children of U.S. Citizens, Even After Divorce or Separation

Until recently, battered spouses of U.S. citizens were left with a tough choice: They could stay in an abusive marriage for three years so that they could obtain U.S. citizenship, or they could leave their spouse—but have to wait longer before applying for citizenship.

Now, permanent residents in physically or emotionally abusive marriages can leave their spouse and still apply for U.S. citizenship three years after obtaining their permanent residence. Children are also eligible under this section, though the child must still reach age 18 before applying for citizenship. If you want to use this rule, the law requires that you got your green card through your marriage to the U.S. citizen—and that in getting the green card, you used special legal provisions that allow the battered spouse to file portions of the paperwork without the abusive spouse's cooperation (either through a self petition on Form I-360 or through cancellation of removal). (See I.N.A. § 319(a), 8 U.S.C. § 1430(a).)

If you've already suffered through an abusive marriage to your U.S. citizen spouse for three years, you can apply under the rule described in Section A3, above. But, if you're not living with your U.S. citizen spouse now, this new section could help. You won't need to prove the abuse all over again, having already provided evidence of it in the application that got you your green card.

iii. Refugees and Political Asylees

If you got your green card because of your refugee or political asylum status, part of your time as a refugee or asylee can be counted as if you were a permanent resident (known as "rollback").

If you were granted refugee status while you were in another country, you can count the date you entered the United States as the beginning of your permanent residence. It doesn't matter how many years you lived in the United States as a refugee as long as you eventually become a permanent resident—all those years will count as if you were a permanent resident. (See 8 C.F.R. § 209.1(e).)

> **EXAMPLE:** Seyoum comes to the United States as a refugee in January 2001. He waits until the year 2004 to apply for permanent residence, and USCIS grants it in January 2005. Seyoum can apply for citizenship in January 2006, because his four years of refugee status and one year as an actual permanent resident all count as part of his five years of permanent residence.

The rules differ for immigrants who were granted political asylum after they reached the United States. The maximum rollback for asylees is one year—if you waited longer than a year to apply for your green card, that extra time won't be counted toward your permanent residency period. In summary, you can apply for citizenship four years after your approval for permanent residence. (See 8 C.F.R. § 209.2(f).)

> **EXAMPLE:** Takalin arrives in the United States on a tourist visa in 1997 and applies for and receives political asylum in 1998. In 2000, he applies for

permanent residence, and his application is approved in March 2002. Takalin can apply for U.S. citizenship in March 2006, four years after he qualified for permanent residence. Only one year of his time as an asylee is counted towards his permanent residence.

⚠️ **Despite rollback benefits, refugees and asylees are subject to the same requirements as other applicants regarding how much time they must spend inside the United States—as opposed to traveling abroad—before applying for citizenship (see Section B, below).**

If you take advantage of the rollback rules for refugees or asylees, make it clear to USCIS when you apply. Mention it in your application cover letter, and include a copy of USCIS or State Department documents proving the date you entered the United States (if you're a refugee) or became a permanent resident (if you're an asylee). USCIS should have these dates in its files, but the office that first handles your citizenship application may not have access to those files.

iv. U.S. Military Personnel and Their Widows and Widowers

People serving in the U.S. military and their families make a special commitment to the United States and for that reason, the immigration law provides certain exceptions for those applying for U.S. citizenship. These exceptions cover people who have performed active or reserve service in the U.S. Army, Navy, Marines, Air Force, or Coast Guard, as well as service in a National Guard unit while the unit was federally recognized as a reserve component of the U.S. Armed Forces. (See 8 C.F.R § 328.1.)

People with one year of service. If you have served honorably in the U.S. armed forces for one year (it doesn't have to have been continuous) and your discharge (if any) was honorable, you can apply for citizenship without waiting beyond the date you get your green card.

However, if you have been discharged, you must apply for citizenship no later than six months after your discharge, so don't delay. If six months have already passed, you will—unless you qualify for one of the other exceptions in this chapter—most likely have to prove five years of permanent residence before applying for citizenship. (See I.N.A. § 328, 8 U.S.C. § 1439.)

Surviving spouses of U.S. citizens killed in action. If you were married to a U.S. citizen who died while honorably serving on active duty with the U.S. armed forces, and if the two of you were married and living together at the time of your spouse's death, you can apply for citizenship without waiting—provided you

are a permanent resident by the time you apply for citizenship. (See I.N.A. § 319(d), 8 U.S.C. § 1430(d).)

Service people during certain conflicts. If you served honorably and on active duty with the U.S. armed forces during one of the conflicts listed below, and enlisted (signed up) while you were still on U.S. territory (including the Canal Zone, American Samoa, Swains Island, or a noncommercial U.S. ship), you don't even need a green card or permanent residence to apply for U.S. citizenship. You can, if your citizenship application is approved, go straight from having no legal status to becoming a citizen—a rare opportunity in the immigration law world. (See I.N.A. § 329, 8 U.S.C. § 1440.) The conflicts that qualify include:

- World War I
- World War II
- the Korean hostilities
- the Vietnam hostilities
- the Persian Gulf War
- the "War on Terrorism" (also called "Operation Enduring Freedom," which began on September 11, 2001, and will end on a date to be determined by the U.S. president.

To take advantage of your right to apply immediately, you'll need certification from the military showing when and where you served and that your service and discharge (if any) were honorable. If you are currently serving in the military and at some later date you are dishonorably discharged, your citizenship can be taken away.

 In addition to the conflicts listed above, the U.S. president can later add more by executive order. Check for new additions in the Legal Updates section of Nolo's website (www.nolo.com).

 Put proof in your application packet. If you plan to claim one of these conflicts exceptions, include an explanation in your application cover letter and a filed Form N-426, which USCIS will use to request proof of your military service and discharge. You also need a separate letter saying your service and discharge were honorable.

Posthumous Citizenship for Soldiers Killed in Action

The law allows family members of noncitizens who died from injury or disease caused during active duty with the U.S. Armed Forces during specified periods of military hostilities—most recently, the war in Iraq—to apply for citizenship for their dead relative. The closest relative should be the one to file the application—in other words, first choice would be a spouse, then a child, a parent, and last choice a brother or sister. You must apply within two years of the military person's death. To apply, fill out and send Form N-644, together with an $80 fee, to the USCIS Service Center that handles your geographical area. Form N-644 and more detailed instructions are available on the USCIS website at www.uscis.gov.

Immediate family members (spouses, parents, and children) of the deceased soldier may apply for green cards as the relative of a U.S. citizen. However, they must file a visa petition within two years of the person's death. (This represents an amendment to the original law, which specifically refused immigration benefits to family members. See Public Law 108-36 §§ 1701-1703, enacted November 24, 2003.)

v. Spouses of U.S. Citizens in Certain Overseas Jobs

If your spouse has a job requiring the two of you to live overseas, you may be able to apply for citizenship without five years of permanent residency. If you're willing to come back to the United States to apply, you can file your application any time after you receive your permanent residence.

There are a number of limitations on who can use this provision:

- You must be regularly stationed abroad because of your spouse's job.
- You must declare your intention to live in the United States as soon as your spouse's job ends.
- Your spouse's employer must be:

- the U.S. government (for example, the CIA, the military, the American Red Cross, or the Peace Corps)
- a U.S. institution of research recognized as such by the attorney general (listed at 8 C.F.R. § 316.20(a))
- a U.S. firm or corporation (or a subsidiary) engaged wholly or partly in the development of U.S. foreign trade and commerce
- a public international organization in which the United States participates by treaty or statute (listed at 8 C.F.R. § 316.20(b) and (c)), or
- a religious denomination with an organization within the United States, for which your spouse performs ministerial or priestly functions or works solely as a missionary.

For more information, review I.N.A. § 319(b), 8 U.S.C. § 1430(b), as well as 8 C.F.R. § 319.11, and consult with an attorney.

 If you plan to claim this overseas job exception, make sure to raise it in your application packet. Include an explanation in your cover letter and proof that you qualify for the exception.

B. Your Physical Location During Permanent Residency

In this section, we discuss three separate but overlapping citizenship requirements concerning your physical location—that is, where your feet were planted (on U.S. soil or overseas)—during the required years of permanent residence leading up to your citizenship application. The three requirements are:

- You spent most of your time during your required years of permanent residence on U.S. soil—called the "physical presence" requirement (discussed in Section B1).
- None of your absences from the United States lasted longer than six months—called the "continuous residence" requirement by USCIS (but we've renamed it the "continuous U.S. stay" requirement, as discussed in Section B2).

Tallying Up Your Time in and out of the United States

You'll need to know exactly when you were inside and outside the United States—preferably with exact dates.

Unless you have a fabulous memory or haven't taken many trips, you probably can't figure this out without a little research. Get out your passport, your calendar, your credit card receipts, and your frequent flier records and fill in the table below. This table is taken directly from the citizenship application, so skipping over it will only postpone the inevitable.

If your records don't reveal the information, be creative. For example, ask your employer for your time sheets and look for the vacation dates. Try to remember details of your trips that will help establish the dates. For example, think about which house or apartment you were living in when you took each trip and whether any trips were for special occasions that you can attach dates to, like your father's 60th birthday or your brother's wedding.

On the table below, enter every trip that lasted 24 hours or longer. Day trips—if you got there and back within 24 hours—don't count. If you can't determine the exact date, approximate (for example giving the month and year). If you really can't remember the dates, write down what you can remember, such as "traveled to Mexico for the Christmas holiday every year—spent no more than two weeks each trip." (Although some USCIS officers will not accept approximations, it's better to provide some information than to hide the fact that you took trips.)

Date You Left the U.S. (Month/Day/Year)	Date You Returned to the U.S. (Month/Day/Year)	Did Trip Last Six Months or More?	Countries to Which You Traveled	Total Days out of the U.S.
		☐ Yes ☐ No		
		☐ Yes ☐ No		
		☐ Yes ☐ No		
		☐ Yes ☐ No		
		☐ Yes ☐ No		
		☐ Yes ☐ No		
		☐ Yes ☐ No		
		☐ Yes ☐ No		
		☐ Yes ☐ No		
		☐ Yes ☐ No		
		☐ Yes ☐ No		

- You lived in the same U.S. state or USCIS district for three months before submitting your citizenship application (which we've named the "state stay" requirement, as discussed in Section B3).

We'll refer to these three requirements collectively as the "location" requirements.

1. Time Requirements for Physical Presence in the U.S.

In Section A3, we discussed how many years of permanent residence are required before applying for citizenship. But having a green card for the right number of years isn't enough to qualify you for citizenship. You must have spent as much time inside the United States as outside of it during those years. This is the "physical presence" requirement, the purpose of which is for you to strengthen your ties to the United States. During those years, you'll become an active participant in U.S. society, start to understand its system of law and governance and make a transition away from your old country.

If you are required to complete five years of permanent residence before applying for citizenship, then you must have spent two and a half of those years (30 months) in the United States. (This applies to refugees and asylees, too.) If you're required to complete three years of permanent residence, then you must have spent one and a half of those years (18 months) physically present in the United States.

EXAMPLE 1: Jorge was approved for his green card as a skilled worker. He has a five-year wait before he's eligible for U.S. citizenship. During those five years, he takes several business trips outside of the United States, adding up to two year's total time. He is eligible for citizenship, because he was physically present in the United States more than two and a half years.

EXAMPLE 2: Graciela received her green card as a result of her marriage to a U.S. citizen (she is still married to him). She has a three-year wait from the date she got her green card before she's eligible for U.S. citizenship. She and her husband love to travel, and have spent a total of two of the last three years outside of the United States. This leaves her with only one year's physical presence since getting her green card—she has a physical presence requirement of 18 months. She'll need to spend another six months within the U.S. before she can apply for citizenship.

⚠ **Your sleeping hours must have been spent in the U.S., too.** If you've been working in the U.S. but commuting back and forth to your home in Canada or Mexico, you can't fulfill the continuous residence requirements.

If you fall into one of the exceptional categories of applicants who don't have to spend a specific number of years as a permanent resident, then you probably won't have to worry about the physical presence requirement. We'll talk more about these exceptional categories in Section 4, below.

The physical presence requirement is not the only way you have to prove that you made your home in the United States. Next, we'll discuss the requirement that you've lived here "continuously."

2. Continuity: Living Outside the U.S. for More Than Six Months at a Time

Taking short trips outside the United States is fine—in fact, it's one of your rights as a permanent resident. However, if during the required years of permanent residence leading up to your citizenship application, any of your trips lasted six months or more, you've got an eligibility problem.

USCIS presumes that a six-month trip (or longer) means that you made your main home in another country and that your period of U.S. permanent residence is no longer "continuous." Even one day more than six months may raise USCIS's concern (though some USCIS offices are less strict than others).

That doesn't mean you're ineligible for citizenship. If your trip was under one year in length, you may be able to persuade USCIS that its presumption was wrong, and that you always intended to make your home in the United States. Your chances are improved if—during your trip—you maintained your primary residence in the U.S. But a trip of more than one year breaks the continuity of your U.S. stay automatically and you are ineligible to apply for citizenship until you have completed a continuous permanent residency period.

Although this requirement is formally known by USCIS as the "continuous residence" requirement, we're going to call it the "continuous U.S. stay" requirement to avoid confusing it with the requirement concerning the number of years you've been a permanent resident.

 USCIS could decide that you broke the continuity of your U.S. stay and abandoned your U.S. residence altogether. If USCIS believes you planned to make your primary home elsewhere, it can deny your citizenship and send you to immigration court for a decision on whether you should be deported. It can take this action for any trips you took during your years of permanent residence. For example, if you've been a permanent resident for 25 years, USCIS could review a trip you took 20 years ago and determine you took that trip with the intention of abandoning your life in the United States. The USCIS officer at your citizenship interview has the power to decide that the border patrol—when they let you back into the country—was too easy on you. Your case may then be handed over to a judge. If this could be an issue for you, see a lawyer.

Tax breaks = continuity breaks! If you claimed to be a nonresident of the United States in order to avoid paying U.S. income taxes, USCIS will determine that you have broken your continuous U.S. stay. This doesn't happen often, so we don't cover it in further depth here. If this is an issue in your case, see a lawyer.

Though their underlying theme is the same— USCIS wants you to live in the United States—the physical presence and continuous U.S. stay requirements are different. Keep in mind that you could meet one while failing to meet the other.

EXAMPLE 1: During his five years as a permanent resident, Kelepi takes 25 vacation trips outside the United States. Each trip lasts 40 days. His total absence from the U.S. is 1,000 days (about two years and nine months). Although he has broken the physical presence rule—he's permitted to spend only two and one half years outside the U.S.—he has not broken the continuity rule, since no single trip was longer than six months.

EXAMPLE 2: During her five years as a permanent resident, Manawune spends eight months abroad with her ailing mother. Manawune has met the physical presence requirement—having spent over two and one half years in the United States—but she has broken the continuity of her U.S. stay. Unless she can persuade USCIS that she didn't intend to make her home outside the United States, she is ineligible for citizenship until she completes a continuous five years of permanent residency.

There are exceptions to the continuity rules. Certain people who are working or stationed overseas can spend longer than six months outside the United States without hurting their eligibility for citizenship. These are discussed in Section 4, below.

In summary, your options if you have broken the continuity of your U.S. stay include the following:

- If your trip was more than six months but less than a year, provide evidence arguing that you didn't mean to break the continuity of your U.S. stay. (See Subsection a, below.)
- If you obviously broke your continuous U.S. stay or if you lived outside the United States for a year or more (but you didn't go so far as to abandon your U.S. residence), wait for a certain amount of time from the date you returned before applying. (See Subsection b, below.)

If you haven't yet spent six months outside the United States, but you know that you'll need to because of a job, you may have an additional option: to apply for advance permission to take a long trip. This is discussed in Subsection c, below.

a. Proving You Didn't Break Your Continuous U.S. Stay

As long as you were not outside the United States for more than one year at a time, you can argue that you didn't intend to break your continuous U.S. stay.

 If you were gone for more than a year at a time, there's no point in arguing with USCIS or providing the documents described in this section—go straight to Subsection b, below, to find out how long you'll have to wait before you'll be eligible for citizenship.

The key facts that will convince USCIS that you didn't intend to break your continuous U.S. stay are that you:
- kept a job with an employer in the United States (whether you were on leave, sent to work for an overseas office, or otherwise)
- continued to pay U.S. taxes
- left close family members in the United States
- kept a home or apartment in the United States to which you still had full access (that is, didn't rent out)
- continued car registration, health insurance, and other such protections
- didn't take a new job overseas, or
- were prevented from returning to the United States by unexpected circumstances.

The more factors you match, the better. You'll need to provide supporting documents, and we've created a checklist below to help you. This is not an exhaustive list. Provide any relevant documents to prove that the United States remained your home during your absence.

Documents Demonstrating an Unbroken Stay

The following documents can help demonstrate an unbroken stay in the U.S.:
- copies of pay stubs showing you kept a job with a U.S. employer
- original IRS Form 1722 listing your tax information for the past three years or, if you can't obtain this, copies of your last three years' U.S. income tax returns
- copies of rent or mortgage payments showing you kept a home or apartment in the United States
- evidence that your family remained in the United States while you were away, such as copies of school, medical, and employment records, and rent or mortgage receipts
- copies of your U.S. car registration, health insurance, and other contracts and receipts
- your written explanation of the purpose of your trip and the reason it lasted so long, or
- if you were prevented from returning by unusual circumstances (for example, you broke your hip and couldn't travel), a letter from your doctor or other authority who can verify what happened.

Include these documents with your citizenship application. (We describe the application process in Chapter 3.)

Put the proof in your application. If you're explaining your continuity break to USCIS, describe what happened in your cover letter and include proof that you didn't break the continuity of your U.S. stay in your citizenship application packet.

b. Dealing With Continuity Breaks

Unless you were kidnapped or forcibly removed from the United States—rare exceptions—any stay of over one year outside the U.S. will break your continuity. If you've stayed over a year, or if USCIS rejects your arguments regarding trips of six months to a year, you'll need to redetermine your years of U.S. residence. If you were required to have five years' permanent residence and were away for a year or more, you'll have to live in the United States for four continuous years and one day after the date you returned from your trip before applying for citizenship. USCIS treats your year away (minus one day) as if it was spent in the United States—but doesn't count any of the time before you left the United States. Oddly enough, if you were away for between six months and one year, you'll have to wait a full five years after your return to apply for citizenship.

If you qualify to apply for citizenship after three years, you must wait two years and one day after returning from the trip that broke your continuous U.S. stay to submit your citizenship application.

If you're applying after one of these waiting periods, don't count on using the 90-day early submission policy described in Section A3. Under these circumstances, most USCIS offices won't allow you to submit your application early.

⚠ **Even the fixes described in this section won't help you if you not only broke the continuity of your U.S. stay, but abandoned your U.S. permanent residence altogether.** If there's any strong basis upon which USCIS could claim that you meant to make your home outside the United States, consult with an immigration attorney before submitting your application. For instance, if you didn't merely divide your life between two places, but actually sold your U.S. home and car, took your children out of school, and gave your dog to a neighbor before leaving, USCIS is likely to suspect that you abandoned your U.S. residence.

c. Applying for Permission to Take a Long Trip

With a little advance planning, you can—under some circumstances—apply for USCIS permission to stay outside the United States for a year or more without breaking your continuous U.S. stay. You are allowed to do so if you have a job that takes you

out of the United States for long stretches of time. You will, however, need to have lived in the United States as a permanent resident for one year before leaving (except religious workers, who can do their one year after returning). And you'll need to come back after two and a half years or else start over counting your years of permanent residence when you return to the United States. Upon return, you will need to prove that you really spent the time doing the designated job.

You are eligible to apply for permission if you are an employee of:
- the U.S. government
- a U.S. research institution (if the institution is recognized by the U.S. attorney general)
- a U.S. firm or corporation (more than 50% U.S. owned) involved in the development of U.S. trade and commerce
- a public international organization of which the United States is a member by treaty or statute, or
- a religious denomination or interdenominational mission organization having a bona fide organization within the United States, where you are authorized to perform ministerial or priestly functions or serve as a missionary, brother, nun, or sister.

(See I.N.A. § 317, 8 U.S.C. § 1428; 8 C.F.R. § 316.5(d)(2).)

You can file an application to preserve your continuous U.S. stay *after* you've left the United States, but you must turn it in *before* you've been away for a whole year. (Religious workers again receive an exception—they can file their application after returning to the United States.) Use Form N-470, Application to Preserve Residence for Naturalization Purposes, to apply. (We do not cover this application process in this book.) For the form and further instructions, see the USCIS website (www.uscis.gov).

📊 **If you've already filed a Form N-470 application and received permission from USCIS to stay away for more than a year, include this proof in your citizenship application packet.** Also include evidence that you actually returned on time, such as a copy of your plane ticket.

⚠️ **Don't confuse applications to preserve your continuous U.S. stay for citizenship purposes (Form N-470), with the Application for Advance Permission to Return to Unrelinquished Domicile (Form I-191).** The latter application allows permanent residents to obtain permission to reenter the United States after a long trip. Such permission does nothing to maintain your continuous U.S. stay for citizenship purposes—it merely protects you from being refused reentry at the U.S. border.

3. State Stay: Three Months of Residence in the State or District Where You Will Apply

You must live in the same U.S. state or USCIS district for three months before submitting your citizenship application to USCIS there—we'll call this the "state stay" requirement. In other words, if you live in Maine but move to Arkansas, you'll have to wait for three months before sending your citizenship application to the Arkansas USCIS. A few people who move to another state won't have to worry, because they'll remain in the same USCIS district. But this occurs only in smaller states, where USCIS serves several states with just one district office. If, for example, you move from Maine to Vermont, you will remain in the same USCIS district and won't have to worry about the three-month requirement.

If you have already submitted your citizenship application and then move to a different state or district, your case can no longer be considered by USCIS in the state or district you left behind. Your file must be transferred (which can delay it by many months, as we'll discuss in Chapter 4). Make sure you're comfortably situated somewhere before sending in your citizenship application.

Military personnel can submit their citizenship application in the state in which they're stationed, in the one where their spouse or minor children live, or in the one where their home address is (as shown in their military file). (See 8 C.F.R. § 316.5 (b)(2).)

College students can apply in their home state or in the state where their school is located. (8 C.F.R. § 316.5 (b)(2).)

4. Exceptions to the Location Requirements

If you're stationed or working overseas, meeting the various location requirements—physical presence, continuity, and state location—can be difficult. The government understands the difficulty and has made special exceptions for:

- U.S. military personnel (see Subsection a, below)
- widows and widowers of U.S. military personnel (see Subsection b, below)
- employees of the U.S. government and certain religious and other organizations (see Subsection c, below)
- spouses of U.S. citizens in certain occupations (see Subsection d, below)
- employees of certain U.S. nonprofits (see Subsection e, below), and
- service people on nonmilitary U.S. ships (see Subsection f, below).

💼 **We briefly discuss each of the location exceptions in this chapter.** If you need more detailed information, consult with an attorney who is an expert in immigration matters.

a. U.S. Military Personnel

If you've served honorably with the U.S. military for a total of one year and you're either still serving or ended your service no more than six months ago, you can apply for citizenship without worrying about location requirements. If it's been more than six months since you left the military, you'll have to follow the rules for ordinary permanent residents—except that USCIS will count your overseas service as residence within the United States for purposes of the location requirements.

📊 **If you want to claim this military service exception, include a filled-out Form N-426 and a certified statement from the appropriate military authorities showing that each period of your service during the required year was honorable and that you've never had a dishonorable discharge—not even**

outside the one year. You'll also have to show that you made your primary home in the United States during any breaks in your military service. Use the types of evidence described in Section 2, above.

b.   Widows and Widowers of U.S. Citizens in the Military

If your U.S. citizen spouse was killed during honorable service on active duty with the U.S. armed forces and you and your spouse were married at the time of death, you can apply for U.S. citizenship without worrying about location requirements. (See 8 U.S.C. § 1430(d), I.N.A. § 319(d).) (And as you already know from Section A3, you don't need to worry about how long you've been a permanent resident, either.) You can submit your citizenship application as soon as you have a green card.

To claim the widow/widower exception, obtain a statement from the military authorities stating that your spouse's service was honorable and that he or she was killed during the course of this service. Include this and a copy of your marriage certificate with your citizenship application.

c.   Employees of the U.S. Government or Research, Religious, and Other Organizations

You may, through an application process, avoid the continuous U.S. stay requirement if you work for:

- the U.S. government
- a U.S. research institution (if the institution is recognized by the U.S. attorney general; see the list at 8 C.F.R. § 316.20)
- a U.S. firm or corporation (more than 50% U.S. owned) involved in the development of U.S. trade and commerce
- a public international organization of which the United States is a member by treaty or statute, or

- a religious or missionary organization for which you work as a priest, missionary, brother, nun, or sister.

(See I.N.A. § 316(b)(1), 8 U.S.C. § 1427(b)(1).)

To apply for advance permission to spend more than six months outside the United States without breaking the continuity of your residence, you'll need to fill out Form N-470. Regardless of this exception, you will still need to meet the physical presence and state stay requirements for citizenship.

d.   Spouses of U.S. Citizens in Certain Overseas Occupations

If your spouse is a U.S. citizen whose job requires that the two of you regularly live overseas, you may be able to avoid the location requirements. (See I.N.A. § 319(b), 8 U.S.C. § 1430(b).) Specifically, your spouse must be:

- employed by the U.S. government
- employed by a U.S. research institution recognized as such by the attorney general
- employed by a U.S. firm or corporation (or its subsidiary) that is engaged wholly or partly in the development of U.S. foreign trade and commerce
- employed by a public international organization in which the United States participates by treaty or statute, or
- serving as a priest, minister, or missionary on behalf of a religious denomination or inter-denominational mission that is organized within the United States.

If any of these employment descriptions apply, you don't have to worry about the physical presence, continuous U.S. stay, or state stay requirements. You'll have to come to the United States to claim your citizenship and must declare your intention to take up residence within the United States as soon as your spouse's employment is over.

You'll need to seek personalized advice from an experienced immigration attorney to take advantage of this overseas employment exception.

e. Employees of Nonprofits That Promote U.S. Interests

If you work for a nonprofit that requires you to live overseas, and you've worked for that nonprofit for at least five years after becoming a permanent resident, you may be able to avoid the location requirements. (See I.N.A. § 319(c), 8 U.S.C. § 1430(c).) You must work for a nonprofit that is:

- a bona fide U.S. incorporated nonprofit
- involved in communications media
- primarily involved in disseminating information that significantly promotes U.S. interests abroad, and
- recognized as meeting the above criteria by the attorney general.

If this section applies to you, you don't have to worry about any of the location requirements—physical presence, continuous U.S. stay, or state stay. You must come to the United States to claim your citizenship, and you must declare your intention to take up residence within the United States as soon as your employment is over.

 You'll need to seek personalized advice from an experienced immigration attorney to take advantage of this nonprofit exception.

f. Workers on Nonmilitary U.S. Ships

If you were living outside the U.S. while working on a nonmilitary U.S. ship, your time on board won't be subtracted from the time you were physically present in the United States and won't break the continuity of your U.S. stay. However, you will still have to remain in one U.S. state or USCIS district for three months before submitting your citizenship application.

A qualifying nonmilitary ship is one that's:

- operated by the U.S. government, or
- registered under U.S. law to a U.S. citizen or corporation and has its home port in the United States.

Time spent working on a *foreign* vessel doesn't count toward your U.S. physical residence requirements. To take advantage of this section, you must also have demonstrated good conduct and honorable service on the ship. (See I.N.A. § 330, 8 U.S.C. § 1441.)

 You'll need to seek personalized advice from an experienced immigration attorney to take advantage of this U.S. ship exception.

C. The Age Requirement

To use the naturalization process described in this book, you must be at least 18 years old at the time you apply. If you're younger than 18, there's an alternate route to U.S. citizenship. If one of your parents is or becomes a citizen, you may qualify for citizenship through your parent. For details, see Chapter 11. You can also refer to "U.S. Citizenship by Birth or Through Parents," in Nolo's online Legal Encyclopedia (www.nolo.com). To find this article, click "Immigration and Green Cards" on the left side of the Nolo home page. Then look under "U.S. Citizenship."

D. Demonstrating Good Moral Character

To qualify for citizenship, you must demonstrate good moral character during your permanent residency, with a particular focus on the last five years (or fewer, if you fall into one of the exceptional categories that can apply earlier). The longer you've shown good moral character, the stronger your case.

What is good moral character? According to USCIS, it's the moral standard of an average member of the U.S. community.

As a general rule, USCIS doesn't ask for proof that you're good; it looks for evidence you've been bad. So, if you've gone about your everyday business, paid taxes and child support, and avoided trouble with the law (either in the United States or abroad), you should have no problem establishing your good moral character.

However, if you have some minor negative behavior to account for—for example, a series of traffic tickets or a past drinking problem—you will need to balance out your bad acts by providing specific evidence of the good things you've done (as discussed in Section D16). Keep in mind that the USCIS determination of your moral character is a subjective, unscientific analysis in which the interviewing officer weighs your good and bad actions and decides which show the real you.

If you've committed more serious transgressions—for example, murder or another serious crime—you may not be able to outweigh them with your good deeds. Immigration laws detail a variety of actions that can destroy your good character. Certain actions will permanently prevent you from becoming a U.S. citizen; others will delay your citizenship, at least until you take some other corrective action. If the law requires, the USCIS officer may be forced to deny your citizenship, no matter how sympathetic your case.

If you have a criminal conviction, see an attorney before applying for citizenship. If USCIS discovers your criminal convictions (and it probably will through your fingerprints), it may not only deny you citizenship, but the agency may send you to immigration court for deportation proceedings. (Note: The USCIS usually won't hold juvenile convictions—when you were younger than 18—against you. Still, it's wise to see a lawyer for a full analysis.)

⚠️ **You may have a criminal record and not know it.** You may have been arrested for something minor and signed a paper saying you're guilty, then never gone to jail. Or you may have received "diversion," with no guilty plea, or perhaps your case was "expunged"—that is, erased from your record years later. Keep in mind that these crimes still count against you for immigration purposes (with rare exceptions). Worse yet, if you state on your citizenship application that your record is clean, you may run into serious problems if USCIS later accuses you of lying. If in doubt, consult with an immigration attorney and ask to run a criminal check on your fingerprints.

The checklist below summarizes the most common ways—but not all the ways—in which moral character can be undermined. Check any boxes for which you answer "yes" and then review the appropriate sections.

Good Moral Character Checklist

☐ Have you committed any crimes?	See Section D1
☐ If you have committed a crime, have you since completed all probation, parole, or similar obligations?	See Section D2
☐ Have you helped or encouraged anyone to enter the United States illegally?	See Section D3
☐ Have you lied to obtain immigration benefits?	See Section D4
☐ Have you pretended to be a U.S. citizen or voted illegally?	See Section D5
☐ Have you received government assistance (such as welfare) through fraud or within five years of any U.S. entry?	See Section D6
☐ Have you paid all court-ordered child support?	See Section D7
☐ Have you paid all your income taxes?	See Section D8
☐ Have you had drinking problems or been arrested for drunk driving?	See Section D9
☐ Have you been a drug addict or abused drugs?	See Section D10
☐ Do you believe in being married to more than one person at once?	See Section D11
☐ If you're male, did you register for the U.S. Selective Service on time?	See Section D12
☐ Have you deserted the U.S. military or evaded the draft or service by claiming to be a non-resident?	See Section D13
☐ Have you advocated Communist or totalitarian systems or attempted to overthrow the U.S. government?	See Section D14
☐ Have you done anything else that society disapproves of, such as committing a minor crime or adultery?	See Section D15

Recent Years of Good Moral Character May Not Be Enough

Although your main task is to prove that your moral character has been good for the required (usually five) years of permanent residence leading up to your citizenship application (I.N.A. § 316(a)(3), 8 U.S.C. § 1427(a)(3)), USCIS is allowed to consider your actions before this time period began. This is especially true if your earlier actions shed light on the type of person you are today (I.N.A. § 316(a)(3), 8 U.S.C. § 1427(a)(3)).

For example, if the USCIS officer suspects that you make a lifestyle out of drinking and brawling, then a disorderly conduct conviction from six years earlier could weigh into the final decision. On top of this, there are certain actions that no amount of time will cure—for example, USCIS will never allow a convicted murderer to become a citizen. Therefore, if you have any criminal or moral issues that arose prior to the last five years of your permanent residency (or fewer years if you're using an exception to apply early), consult an attorney to determine the effect on your citizenship application.

1. You Have a Criminal Record

If you have ever been prosecuted for criminal activity, you'll need to see an immigration attorney for a full check of your record and what it means in immigration law terms. Don't try to interpret what's a serious crime and what isn't.

To give you an idea of what your attorney will need to analyze, we provide a brief overview of the most serious crimes that will permanently bar you from citizenship (Subsection a, below) and of the various other crimes that will block or delay your qualifying for citizenship (Subsection b, below).

⚠ Crimes committed overseas count, too. See a lawyer about any criminal prosecution in your past—even if it occurred overseas. Note, USCIS will not deny citizenship to refugees and political asylees who were victims of inappropriate government prosecution—but talk to a lawyer anyway, just to be safe.

a. Crimes That Permanently Bar You From Citizenship

If you've ever been convicted of one of the following, you are permanently denied U.S. citizenship:

- murder, or
- an aggravated felony (if the conviction was after November 29, 1990).

These bars are automatic—that is, the USCIS officer reviewing your citizenship application will have no choice but to deny your citizenship. In addition, you'll probably be placed in deportation proceedings.

The USCIS's definition of aggravated felonies includes more than rape, sexual abuse of a minor, drug trafficking, firearm trafficking, racketeering, running a prostitution business, child pornography, and fraud of $10,000 or more. It also includes crimes that local and state courts sometimes classify as misdemeanors. For example, any crime of violence, or theft or burglary that resulted in a prison term of one year or more will be considered an aggravated felony.

> **EXAMPLE:** An immigrant who stole a car stereo was sentenced to six years in prison. The federal circuit court decided that this was an aggravated felony—a crime of violence, the court said,

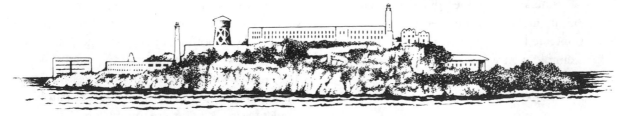

Alcatraz (Former Prison)—San Francisco, California

because the immigrant had pried the car door open first. (See *U.S. v. Alvarez-Martinez*, 286 F.3d 470, 2002 WL 538939 (7th Cir. 2002); 8 U.S.C. § 16.)

Even driving while under the influence of alcohol is sometimes considered a crime of violence by USCIS, particularly if it involves reckless or intentional behavior.

Helping to smuggle an alien into the United States is also considered an aggravated felony—unless it was a first offense to help your spouse, child, or parent. Note this exception doesn't cover smuggling grandparents, brothers, sisters, aunts, uncles, cousins, fiancés, and friends.

There are many tragic stories of immigrants innocently or negligently led into criminal acts that are later classified as aggravated felonies—for example, someone who befriends a drug dealer, buys a fake green card, or has sex with an underage girlfriend. Because this area is so complex, see a lawyer if you believe your criminal record will affect your citizenship quest.

b. Crimes That Temporarily Bar You From Citizenship

Some crimes make you only temporarily ineligible for citizenship. (See I.N.A. § 101(f), 8 U.S.C. § 1101(f).) If, after the date you committed the crime, you wait out the same number of years that you must have to meet your permanent residence requirement, you may be able to receive U.S. citizenship. We say "may" because USCIS can still consider your past actions in reviewing your application—and choose to deny your application. But at least you'll have a chance to prove that the good side of your character outweighs your past bad acts.

Here is a summary list of the crimes that make you temporarily ineligible for citizenship:

- You operated a commercial vice enterprise—for example, you were a prostitute, ran a call-girl ring, or sold pornography.
- You participated in illegal vice activities—for example, you hired a prostitute.

- You have been convicted of or admitted to a crime involving moral turpitude, such as fraud.
- You spent 180 days or more in jail or prison for any crime.
- You committed any crime related to illegal drugs other than a single offense involving 30 grams or less of marijuana.
- You have been convicted of two or more crimes, the combination of which got you a total prison sentence of five years or more.
- You get most of your income from illegal gambling or have been convicted of two or more gambling crimes.

If anything on your record remotely resembles an entry on the list above, see a lawyer. The lawyer can determine whether there's a problem and confirm how many years you should wait after the conviction date before you apply.

c. Other Crimes

If you've committed a crime that is not on any of the lists in the previous sections, you are not automatically barred from citizenship. But USCIS can still use its discretion to claim that your crimes demonstrate your lack of good moral character. USCIS considers such factors as whether anyone was injured, whether or not you cooperated with the police and the courts, and whether you were drinking or carrying an illegal weapon. As with all crimes, you should see an attorney to evaluate the situation.

2. You Haven't Completed Probation, Parole, or Similar Obligations

If, after being convicted of a crime, you are placed on probation or parole, you must successfully complete it before you can be approved for citizenship. (See 8 C.F.R. § 316.10(c)(1).) Your citizenship application will not be approved while you are on probation or parole—no matter how minor the crime. USCIS will either postpone a decision on your application until your probation or parole is completed or ask you to reapply later.

3. You Helped Someone Enter the U.S. Illegally

If USCIS finds out that you helped someone enter the United States illegally (often called "alien smuggling"), your application for citizenship will be denied—and if you smuggled the alien within five years of your last entry into the United States, you can be deported.

Alien smuggling doesn't just refer to what professional lawbreakers, sometimes called "coyotes," do in escorting someone across the U.S. border for a fee. It can also refer to someone who gives friendly assistance or encouragement to another—for example, by pretending a cousin is part of the family on a car trip back from Mexico, or by lending a green card to one's twin sister. Even if the friend or relative fails in the attempt to enter the United States, the people who tried to help will have a problem obtaining citizenship.

If you weren't convicted, how might USCIS find out that you helped someone enter the United States illegally? Apart from the fact that you'll be asked about this on the application form, USCIS may pick up other clues during your interview—for example, the USCIS officer may inquire about the immigration status of friends or family members.

Not all USCIS interviewers are nosy. In fact, USCIS interviewers often see cases where undocumented family members live in the same house as the applicant, and they let the issue pass. Also, USCIS has not shown any pattern of arresting family members whose undocumented status is revealed on citizenship applications (though in light of recent terrorist activities and the U.S. response, this could change). Again, as with all issues of moral character, see an immigration lawyer if in doubt.

4. You Lied to Obtain Immigration Benefits

If you lied to obtain an immigration benefit, you will not be granted U.S. citizenship. For example, if you pretended to have a job offer in order to show USCIS that you wouldn't go on welfare or pretended to qualify for amnesty as a farm laborer when you really worked in a bank, these false statements—if discovered—could ruin your chances for citizenship.

Because USCIS takes lying so seriously, it's better to be truthful about something you're ashamed about than to lie about it. Not all past lies will bar you from citizenship. After you've finished your required period of permanent residency, you may be able to overcome the problem with evidence of your recent good moral character. A lawyer can help and may also prevent you from losing your green card.

5. You Pretended to Be a U.S. Citizen or Voted Illegally

If you've told any government agency that you're a U.S. citizen, or if you have registered to vote or voted illegally in a federal, state, or local U.S. election, you are barred from U.S. citizenship. A noncitizen who votes in a federal election can also be prosecuted criminally. See 18 U.S.C. § 611. However, voting illegally will neither be considered a deportable offense nor a crime if the person's parents were or are U.S. citizens, the person permanently resided in the U.S. prior to age 16, and the person reasonably believed at the time of voting that he or she was a U.S. citizen. You can also be deported. (See I.N.A. § 237(a)(3)(D), (a)(6); 8 U.S.C. § 1227(a)(3)(D), (a)(6).)

This rule won't affect you if you told an employer or other private party that you were a citizen (although such lies could affect a determination as to your moral character or lead to criminal proceedings).

Beware of state "Motor Voter" registration. Think back to when you got your driver's license—many states offer you a voter registration form at the same time, without checking to see whether you're actually eligible to vote. If you filled out the voter registration form, you may have disqualified yourself from U.S. citizenship.

If you registered to vote or voted illegally and didn't realize at the time that you weren't allowed to vote, get a lawyer's help. If you don't fit the exception described above, your lawyer can check whether your state punishes only those people who knew they were voting illegally, rather than punishing those who voted through a misunderstanding of their rights. That will help with your citizenship application.

6. You Obtained Government Assistance Through Fraud or Within Five Years of Any U.S. Entry

If you ever lied in order to get or keep welfare or disability benefits—for example, by pretending that a boyfriend or girlfriend was not supporting you, or by hiding a job or other source of income—you can run into problems. There are two ways in which your fraudulent receipt of government benefits can hurt your citizenship application:

- It can destroy your showing of good moral character.
- You can be deported if it occurs within five years of your U.S. entry.

If a small-scale fraud was committed—for example, you took a trip while on welfare but didn't realize your benefits program prohibited traveling—you can sometimes clear your name for citizenship purposes by arranging to pay back amounts you shouldn't have received. If you wait until your citizenship application to deal with this, the USCIS officer will probably refuse to approve your application until you've paid back the money and obtained a letter of proof that you can send to USCIS.

Under a little-noticed provision of the immigration laws, becoming a "public charge"—that is, receiving need-based government assistance—within five years of entering the United States can make you deportable and therefore ineligible for citizenship. (See I.N.A. § 237(a)(5), 8 U.S.C. § 1227(a)(5).) In other words, you can be a green card holder for 20 years, leave the United States for a short vacation, then be at risk of deportation if you receive any government assistance during the next five years.

EXAMPLE 1: Jurgen has been a permanent resident since 1997. He worked repairing VCRs until 2004, when many consumers began buying new VCRs rather than repairing the broken ones, and so he ran out of customers. Jurgen has three children. In early 2005, he took a trip to see his parents in Scandinavia. He hoped they would help him out with some money, but they refused. Soon after Jurgen's return, he signed up for food stamps and other assistance. This makes Jurgen deportable—he should see an attorney before applying for citizenship.

Many citizenship manuals don't mention this—perhaps because USCIS rarely seems to invoke this part of the law. Also, many people can take advantage of an exception built into the law, stating that if the cause of needing the welfare arose after your last entry, you're safe from deportation.

7. You Haven't Paid Court-Ordered Child Support

If you have refused to pay court-ordered child support, you are barred from receiving U.S. citizenship and should consult with a lawyer before applying. The lawyer may be able to show that you didn't really "refuse" to pay child support, but simply couldn't pay for reasons beyond your control.

A second possibility is for the lawyer to help you prove to USCIS that the good side of your character outweighs the bad. In that case, however, you'll have to wait for the same amount of time that you are required to have been a permanent resident before applying for citizenship (five years for most people), and the clock won't start ticking until the date of your last failure to send a child support check.

8. You Haven't Paid Income Taxes

Unless you qualify under an exemption, you are required to pay U.S. income taxes. If you haven't paid them during any one of the required years of permanent residence leading up to your citizenship application, see a tax accountant or attorney before going any further. You'll need to pay any back taxes and clear your record with the Internal Revenue

Service (IRS) before USCIS will grant your citizenship. This is not in the immigration laws—it's a case of the IRS and USCIS working together to make sure you've paid your taxes. However, if you've actively committed tax evasion, that's a crime and a separate immigration law concern.

9. You Had a Drinking Problem

Your citizenship can be denied if you've been convicted of driving while under the influence of alcohol or drugs (commonly referred to as a "DUI" or "DWI") or if you are or have been a "habitual drunkard."

DUI is a crime, and the advice that we gave about crimes in Section D1, above, applies here too: Get a lawyer. The ordinary DUI case does not automatically bar someone from establishing good moral character, but since USCIS takes a very dim view of DUIs, you have to present strong evidence that you've reformed and have many positive character traits in order to convince USCIS that you deserve citizenship.

On top of this, a few additional circumstances can turn an ordinary DUI case into something far more serious. For example, in some parts of the United States, USCIS considers DUIs to be crimes of violence if committed recklessly or intentionally. In these situations, a DUI may escalate to an aggravated felony and become a permanent bar to citizenship.

It's not a crime to be a "habitual drunkard," but if USCIS decides that you've made a lifestyle of heavy drinking—for example, based on arrests for disorderly conduct or domestic violence, or by asking for a doctor's report—you will have to demonstrate that you've gotten over your drinking problem in order to qualify for citizenship.

If you've had drinking problems but have gotten over them, wait from the date of your last drink until the number of years you're required to have held permanent residence have passed to apply for citizenship. Also, be prepared to show USCIS that you took steps to address the problem, such as consulting with a doctor or successfully completing a treatment program.

10. You Abused Drugs

If you have abused or been addicted to illegal drugs at any time since coming to the United States, you are barred from U.S. citizenship and could be deported. You do not have to have been arrested or convicted to fall into this category. In the eyes of USCIS, trying an illegal drug more than once is abuse. This hasn't been named as a permanent bar to citizenship, but its temporary nature won't help you much if you're placed in deportation proceedings—so see a lawyer if you have a history of drug use or if you are addicted to drugs.

Of course, if you've been arrested for a drug crime, you've got a separate problem and should already be looking for a lawyer.

11. You Believe in Polygamy

In certain cultures and religions, polygamy—the practice of taking multiple husbands or wives—is considered acceptable and normal. However, it is illegal in every U.S. state, and if you have committed or believe in polygamy, you are barred from receiving U.S. citizenship.

Even if you have only one spouse now, USCIS will deny citizenship if it believes you intend to enter into additional marriages later. In other words, what you believe is as important as what you do. On the other hand, if you accidentally married a second person—for example, you incorrectly believed that your divorce was final when you remarried—you are not barred under this rule. See an attorney if you think USCIS might doubt your intentions, particularly if you come from a religion or culture in which polygamy is an accepted practice.

12. You Fail to Register With the Selective Service

If you're a man who lived in the U.S. or got your green card at any time between the ages of 18 and 26, you were expected to register with the U.S. Selective Service System. The Selective Service collects the names of young men who are available to be called up in a military draft. The only exception likely to help you is if your entire time in the United States between ages 18 and 26 was covered by an unexpired student, tourist, or diplomatic visa. Notice, however, that no exception is made for undocumented or illegal aliens, who are expected to register. Another, less widely applicable exception is made for men born between March 29, 1957, and December 31, 1959—they were never under any obligation to register. For more information, see the Selective Service website at www.sss.gov.

Registering for selective service doesn't mean that you have to have actually joined the military. However, like all men who already are U.S. citizens, you are expected to be ready to join if a large-scale war or similar emergency arises.

If you knew about the requirement and refused to register, USCIS can deny your citizenship. But if you didn't know about this requirement, you're not alone. In fact, the average American is surprised to find out that noncitizens are on call to serve in our military. If you haven't registered, and you're younger than 26, see Subsection a, below. If you're between 26 and 31, see Subsection b, below. If you're older than 31, see Subsection c, below.

a. You're Younger Than 26

If you didn't register for the Selective Service and you're not yet age 26, it's not too late—pick up the registration form at a U.S. post office, fill it out, and submit it.

b. You're Between 26 and 31

If you've passed age 26, it's too late for you to register for the Selective Service. Your chances of qualifying for U.S. citizenship depend on how many years have passed (after five years, you'll probably be okay) and how strict your local USCIS office is—they vary from sympathetic to unyielding. Nevertheless, many young men are able to show USCIS that

they had no idea that registering was expected of them, and therefore didn't "wilfully" fail to register, using a combination of:

- a Status Information Letter from the Selective Service System (Subsection i),
- your sworn declaration (Subsection ii), and
- where appropriate, sworn declarations from people who knew you (also discussed in Subsection ii).

i. Obtaining a Status Information Letter

A Status Information Letter from the Selective Service doesn't really help your case much—it simply states that you are over age and therefore no longer required to register—but USCIS won't look at the rest of your materials without this letter.

In order to request the Status Information Letter, you'll need to visit the Selective Service System website (www.sss.gov). Click "Registration Info," then click "Men Over the Age of Eligibility to Register" and look for the link to the "Request for Status Information Letter." You can also get the request form by calling 847-688-6888. (If you were born before March 29, 1957, the number you must call is 703-605-4047.) After you receive the Status Information Letter, send the original to USCIS with your citizenship application and keep a copy for your records.

ii. Using Sworn Declarations to Explain Your Failure to Register

Next, write a sworn statement explaining your failure to register. You'll find an example below. (Don't just copy the sample—insert facts that apply to your own life.)

Your sworn statement should offer reasons why you failed to learn about registration. If you attended high school in the United States—most U.S. high schools tell students about this requirement—explain why the information didn't prompt your registration. For example, you might have heard about the requirement but assumed it only applied to U.S. citizens. If possible, get letters from other people who knew you, such as a high school teacher, backing up your account of events.

Sample Sworn Statement

I, Jean-Paul Mercredi, hereby say and declare as follows:

1. I am a French citizen and lawful permanent resident of the United States, residing at 432 Lake Place, Detroit, MI, 12345.

2. I was born on March 4, 1974. I was approved for permanent residence on April 10, 1998, when I was 24 years old.

3. I didn't register for Selective Service because I didn't know I was expected to. When I was approved for permanent residence, neither the INS nor my lawyer said anything about my obligation to register—or if they did, I didn't understand it, because my English was rather weak then. Nor did I learn about the requirement independently.

4. I became a resident through marriage to a U.S. citizen. My wife did not know about the Selective Service requirement—she doesn't have any brothers, so registering for the draft is not something she has had to think about. Nor was Selective Service registration a topic of discussion among any of our friends. I have a few friends who have green cards, but they didn't say anything to me about this requirement—many of them are women or older than age 26, so they probably didn't know or remember.

5. Even when I first read about the Selective Service requirement in preparing my application for U.S. citizenship, I was surprised, thinking that someone would have contacted me if I was required to register. I was certainly never contacted by the U.S. military authorities or by anyone else.

6. I had no intention of avoiding my obligations, I was simply completely unaware that I was supposed to register for the Selective Service.

I swear, under penalty of perjury, that the contents of the foregoing statement are true and correct to the best of my knowledge.

Date: _March 12, 2006_

Signed: _Jean-Paul Mercredi_

⚠️ **You'll have trouble claiming ignorance of the registration requirement if …** If you got your green card through the amnesty program in the 1980s, or if you got your green card more recently, during or after the year 2001, you'll have a harder time claiming ignorance of Selective Service registration. In both cases, participants were alerted as to the registration obligation or were registered automatically.

📊 **When explaining your failure to register, include your sworn statement and any additional letters with your citizenship application.** Prepare these documents no matter how old you are now—even though USCIS is far more likely to deny your citizenship if only five years or fewer have passed since your failure to register.

c. You're Older Than 31

If you have passed the age of 31, it's a mathematical certainty that five years have passed since you were last required to register for Selective Service. And as you'll remember, it's the five years leading up to your citizenship application that are the most important in proving your good moral character. So, once these years have passed, even a knowing and willful failure to register for Selective Service is not an absolute bar to citizenship. You can overcome any remaining concerns are USCIS might have with other proof of your good moral character. However, if you want to be on the safe side, also provide documents showing that you didn't know about the Selective Service requirement, as described in Subsection B, above.

13. You Deserted or Avoided the U.S. Military During Wartime

If, during wartime, you deserted from the U.S. military, left the United States in order to evade the draft, or asked to be exempted from service based on being a noncitizen, you are permanently ineligible for U.S. citizenship. (See I.N.A. §§ 314, 315; 8 U.S.C. §§ 1425, 1426.) If you believe you might fit into this category, see an immigration lawyer before going any farther with your application. Vietnam War draft dodgers who received amnesty from President Jimmy Carter do not fall into this category.

14. You've Been a Communist, or Totalitarian, or Opposed the U.S. Government

If, during the ten years before you apply for citizenship, you were involved in or advocated certain political activities, you are automatically (though not permanently) barred from receiving U.S. citizenship. More specifically, if you've shown support for activities involving anarchism (you oppose rule by government or law), world communism, totalitarianism, the overthrow of the U.S. government, or violence against the officers or property of the U.S. government, whether in the United States or abroad, you face a serious problem getting citizenship. (After ten years have passed from your date of involvement, this bar no longer applies—though if you committed any crimes based on your beliefs, separate bars may apply. See I.N.A. § 313, 8 U.S.C. § 1424.)

There are exceptions—for example, you were too young to understand, your involvement was against your will or without your understanding of the group's true aims—but in general, you're facing an uphill battle if USCIS suspects you of support for, or involvement in, such a group.

If you know you may be suspected of such involvement, get the help of an immigration attorney before you apply for citizenship. The attorney will help you draft an affidavit explaining your membership and activities.

15. You've Done Something That Society Frowns Upon

If you've done something that a USCIS officer might consider "bad," even if it's not listed in the law or mentioned in this book, you can still be denied citizenship. This vague standard is not commonly used to deny citizenship, and USCIS officers rarely ask prying personal questions.

In general, living with someone outside of marriage, having a child out of wedlock or with a person other than your spouse, or engaging in homosexual relationships are not a basis for denying citizenship. So don't be fearful about your personal life just because conservative members of society might frown on your actions. But keep in mind that when your personal behavior harms others—for example incest, prostitution, or having sex with minors—USCIS is more likely to find bad moral character.

For example, one INS officer barred an applicant from citizenship for having an extramarital affair that destroyed an existing marriage. Another officer barred an applicant who sold liquor illegally in a restaurant.

In summary, you should primarily be concerned about antisocial behavior if a USCIS officer believes that your actions will harm others.

16. Showing Your Good Side

As your grandmother may have told you, everyone has some goodness inside of them. USCIS recognizes this, too. So, if you've done anything that you think a USCIS officer might take as a bad sign (and you've made sure the issue doesn't require a lawyer's help), get ready to show all your good deeds. Your goal is to show so many positive parts of your character that they outweigh the negative.

Here are some ideas to get you started:
- regular attendance at a church, temple, or mosque
- volunteer work
- caring for an ill or elderly friend or relative
- assisting with events at your child's school or with organized after-school activities, and
- winning community awards.

Gather written materials to prove your activities—for example, a copy of your award certificate or a newspaper article discussing your achievements. Ask friends and community contacts to help. Once they hear that you're applying for U.S. citizenship, you'll probably be surprised at their willingness to help. Show them a sample of the type of document you need (we provide one below) and ask them to make their letter personal to you, including your name, the dates you worked, volunteered, or attended services with the person, and anything else that you want USCIS to hear about.

Sample Good Moral Character Letter

Bayshore Elementary P.T.A.
222 Bayshore Drive
Coasttown, CA 12345

November 9, 2005

To Whom It May Concern:

I am the president of the Bayshore Elementary P.T.A. It is my pleasure to write this letter in support of Marta Rivera's application for U.S. citizenship.

I have known Marta for four years. Our children both attend Bayshore Elementary. Marta has regularly attended P.T.A. meetings and enthusiastically participated in some special projects.

For the past two years, Marta has helped organize the holiday play, including helping supervise rehearsals and designing costumes. Everyone was amazed by her fir tree and elf costumes. She has also regularly baked cookies for our fundraising bake sales.

We particularly appreciate Marta's contributions since she, like many parents, works during the day. She obviously cares about her children a great deal. I never fail to see her at parent-teacher conference nights. Her children are lovely, always well dressed and well behaved.

Very truly yours,

Pat Pennyroyal

Pat Pennyroyal
P.T.A. President

Once you've gathered these written materials, you should include copies of them with your citizenship application packet.

E. English Language Skills

To qualify for citizenship, you must have "an understanding of the English language, including an ability to read, write, and speak words in ordinary usage … ." (I.N.A. § 312(a)(1), 8 U.S.C. § 1423 (a)(1).) You'll need to demonstrate your English skills at your citizenship interview. To more fully address this topic, and to help you prepare for the exam, we've devoted a separate chapter to it—see Chapter 5. USCIS recognizes that age and physical disabilities can affect your ability to learn English, and permits various waivers of the English requirement, discussed below.

1. Waiving the English Requirement for Advanced Age

Two separate rules allow older people to avoid the English requirement. If you're older than age 50 and have lived in the United States as a green card holder for at least 20 years, you can have the entire citizenship interview conducted in your native language. (This is commonly known as the "50/20" waiver.) Your 20 years of residence do not need to have been continuous—if you've been away for short periods (fewer than six months at a time, to be safe), that's okay, so long as your total time living in the United States reaches 20 years.

The second rule—known as "55/15" waiver—applies as follows. If you're older than age 55 and have lived in the United States as a green card holder for at least 15 years, you can have the citizenship interview and exam conducted in your native language. Your 15 years do not need to have been continuous.

To avoid delays, make sure the interviewer knows in advance you are requesting a waiver and whether you need an interpreter. Mention this in your cover letter and write "50/20" or "55/15" in big red letters at the top of your application form. There will still be plenty to cover at your interview. In Chapter 8, we discuss what happens at the interview.

2. Waiving the English Requirement for Disability

If you have a physical or mental disability that prevents you from learning English—for example, an ailment that requires regular medication making you severely drowsy, a developmental disability, or deafness—you may qualify for a waiver of the English requirement. In such a case, you would be allowed to have the citizenship interview done in your native language.

You can't just request this waiver; your doctor must fill out a form explaining your disability and why it prevents you from learning English. We cover the precise procedures for requesting this waiver in Chapter 7.

Special Exam Waivers for Laotian Refugees

For a limited time, certain refugees from Laos were able to request that their naturalization interview be conducted in their native language and that they be permitted to take an easier form of the U.S. history and government exam (the same one offered to 65-year-old applicants, as described in Section 1, above).

The law permitting this was called the "Hmong Veterans' Naturalization Act of 2000." This law applied to Laotian refugees who fought in Laotian-based military units in support of the U.S. from 1961 to 1978. It also applied to their spouses—provided they were married when refugee status was sought—and to their widows—if the qualifying veteran died in Laos, Thailand, or Vietnam.

Unfortunately, the application period ended in 2003. However, Congress has been discussing renewing the law. Keep your eyes on the news, and on the legal updates posted on Nolo's website at www.nolo.com.

F. The U.S. History and Government Exam

In order to become a U.S. citizen, you must pass a test showing your "knowledge and understanding of the fundamentals of history, and of the principles and form of government, of the United States." (I.N.A. § 312(a)(2), 8 U.S.C. § 1423(a)(2).) As a practical matter, this means you'll have to memorize the answers to 100 potential questions. We give you all the possible questions, and help you prepare for them, in Chapter 6.

At your interview, the examiner will choose ten questions from the 100 to quiz you on. To pass, you'll need to answer six out of ten questions correctly.

There are some people who, for reasons of age or disability, will find it nearly impossible to learn the answers to these questions. See Section 1, below, for information on age-related waivers and Section 2, below, for information on disability-related waivers of the exam requirement.

Using Past Exam Results

Some years ago, it was possible to take the U.S. history and government exam in advance, at a local adult school or community organization. Applicants could take the exam many times and wait until they had passed to submit their citizenship application. After allegations of fraud, the INS ended this program in the late 1990s. You now must wait until your naturalization interview to take the exam.

The only exception is an applicant who got his or her green card through the legalization program (also called "1/1/82"). If you are one of these applicants and took the citizenship exam during Phase II of applying for your green card, you won't have to repeat the exam. If you have a certificate from the exam, include a copy with your application.

1. The 65/20 Exception for Applicants of Advanced Age

If you are older than age 65 and have lived in the United States as a permanent resident for at least 20 years (these don't need to be continuous years) you can take an easier version of the history and government exam. This is commonly referred to as the "65/20 exception." You will have to study only 25 questions. You'll be asked ten of the questions and will need to answer six correctly in order to pass. For more information on these questions, see Chapter 6. Your 20 years of U.S. residence don't need to have been continuous—if you've been out of the country for short periods (fewer than six months at a time, to be safe), that's okay—so long as your total time here reaches 20 years.

If you qualify for the easier exam, you automatically qualify to avoid the English language requirement as well. Alert USCIS in advance as to which waivers you are claiming in your cover letter. Also write "65/20" in large red numbers at the top of your application form.

2. Waiving the History and Government Exam for Disability

If you have a physical or mental disability that prevents you from learning the required concepts of U.S. history and government, you may qualify for a waiver. As we explained for people seeking to avoid the English requirement, you'll need to have your doctor fill out a form explaining exactly what your disability is and why it prevents you from learning concepts of U.S. civics and government.

We cover the precise procedures for requesting a disability waiver in Chapter 7. This waiver may also qualify you to conduct the citizenship interview in your native language.

Table Summarizing Available Language and U.S. History Waivers

If you are:	USCIS can:	To request the waiver:
Older than age 50, with 20 years permanent residence	Allow you to take the citizenship test and interview in your own language	Alert USCIS in your cover letter and write "50/20" on top of your Form N-400
Older than age 55, with 15 years permanent residence	Allow you to take the citizenship test and interview in your own language	Alert USCIS in your cover letter and write "55/15" on top of Form N-400
Older than age 65, with 20 years permanent residence	Allow you to take a modified version of the citizenship test, with fewer possible questions; and allow you to take the test and interview in your own language	Alert USCIS in your cover letter and write "65/20" on top of Form N-400.
Physically or mentally disabled	Make special accommodations for your interview, and/or allow you to avoid the citizenship test and/or have the interview done in your own language	Mention any needed accommodations in your cover letter. Fill out the appropriate box(es) on the English language or history exam, and have your doctor fill out Form N-648.

G. Loyalty to the U.S.

Several questions on the citizenship application reflect USCIS rules requiring that you be "attached" to the principles of the Constitution and be "favorably disposed to the good order and happiness" of the United States. (8 C.F.R. § 316.11(a).) This means that you should:

- not be hostile to the U.S. form of government
- believe in representative democracy
- believe in the ideals of liberty and equality among people that are described in the Bill of Rights portion of the Constitution, and
- believe that political change should only be carried out only in a peaceful manner and in accordance with the law.

You can, however, still have a sentimental fondness for your home country.

You'll also be asked, on the application, whether you're willing to take the Oath of Allegiance (shown below) to the United States during the "swearing-in" ceremony that formally makes you a citizen. In addition, you'll be asked whether you're willing to serve in the U.S. armed forces (in a combat or noncombat role) or to perform "work of national importance under civilian direction when required by the law."

It's best if you can simply answer "yes" to all of these questions. However, if you have legitimate concerns over taking the Oath of Allegiance or serving in the U.S. military, review the sections below.

The Great Seal of the United States

The Oath of Allegiance

I hereby declare, on oath,

that I absolutely and entirely renounce and abjure all allegiance and fidelity to any foreign prince, potentate, state or sovereignty, of whom or which I have heretofore been a subject or citizen;

that I will support and defend the Constitution and the laws of the United States against all enemies, foreign and domestic;

that I will bear true faith and allegiance to the same;

that I will bear arms on behalf of the United States when required by the law; and

that I take this obligation freely, without any mental reservation or purpose of evasion, so help me God.

1. Your Beliefs Forbid Taking Oaths

Some groups, most notably the Quakers and Jehovah's Witnesses, forbid swearing oaths. If you belong to such a group, you may make a modified version of the Oath of Allegiance, substituting the words "and solemnly affirm" for the words "on oath" and leaving out the words "so help me God." For more on the swearing-in ceremony, see Chapter 11.

If you wish to modify the oath, advise USCIS when you submit your citizenship application and include a letter from your pastor or religious leader indicating your religious affiliation.

2. Your Beliefs Forbid Serving in the Military

If your religious beliefs forbid you to carry or use weapons—that is, you are a "conscientious objector" —you can still become a U.S. citizen. You do not have to be a member of a Christian religion, nor do you have to believe in God or a supreme being. However, you will need to show USCIS that:

- you are opposed to all military service
- you hold this objection based on religious principles, and
- you hold these beliefs deeply and sincerely.

As a practical matter, however, USCIS is most willing to recognize conscientious objectors who are formal members of religious communities with a tradition of pacifism, such as Buddhists, Quakers, and Mennonites.

Because you will answer "no" to certain questions on the citizenship application, you must send USCIS a sworn declaration explaining your beliefs. In your declaration, you should request permission to take a modified Oath of Allegiance. If your beliefs forbid you only to fight, then at your swearing-in ceremony, you will be allowed to leave out the words "I will bear arms on behalf of the United States when required by law."

If you can show USCIS that your beliefs also forbid you to serve in any military capacity, you'll also be able to leave out the words "I will perform noncombatant services in the Armed Forces of the United States when required by law." For more on the swearing-in ceremony, see Chapter 11.

Explain your conscientious objector status in your application cover letter and include your sworn statement with your citizenship application packet.

For more information and support, contact the Center on Conscience & War (CCW), at www.nisbco.org, or 800-379-2679.

H. Overview: Are You Ready to Apply?

Use the list of questions below to confirm your citizenship eligibility. Check the box if your answer is "yes." For any unchecked boxes, review the appropriate section of this chapter and familiarize yourself with the rules. Once you are certain of your eligibility—that is, you have checked all the boxes—you're ready to prepare and submit your application.

Citizenship Eligibility Checklist

☐ Have you had valid lawful permanent U.S. residence for the last five years (or less if you fall into an exception)? (See Section A.)

☐ Have you spent at least half of your required permanent residence period inside the United States (unless you qualify for an exception)? (See Section B1.)

☐ Has your U.S. stay been continuous—that is, unbroken by trips of six months or longer? (See Section B2.)

☐ Have you lived for at least three months in the state or USCIS district where you plan to submit your citizenship application? (See Section B3.)

☐ Are you at least 18 years of age? (See Section C.)

☐ Have you behaved in a way that shows your good moral character during your required years of permanent residence? (See Section D.)

☐ Can you speak, read, and write English (unless you fall into a group that can request a waiver of this requirement)? (See Section E.)

☐ Can you pass an exam in U.S. history and government (unless you fall into a group that can request a waiver of this requirement)? (See Section F.)

☐ Are you attached to the principles of the U.S. Constitution and willing to swear loyalty to the United States? (See Section G.)

■

Preparing and Submitting Your Application

You'll find that applying for U.S. citizenship is far easier than getting your green card. The application process involves only one form and very few accompanying materials. As with any application to USCIS, however, the form can be deceptive—a seemingly innocent question can be dangerously significant. And the USCIS bureaucracy is as frustrating as it has ever been—delays are normal and lost applications are common.

This chapter will show you how to get through the application process with the least possible frustration and difficulty. We explain to you:

- what goes into your application packet (see Section A)
- what to tell USCIS in your cover letter (see Section B)
- how to fill out Form N-400 (see Section C), and
- how to submit the application (see Section D).

Some time after submitting your citizenship application, you will be notified when to appear for a personal interview at your local USCIS office. During that interview, a USCIS officer will review your application and approve or deny your citizenship. However, you're likely to wait a long time for this notification of your interview. What to do during this waiting period and during the interview itself are explained in Chapters 4 and 8, respectively.

A. What You'll Put in Your Application Packet

The most important part of your citizenship application is Form N-400. However, along with this form you'll need to prepare and assemble a few other items, listed below and summarized within the checklist in Section D1.

Your citizenship application packet will need to include the following:

- cover letter (see Section B, below)
- Form N-400 (see Section C, below)
- fee payment (currently $320 for the application plus $70 for fingerprints, but check for current fees at the USCIS website (www.uscis.gov)). U.S. military personnel don't have to pay the

fees. If you're age 75 or older, you don't have to be fingerprinted, and don't have to pay the fingerprinting fee. To pay the fees, a personal check is best, because after it's cashed the USCIS stamp on the back can be used to trace your application if it's lost. A money order is okay, but harder to trace. Do not send cash. Make checks or money orders payable to USCIS. If you're living overseas, don't send the $50 for fingerprints—you can have your fingerprints done at a local U.S. consulate

- two photos, passport style. It's too difficult to take a snapshot that meets USCIS's specifications, so find a shop that does passport photos. Write your name and your A-number (from your green card) on the back of each photo, in pencil, and
- a photocopy of your green card (both sides of the card, on two sheets of regular 8½-by-11-inch paper). If your card has expired or you've lost it, see "How to Renew or Replace a Green Card," below.

If you plan to take advantage of one of the various exceptions described in Chapter 2, you may also need to include one or more of the following:

- If you've been married to a U.S. citizen for three years and you're applying after only three years of permanent residence on this basis, furnish proof of your eligibility for this exception—for example, copies of your spouse's citizenship certificate, your marriage certificate, proof that your spouse's previous marriages ended legally (certificate of death, divorce, or annulment), and copies of your tax returns for the last three years, as well as recent credit card bills in both your names and copies of your joint home title or rental receipts to show that you live together or share financial matters.
- If you've served in the U.S. military, furnish Form N-426, Request for Certification of Military or Naval Service, and Form G-325B, Biographic Information. Both of these forms are included in Appendix C. When completing these forms, follow USCIS's instructions, provided on the forms and at the USCIS website (www.uscis.gov). Consult a lawyer if you need more help.

- If you are disabled and are asking for a waiver of the English and/or U.S. history and government exam requirements, furnish Form N-648, filled out by your doctor (see Chapter 7).
- Include any other items applicable to you as recommended elsewhere in this book and denoted by the application reminder icons—for example, a sworn explanatory statement if you're a male who forgot to register for the Selective Service, or a letter from your church if you're a Jehovah's Witness who can't swear the full Oath of Allegiance.

⚠️ **Always make your photocopies on one-sided, 8½-by-11-inch paper.** Don't create exact copies of small documents by making a copy on normal paper and cutting out the image—creating, for example, a tiny photocopied green card. The government doesn't appreciate mini-copies, which it will have to recopy onto a full-size sheet of paper. By the same token, 8½-by-11-inch paper (or larger) doesn't fit well into the government's files—if you have oversized documents, reduce them to 8½-by-11, if possible.

How to Renew or Replace a Green Card

It's possible your green card has expired or been lost. That doesn't mean that you've lost your permanent residence, but it's best to get a new green card before applying for U.S. citizenship. A few USCIS offices will allow you to apply without your green card, but most are not so accommodating. In any case, the law requires you to carry your green card with you at all times until you're a citizen. In these security-conscious times, it's likely that you'll be asked for your card by USCIS, the police, or airport authorities.

To renew or replace your green card, obtain Form I-90 from the USCIS website or by calling 800-870-3676. Follow instructions that come with the form.

💡 **Report stolen green cards to the police.** There is a hot market for illegal green cards. If yours is stolen, file a police report immediately. You may not get your card back, but when you apply for a replacement card, the police report will demonstrate your diligence and reduce suspicions regarding the loss.

B. Preparing Your Cover Letter

Including a cover letter with your citizenship application is not required, but it's a good idea. You can use the letter to list what's in your application, making it easier for USCIS to understand and organize your file. And the cover letter reminds you to include everything. The cover letter is also a good place to advise USCIS of any special circumstances in your case—for example, that you're claiming a right to apply early based on an exception, or that you're requesting a waiver of the exam requirements based on age or disability.

The cover letter provided below covers the basic circumstances that apply to all applicants. Use it as a starting point, and if you determine that special circumstances exist in your case, mention these in the letter as well.

💡 **You can't over-advise USCIS.** Even with a cover letter, USCIS frequently fails to notice important circumstances in applicants' cases—and therefore may not be adequately prepared for your interview. For example, people who've asked to take the interview in

Grand Canyon—Arizona

their own language often find that USCIS didn't notice, and didn't arrange for an interpreter. That's why it's also important to follow any instructions we've given you in this book about writing things in red pen on the top of the Form N-400. Bolding or highlighting important parts of your cover letter is also a good idea.

Cover Letter Template

[*Your address*]

[*Today's date*]

Re: A-number: [*Your eight-digit Alien number, from your green card*]

Application for Naturalization

[*Address of USCIS Service Center; see Section D4, below, for the one serving your geographic region.*]

Dear Sir or Madam:

Enclosed please find my application for naturalization, including the following items:

- Form N-400

- Application and fingerprint fees, totaling $_____ [*or your request for a fee waiver*]

- Two photos

- A photocopy of my green card

- [*Any other needed documents as described elsewhere in this book*].

In addition, please note [*Describe any special circumstances in your case, any accommodations that you need for disability, or any waivers of the English language, U.S. history and government exam, or oath-taking requirements that you're claiming based on age or disability. See Chapter 7 for details*].

Thank you for your attention to this matter.

Very truly yours,

[*sign your name*]
[*print your name*]

C. Filling Out USCIS Form N-400

Form N-400 is the central and most important form that you will fill out in order to apply for U.S. citizenship. Everyone applying for citizenship through the naturalization process described in this book must fill out Form N-400. The form collects basic biographical information about you and asks questions to make sure that you meet all the citizenship eligibility requirements (discussed in Chapter 2).

Form N-400, pictured blow, is available as a tear-out in Appendix C, by telephone at 800-870-3676, and on USCIS's website (including a version that—although it can be filled out on the computer—can't be submitted online). You can print out or photocopy the official version for your use.

Before you fill out the form, read the general tips in Section C1, below. Then, once you've got a copy of Form N-400 in hand, follow the line-by-line instructions in Section C2 on how to fill it out.

1. Tips on Filling Out USCIS Forms

How clearly and carefully you prepare your paperwork can affect how your application is judged. This doesn't mean you have to hire someone to do it professionally—USCIS receives plenty of handwritten applications. But following these instructions will avoid confusion and make your application stand out.

a. Typing or Ink?

This isn't the time to express your individuality with purple ink. Complete the form on a computer, as described below, or use a typewriter. If you cannot use a computer or typewriter, prepare it by hand, using black ink.

You can download Form N-400 and complete it on your computer, using Adobe Acrobat. (If you don't have Adobe Acrobat, download a free copy from www.adobe.com.) You can download Form N-400 at the USCIS website (www.uscis.gov). Click

"Immigration Forms, Fees and Fingerprints," then click "Forms and Fees." Scroll down and click "Form N-400." You'll find instructions and links for both the fillable and the nonfillable versions of the form. After you fill out the form you can print it, but you cannot save the data. So, don't turn off until you've printed the form properly. Otherwise you'll have to start all over again at your next session.

b. Inapplicable Questions

If you know that a question on Form N-400 doesn't fit your situation, write "N/A" (not applicable) or "none" rather than leaving the space blank. If you're not sure how or whether to answer a question, contact an attorney.

c. Tell the Truth

Lying to USCIS can get you in bigger trouble than the problem you are lying about. When a USCIS officer discovers that you've lied, he or she will not only become angry, but you might have your citizenship application denied on moral character grounds, no matter how minor the lie. Even if undetected at your interview, a lie can result in your citizenship being revoked if USCIS finds out about it later—even many years later.

If you are torn between hiding and disclosing information on the form, now is the time to see a lawyer. An attorney can advise you how to complete the form honestly and protect your interests.

d. Be Consistent With Previous USCIS Applications

Pull out other applications or paperwork that you've submitted to USCIS and double check that the information you're providing now matches what you've stated in previous applications. Failure to do this could lead to trouble.

U.S. Department of Justice
Immigration and Naturalization Service

OMB No. 1115-0009
Application for Naturalization

Print clearly or type your answers using CAPITAL letters. Failure to print clearly may delay your application. Use black or blue ink.

Part 1. Your Name *(The Person Applying for Naturalization)*

Write your INS "A"- number here:

A _ _ _ _ _ _ _ _ _

A. Your current legal name.

Family Name *(Last Name)*

FOR INS USE ONLY

Given Name *(First Name)*   Full Middle Name *(If applicable)*

Bar Code   Date Stamp

B. Your name **exactly** as it appears on your Permanent Resident Card.

Family Name *(Last Name)*

Given Name *(First Name)*   Full Middle Name *(If applicable)*

Remarks

you have ever used other names, provide them below.

e *(Last Name)*   Given Name *(First Nam*

Form 400, Application for Naturalization

EXAMPLE: When Sarita applied for her green card in 1995, she was 17 and had a juvenile conviction for shoplifting. She mentioned the conviction on her green card application, but since USCIS doesn't ordinarily count juvenile arrests against applicants, Sarita got her green card. After becoming an adult, Sarita's juvenile record was sealed, and she figured the matter was far behind her. On Sarita's citizenship application, she answers "no" to the questions about whether she'd ever been arrested or convicted for a crime. The USCIS officer notices that this doesn't match the information on her green card application and because of her "lie," he denies Sarita's citizenship application on the grounds that she lacks good moral character. Sarita must wait for her full period of required permanent residence (in her case, five years) to rebuild her moral character before reapplying.

You can request a complete copy of your immigration file from USCIS. If you've misplaced copies of your previous immigration applications, you can get your file by downloading Form G-639 from the USCIS website or calling 800-870-3676. Send the completed form to your local USCIS District Office. (You can locate the address for your local office at the USCIS website.)

Of course, if you've found a harmless error in a previous application—such as a misspelled name or a wrong address—don't feel you have to stick to it. Insert the correct information on your citizenship application, but be prepared to explain the error and provide evidence of the true situation.

e. Use Extra Pages If Needed

In a few places on Form N-400, you may need more space for your response. In that case, attach a separate piece of paper and write "Please see attachment" in the appropriate space on the form. At the top of each attachment page, print your name, your A-number, and the words "Attachment to Form N-400."

Then indicate which question(s) from which part(s) of the form you're answering. If you need more than one attachment page, add page numbers to them as well.

2. Line-by-Line Instructions for Form N-400

To follow instructions in this section, you'll need to have a copy of Form N-400 in front of you. (Tear or copy it from Appendix C or get a copy from USCIS.) Below, we'll go through the form, question by question.

Part 1. Your Name

Question A. Your current legal name. Enter your full name. If your name has changed during your life— for example, because of adoption, marriage, or a court-ordered name change—include legal documentation as proof.

Question B. Your name exactly as it appears on your Permanent Resident Card. This question serves to match your application to your green card, so copy your name exactly as it appears on your green card, even if there are mistakes or your name has or will be changed.

Question C. If you have ever used other names, provide them below. Here you should provide alternate versions of your name as well as names by which you've been commonly known. For example, if your legal name is Alexander but your nickname is Sasha and it appears on some of personal records and documents, mention Sasha on this part of the application. If, however, only your mother or a few friends affectionately call you Sasha, then you don't need to enter it here. If you aren't sure, go ahead and include the nickname or alternate name, to be safe.

Question D. Name change. If you've wanted to change your name, this may be your chance. You can legally change it without any extra court procedures by simply filling in your chosen new name on the form. However, there's one catch. This service is available only at USCIS offices where the swearing-in ceremonies are held in a courtroom, presided over by a judge, not a USCIS officer. Contact your local USCIS office and ask if a judge performs the ceremony, or wait until your USCIS interview and ask the officer who will preside. If you're in luck, the officer will have you fill out a form called a Petition for Name Change during your interview.

For information on changing your name in California, see *How to Change Your Name in California*, by Lisa Sedano and Emily Doskow (Nolo).

The judge will not approve your name change if:

- You changed your name for fraudulent reasons, such as to escape capture for a crime or to avoid paying a debt.
- Your new name interferes with someone else's right to a name, particularly a famous person, such as Bill Clinton or Cher, or of a company, such as Charles Schwab.
- Your name is intentionally confusing, such as "P.O. Box 2000" or "Boeing Jet."
- Your name is threatening, obscene or likely to incite violence. "Beat U. Up," for example, is not likely to be allowed.

Part 2. Information About Your Eligibility

Check the box indicating the number of years of permanent residency you are required to have completed. Most people check box A (five years of permanent residence). However, some applicants (for example, spouses of U.S. citizens or people in military service) will check a different box indicating they qualify for an exception to the five-year rule. (These applicants must remember to provide proof that they fit in this alternative category.)

Refugees and those who obtained political asylum should check the first box (five years of permanent residence). Although they are permitted to credit some of their years as refugees or asylees toward the five-year requirement, they aren't exempt from the requirement itself, as discussed in Chapter 2, Section A3.

Part 3. Information About You

Most of this section is self-explanatory, but we'll discuss certain questions that may not be.

For Question C, you can find the date you became a permanent resident on your green card. On the old-style green cards, the date begins with the year—so, for example, 870723 would be July 23, 1987.

For Question F, USCIS wants to know whether your parents are U.S. citizens in the event they transmitted their citizenship to you. They may have done this automatically, but it depends on a variety of factors, such as your date of birth, how long they lived in the United States, and whether one or both of them were citizens. For more information on the complex rules surrounding transmission of citizenship, see Nolo's Legal Encyclopedia, online at www.nolo.com.

Date of Residency

Old-Style Green Card (Front)   **Old-Style Green Card (Back)**

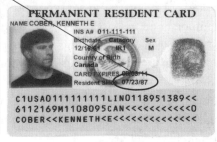

New-Style Green Card (Front)

In Questions H and I, you have an opportunity to alert USCIS as to any physical or mental disabilities. USCIS wants to know two things: (1) whether you're seeking a reduction or waiver of the English language and/or U.S. history and government exam requirements because of your disability, and (2) whether there's anything USCIS can do to make your interview more comfortable, such as ensuring wheelchair access or providing a sign language interpreter. It's okay to say yes to both. Chapter 7 explains what it takes to qualify for a disability waiver or accommodation and what documents you'll need to add to your application.

In fact, there's a third issue regarding your disability that Form N-400 fails to address. Applicants whose conditions are particularly severe may, even after being approved for citizenship, be unable to understand or repeat the Oath of Allegiance that actually makes them a citizen. But, the applicant won't automatically be allowed to skip this oath—a separate waiver of the oath requirement must first be requested. USCIS suggests that you use the space under this question to request this waiver. (Alternately, the request can be made in the cover letter or in a separate statement.)

USCIS will conduct the interview in English unless you qualify to avoid the exam requirements based on disability or age.

Part 4. Addresses and Telephone Numbers

Section A. Enter your current home address. If you do not want to receive mail there, indicate where to send mail in the next section.

Section B. Care of. Fill in this section only if you want someone else to receive your mail for you or you'd prefer that it be sent to a post office box or temporary address. (Even if you complete this section, you must enter your home address in Section A.)

Section C. This section asks for your phone numbers and email address. If you don't have a telephone or email address, answer "none." Alternately, you could use a friend or neighbor's phone number—USCIS is unlikely to call you.

Part 5. Information for Criminal Records Search

Fill in this information precisely and honestly. If you don't believe you fit into any of the categories, either choose one that is close or check "unknown" or "other." Under "Race," people of Latin American or Hispanic background ordinarily check "white." If you have a criminal history, you'll have a hard time hiding the truth—USCIS separately checks your fingerprints. If you are concerned about what USCIS may turn up in its check of your records, consult a lawyer.

Part 6. Information About Your Residence and Employment

Here, you must provide information about where you worked and lived for the last five years. If you can't remember an exact address from years past, enter as much information as you can remember.

If you had periods of unemployment, unpaid work, self-employment, or taking care of home or children, list these too. (Be specific—don't just write "none" in the employer box.) Include time spent working here illegally before you got your green card, if any (but make sure that it matches the information on your green card application forms).

Part 7. Time Outside the United States

As discussed in Chapter 2, Section B, you'll need to prove that you spent the required minimum amount of time in the United States in the years before your citizenship application and that your visits outside the United States didn't last too long.

For Question C, copy the information from the box you filled out in Chapter 2, Section B, under "Tallying Your Time in and out of the United States." If you cannot determine the information, put down as much as you can. For example, some people may write in the space (or on an attachment page) something like, "I crossed the border into Mexico to spend time with my mother approximately once a month for the last five years. Most of my visits were three days long, except for visits at Christmas, which usually lasted one week."

Part 8. Information About Your Marital History

Most of the questions about your marital history are self-explanatory. However, the first question in Question G may confuse you: It asks "How many times has your current spouse been married?" Many applicants wonder whether their current marriage counts in adding these up. The answer is yes: If, for example, your spouse has been married once before, you'll need to answer "two" here. (This makes sense when you realize that, if you didn't add your current marriage to the count, anyone whose spouse had not been married before would have to answer "zero.")

Information about marriages may not be relevant to all citizenship applications, but USCIS prefers to gather a wide range of information and decide what to do with it later. You may have one of three concerns:

- What happens if you've divorced the person who was the basis for getting your green card?
- What happens if you reveal that your spouse is living in the United States illegally?
- Why does USCIS need to know about your and your spouse's previous marriages?

Divorce. Some people worry that if they got their green card through marriage, but have since divorced, they won't qualify for citizenship. As long as your marriage wasn't a sham (meaning the whole purpose of the marriage was for you to get a green card), your divorce should not pose an obstacle to citizenship. However, USCIS may ask some additional questions to double check that your marriage wasn't a sham.

To be ready for these questions, review the material in Chapter 1, Section A1.

Undocumented spouses. Another concern for applicants is listing a spouse who has no legal status in the United States. As you can see on the form, question E3 specifically asks for your spouse's immigration status. If your spouse has no status at all, you can simply write "alien" in the box for question E3. If you have filed applications with the INS or USCIS to help your spouse immigrate, then you can write "pending" in the box (meaning that your spouse is awaiting his or her green card or other status). Historically, USCIS has not used this information to try to track down spouses living here illegally. The USCIS officer may, however, question you as to whether you helped smuggle your spouse into the country—see Chapter 8 for details.

Previous marriages. One of the main reasons that USCIS asks about previous marriages is to make sure that you aren't married to more than one person and that your current marriage is valid. Some people discover that their or their spouse's divorce wasn't legally final until after their current marriage took place—or even that they are married to two people at the same time.

Being intentionally married to more than one person is "polygamy," which USCIS considers as a sign of bad moral character. Even if the double marriage was an accident, it can create a problem if you got your green card as a result of your recent marriage. Applying for citizenship will give USCIS a chance to discover this problem and could result in the loss of your green card. If you find yourself in one of these situations, see a lawyer.

Part 9. Information About Your Children

As indicated in the N-400 instructions, you must list *all* of your children, whether they are:

- alive, missing, or dead
- born in other countries or in the United States
- younger or older than 18 years
- married or unmarried
- living with you or elsewhere
- stepsons or stepdaughters not legally adopted, or
- born out of wedlock.

Carefully comply with this instruction, as it may help one of your children immigrate to the United States later. If you fail to mention a child on your citizenship application, then come back later with a petition to immigrate that child, USCIS may suspect that you're just trying to help someone else's child immigrate.

Part 10. Additional Questions

These questions relate to your eligibility for citizenship, focusing in particular on your moral character and the amount of time you've lived in the United States. (To review eligibility requirements, see Chapter 2.)

Notice that in Part D, the questions regarding your criminal history are very broad—so broad that you'll even need to disclose any traffic tickets that you've received (in Question 16), although traffic stops or tickets ordinarily will not disqualify you from citizenship. (Don't worry about parking tickets—it's the incidents that happened while you were behind the wheel that USCIS is worried about. If your answer to any of the questions is "yes" (with the exception of Questions B, G, and H, discussed below), there's a risk that your application could be denied. See a lawyer before going further.

Don't guess! If you aren't sure how to answer one of these questions, see a lawyer. For example, if a department store once accused you of shoplifting and you went to court, but you don't remember whether you were convicted or not, since you didn't actually serve any jail time, a lawyer could help clarify matters.

Incorrect answers on this set of questions can have devastating consequences, including denial of citizenship or deportation.

Question B, Affiliations. Don't fear listing your membership in community organizations such as a social club, church group, P.T.A., volunteer corps, or other volunteer group. These memberships demonstrate you have good moral character. Not so, if you belong to a group that advocates world communism, violence, terrorism, or other perceived dangers to the United States, or if you were involved with Nazi activities in Germany. If you belong to a controversial group, consult with a lawyer before going further. See Chapter 2, Section D14, for more on the effects of such group memberships on your citizenship eligibility.

Question G. Selective Service. Here, you must indicate whether you are a male who was living in the U.S. or got your green card before or between the ages of 18 and 26. If you are, you were probably required to register for Selective Service, a list kept in preparation for a U.S. military draft. See the full discussion of this requirement in Chapter 2, Section D12, and on the Selective Service website at www.sss.gov. If you answer "yes" here, you must either register with the Selective Service now (which you can only do if you're younger than age 26) or attach a statement explaining why you didn't register. We provide a sample statement in Chapter 2.

Mount Rushmore—South Dakota

Question H. Oath Requirements. Here, you must show that you're loyal to the United States and will fight for it if necessary.

If you are a conscientious objector, meaning that for religious or moral reasons you refuse to take up weapons or join in a war, answer "no" to Question H.37, which asks whether you'll bear arms for the United States. If your beliefs would prohibit you from providing any support to a war effort, answer "no" to Question H.38, which asks whether you're willing to provide noncombatant services. (As covered in Chapter 2, Section G, you'll need to attach proof of your conscientious objector status and ask to take a modified oath of allegiance.)

If you're a member of a religion that prohibits taking any sort of oath (for example, the Quakers and the Jehovah's Witnesses fall into this category), answer "no" to Question H.36—but you must provide a letter from your church or other religious body confirming your membership. (Include this letter when you send in your citizenship application.)

Part 11. Your Signature

If possible, sign your name in cursive, not printed letters. Cursive means a flowing style, usually slanted to the right, where the letters are connected: it looks like this: *Vida Karalis*, rather than this; Vida Karalis.

If you're disabled and can't sign your own name (for example, because your hands don't work, or because of cognitive difficulties), you have two choices. You can either mark an "X" in place of your signature, or your legal guardian can sign for you. (After the signature, guardians should put in parentheses "signed by [*guardian's name*], designated representative.")

Part 12. Signature of Person Who Prepared This Application for You

If a lawyer, paralegal, or other preparer (including the "designated representative" of a disabled person) completes this form for you, that person must sign this section. If you completed the form on your own, however, or if you received some advice or assistance from a friend, neither you nor your friend need to complete this section.

Parts 13 and 14. Signature and Oath

You won't fill these out until your interview. Look again at instructions under Part 11, above: The officer may require you to sign your name in cursive. If you're not used to writing in cursive, practice this until you can do it smoothly.

D. Submitting the Application

After you've filled out your Form N-400, obtained your photos and assembled the materials described in Section A, you're almost ready to send your application.

Here are some final suggestions:

- See our suggestions in Section D1, below, to ensure you have included everything in your application packet. Forgetting something probably won't disqualify you from citizenship, but it could delay the process. Double check the USCIS website to make sure the fees haven't gone up.
- Take precautions against your application being lost, as discussed in Section D3, below.
- Be careful about where you mail your application—not all USCIS offices are authorized to accept citizenship applications. Don't waste your time trying to walk it in to the USCIS office in your city. You'll need to mail it to the USCIS Service Center listed in Section D4, below—and Service Centers never take walk-ins.

⚠️ **Make sure you're not applying too early.** If you haven't already done so, read Chapter 2, Section A, to determine when you are eligible to file your citizenship application. Most applicants must wait four years and 275 days (five years minus 90 days) from when they were granted lawful permanent residency, but there are some exceptions (as discussed in Chapter 2). Calculate the days to avoid filing early. If you submit your application early—even one day too early—USCIS will send it back—sometimes waiting weeks or months before doing so.

1. Using the Checklist for Citizenship Packet

Use the checklist below when preparing your application. Attach a copy to the file folder or envelope in which you're collecting the various items, and mark off each box as you add the item. That way, you'll ensure that nothing is left out.

Checklist for Citizenship Packet

☐ cover letter

☐ Form N-400

☐ application fee (unless you're in the U.S. military or have requested a fee waiver)

☐ two photos, passport style

☐ photocopy of your green card

☐ if you're applying earlier than five years on the basis of an exception, proof that you're eligible

☐ if you've been in the U.S. military, Form N-426, Request for Certification of Military or Naval Service, and Form G-325B, Biographic Information

☐ if you're requesting a waiver of the testing requirements based on disability, Form N-648, filled out by your doctor, and

☐ any other items applicable to you as recommended elsewhere in this book.

---

2. Asking for a Fee Waiver If You're Receiving Government Benefits

No question about it, applying for citizenship is expensive: $320 for the application and $70 for fingerprints. If your income is below the federally established Poverty Guidelines and you can't come up with this amount, USCIS offers an alternative: You can make a written request to be excused from paying the fee (a "fee waiver").

The Poverty Guidelines are updated annually. For the most recent version, go to the U.S. Department of Health and Human Services' website at http://aspe.hhs.gov/poverty/poverty.shtml.

There is nothing automatic about which cases USCIS will approve for the fee waiver. They consider each case individually, taking into account such factors as:

- whether you have received public benefits such as food stamps, Medicaid, or Supplemental Security Income (SSI)
- your age, particularly if you're elderly (65 or over)
- whether you're disabled
- the age and number of dependents in your household, and
- humanitarian or other reasons.

Most attorneys recommend against using the waiver at all unless it's absolutely necessary. The paperwork is lengthy and complicated. You must prepare a monthly budget of all your income and expenses, an explanation of your living arrangements, a list of your assets, and more—all with supporting documents.

After all your trouble, USCIS may deny your request if the agency is convinced that your expenses are inflated or unrealistic, or that you're spending money on so-called luxuries (items not necessary for your survival). In these cases, USCIS may advise economizing and saving up for a few more months to pay the fee. After all, no one is forcing you to apply for citizenship right now. Also keep in mind that a little mistake could raise suspicions of lying—which could destroy your chances of obtaining citizenship.

Even if USCIS grants your fee waiver, the time that they take to make this decision will add to the time that you wait for your interview. For example, at the California Service Center, it typically adds about a month to your wait. If USCIS denies your fee waiver, it will send you back your entire N-400 package for refiling with the appropriate fee.

If requesting a fee waiver, don't attach a check as a "backup." In hopes of saving time, some people have tried sending both a fee waiver and a check, with instructions to use the check only if the fee waiver is denied. However, this approach doesn't work. As soon as USCIS sees the check, its policy is to cash it, and pay no attention to the fee waiver request.

As if these reasons weren't enough, when you later attend your naturalization interview, your case may be reviewed by a USCIS officer who, consciously or subconsciously, judges people based on their income. USCIS cannot use poverty as the basis for a bad moral character judgment—but an officer may ask unpleasant questions if, for example, he or she believes that you're refusing to get out and find a job.

If you must apply for a fee waiver, you have two choices:

- If you are receiving need-based public benefits, see our instructions in Subsections a and b, below.
- If you're not receiving public benefits, seek help from a legal services agency serving immigrants and refugees, as discussed in Chapter 10.

a. Public Benefits Recipients: What You'll Need to Prove to Qualify for a Fee Waiver

If you provide proof that you're receiving need-based public benefits—such as SSI, food stamps, Medicaid, or Temporary Assistance for Needy Families (TANF)—you'll improve your chances of getting your fee waiver approved. Based on your proof of public benefits, USCIS will presume that your income level is below the federal Poverty Guidelines and won't ask you to provide extensive documentation demonstrating your income and assets.

However, it's not enough to show USCIS that you are receiving public benefits. You must also prove that your benefit check barely covers your monthly expenses—if it covers them at all. Some people manage to live comfortably within the limits of their benefit checks. Other people find that their checks disappear all too quickly—for example, because of family demands or medical expenses. How to supply this proof is covered in Subsection b, below.

b. Documents to Include in Your Fee Waiver Request

As a public benefits recipient, you should include the following information in your fee waiver request and attach any documentation to your citizenship application:

- an explanation in your application cover letter (see Section B, above)
- a photocopy of your most recent tax return, hopefully showing that your income falls below the federal government's Poverty Guidelines
- a photocopy of your benefit check or other evidence that you're receiving assistance
- your sworn statement stating why you're requesting the waiver (see sample below)
- your estimated monthly budget, detailing your income and expenses (see sample below)
- documentation proving the major income and expense items on your budget, such as copies of rent or mortgage payment receipts, and bills for electricity, medical or home care, food, school tuition, and other essentials
- proof of your living arrangements, particularly if you are living in a nursing home or other assisted facility, but also showing whether you are living with others or have others living with you, and
- documentation proving your assets (property that you own, such as a house, jewelry, or bank account) as well as your debts and liabilities, such as your outstanding loans and credit card debt.

Write "Fee Waiver Requested" in red letters on the top of your Form N-400 and all attachments, as well as on the outside of your mailing envelope. This helps to alert USCIS as to your waiver request and may prevent your application from getting bounced back with USCIS claiming you forgot to pay.

The following samples will give you an idea of how to prepare your sworn statement and monthly budget. We do not provide a form for your use because USCIS is suspicious of fee waiver forms. Prepare your own sworn statement and monthly budget, accurately describing you own personal situation, using our samples as general guides.

Be as accurate as possible when calculating your monthly budget. Go through the last four or five months' cancelled checks, credit card bills, and receipts from stores and restaurants. Figure out, if possible, where you spent cash but did not get a receipt—for example, the babysitter, vending machine, public pool, and toll bridge. Add up all of these expenses and figure out a monthly average.

After you've got your monthly average, determine whether you need to add anything that didn't appear during the last few months. Look for irregular but justifiable expenses, such as the hairdresser and the dentist. For an expense like the dentist that happens only once a year, divide the number of dollars by 12 and add the result to your monthly average. For additional regular expenses, calculate the number of months that pass between each time that the expense arises and divide the amount of the expense by that number of months. For example, if you get a haircut every two months, divide the cost of the haircut by two and add that to your monthly average. If you use personal accounting software such as Microsoft Money or Quicken, you can use the software to calculate your monthly averages.

You'll need to supply only the total amount of your monthly expenses in your USCIS documentation. You don't have to explain every item. However, be sure to retain the financial records and notes used to arrive at your final figures, just in case USCIS asks for follow-up information.

You'll also need to tell USCIS how much money you have in the bank and in cash (such as in your wallet and the cookie jar). Add this information to the monthly budget statement. And don't forget to add income you receive from sources such as an ex-spouse ("alimony" payments) or parents.

Sample Fee Waiver Request Statement

Fee Waiver Request Statement

A# 12345678
Social Security # 123-45-6789

Name: Aceline Benicoeur

1. I am submitting an application for naturalization.

2. I am requesting a waiver of the naturalization processing fees of $390 ($320 for Form N-400 and $70 for fingerprinting).

3. I cannot pay the application fees because my income is not enough to cover it after paying my monthly expenses.

4. I am 77 years old and disabled. I receive Supplemental Security Income (SSI) in the amount of $545 per month, along with $50 in food stamps.

5. I have no source of income other than SSI.

6. As the attached budget shows, my monthly expenses total at least $545. I rent a one-bedroom home in an inexpensive neighborhood. I live alone. Though I economize whenever possible—for example, growing many of my own vegetables—I cannot afford anything outside of my usual expenses.

7. I believe that I am otherwise eligible for U.S. citizenship. However, I am unable to pay the naturalization filing fees and therefore request this fee waiver.

I declare, under penalty of perjury that the foregoing, as well as the attached documentation, are true and correct to the best of my knowledge.

Name: Aceline Benicoeur
Signature: *Aceline Benicoeur*
Date: April 3, 2005

Sample Monthly Budget

Budget in Support of Fee Waiver Request

A# 12345678
Social Security # 123-45-6789
Name: Aceline Benicoeur

MONTHLY INCOME

Wages/salaries	$ 0
SSI	545
Food stamps	50
Other public benefits	0
Other income	0
Total income	**$595**

MONTHLY EXPENSES

Housing	$375
Food	90
Utilities	45
Clothing	15
Transportation/travel	35
Medical	20
Child care	0
Spousal support	0
Debts	0
Personal care	15
Total Expenses	**$595**

ASSETS

Cash on hand	$ 17
Checking/savings	$ 44
Property (wedding ring & television)	$220

Signature: *Aceline Benicoeur*

Date: April 3, 2005

3. Protecting Your Application Against Loss

When the INS was reorganized and USCIS became the agency in charge of immigration services, people hoped that the new agency would fix some of the problems of the old one, like long delays and frequently lost applications. However, USCIS so far seems to be just as inefficient as the INS. You must prepare for the very real possibility that you will send in your application and hear nothing back, ever, even after writing many letters and trying to make contact in every other way possible. Here are three tips to help you avoid a USCIS disaster:

- Make copies of everything you send.
- Use a traceable method when mailing your application.
- Don't give USCIS anything you can't replace.

We'll explain the reasons for these maxims—and how to follow them.

Behind the Scenes

Reporters for *The Oregonian* newspaper visited USCIS Service Center of the INS (as it was then called) in Burlington, Vermont, and found "crates of files teeter[ing] along the walkways between overstuffed cubicles." Even with new computers, the center relies on old-fashioned filing techniques. Paul E. Novak, Jr., director of Vermont Service Center, told the reporters: "I don't know what we'd do without hand trucks and milk crates."

The reporters also described a 1998 case in which the INS allowed a storage room containing asbestos to be sealed off—ignoring the fact that 30,000 application files were in the room. The INS didn't bother to notify the applicants, and one waited three years for his citizenship interview. (See "INS Bureaucracy, Blundering Create 'Agency from Hell,'" by Brent Walth and Kim Christensen, *The Oregonian*, Monday, December 11, 2000.)

a. Make Complete Copies

When you've finished preparing your citizenship application, don't mail it until you've made photocopies. Copy every page of the application form, as well as photos, documents, checks, and money orders. This will help you re-create these pages and items if they're lost in the mail or in the overstuffed files of a USCIS office. It may also help convince USCIS to take another look for the lost items.

b. Mail by a Traceable Method

It's not uncommon for applications to be misplaced when they arrive in the USCIS mailroom. If this happens to your application, you'll need proof that you mailed it. For that reason, use certified mail with a return receipt. A return receipt postcard will be mailed back to you, and you can use it to convince USCIS to look for your misplaced application.

⚠️ **You cannot use UPS, Federal Express, or other private delivery services to send your citizenship application to a post office box.** In other words, you must use the U.S. Postal Service, or check the Service Center's website for the address of its special post office box for such purposes.

By taking these steps, you'll have the evidence you need to show USCIS that it was its fault that a file was delayed or mislaid. In some cases, USCIS will rely on your own photocopies to proceed with your application.

c. Don't Send Something If You Want It Back

You may have to include personal documents with your application. Don't send originals of important documents such as marriage certificates or green cards to USCIS. You run a serious risk of losing them. USCIS refuses to give any assurance that you'll get your originals back. Photocopy any document (as long as the original is the official version), and send

the copy. Bring the originals to your interview so the USCIS examiner will have a chance to view them. (If USCIS makes a special request that you mail the original, comply with the demand, but make copies for yourself first!) Add the following text on the front of the copy, if there's room:

Copies of documents submitted are exact photocopies of unaltered original documents, and I understand that I may be required to submit original documents to an immigration official at a later date.

_____
Signature

_____
Typed or Printed Name

_____
Date

4. Where to Mail Your Application

You are required to mail your application to a USCIS Service Center—a large processing facility that will handle your file until it's turned over to a USCIS office near you for your interview. The table below lists the addresses of USCIS Service Centers, including the appropriate post office boxes for citizenship applications. Find the one serving the state where you live and send your application there.

⚠️ **The following addresses are only for citizenship applications.** If you submit other applications to USCIS, such as visa petitions for family members, you can find the correct addresses and post office boxes for those applications at the USCIS website or by calling USCIS at 800-375-5283.

💡 **People applying while serving in active-duty status with the U.S. Armed Forces must use a different address.** Your application should go to: USCIS Nebraska Service Center, Attention N-400 Naturalization Facilitation Unit, P.O. Box 87426, Lincoln, Nebraska, 68501-7426.

USCIS Service Centers	
If You Live In:	Send Your Citizenship Application To:
Arizona, California, Hawaii, Nevada, Territory of Guam, or the Commonwealth of the Northern Mariana Islands	USCIS California Service Center Attention: N-400 Unit P.O. Box 10400 Laguna Niguel, CA 92607-0400
Alaska, Colorado, Idaho, Illinois, Indiana, Iowa, Kansas, Michigan, Minnesota, Montana, Nebraska, North Dakota, Ohio, Oregon, South Dakota, Utah, Washington, Wisconsin, or Wyoming	USCIS Nebraska Service Center Attention: N-400 Unit P.O. Box 87400 Lincoln, NE 68501-7400
Alabama, Arkansas, Florida, Georgia, Kentucky, Louisiana, Mississippi, New Mexico, North Carolina, Oklahoma, South Carolina, Tennessee, or Texas	USCIS Texas Service Center Attention: N-400 Unit P.O. Box 851204 Mesquite, TX 75185-1204
Connecticut, Delaware, Maine, Maryland, Massachusetts, New Hampshire, New Jersey, New York, Pennsylvania, Rhode Island, Vermont, Virginia, Washington, D.C., West Virginia, Commonwealth of Puerto Rico, or the U.S. Virgin Islands	USCIS Vermont Service Center Attention: N-400 Unit 75 Lower Weldon Street St. Albans, VT 05479-0001

■

Between Filing and Interview: Dealing With the Wait

The period between when you submit your citizenship application and obtain your USCIS interview is likely to be long—in most states, more than a year. During this period, you should:

- improve your eligibility by working on your English language skills and American history (see Section A), and
- monitor the processing of your application (to be sure it isn't lost, misplaced, or ignored) (see Section B).

In this chapter, we'll discuss these activities and what you should do if:

- you move or go on vacation (see Section C), or
- you need to request emergency attention from USCIS (see Section D).

How Long Does It Take to Become a U.S. Citizen?

The following chart will give you an idea of how long you might wait between when you file your application and your swearing-in ceremony. (Your interview usually takes place 60 days before the ceremony.) At most USCIS offices, applicants wait more than a year before they're sworn in—and at a few offices, the wait lasts two or more years. But don't make any decisions based solely on this chart, since the average wait may change by the time you read this. This information was compiled by the American Immigration Lawyer's Association in April 2004, and has not been approved by USCIS for publication.

Taos Pueblo—New Mexico

Average Time Between Filing and Swearing In

USCIS Office (by U.S. City)	Average Wait in Days	USCIS Office (by U.S. City)	Average Wait in Days
Albuquerque	330	Memphis	180-365
Atlanta	180	Milwaukee	180-240
Baltimore	90 days after receipt from VSC	Newark, NJ	No report
Boston	240	New Orleans	360-560
Buffalo	180-240	New York	360
Charlotte	345-400	Oklahoma City	300-360
Cherry Hill	No report	Omaha	330-360
Chicago	180	Orlando	420-540
Cincinnati	No report	Phoenix	360
Cleveland	No report	Philadelphia	No report
Dallas	240-360	Pittsburgh	No report
Denver	150	Portland, OR	240
Detroit	360-540	Sacramento	No report
El Paso	166	Salt Lake City	No report
Harlingen, TX	No report	San Antonio	150-210
Hartford	300-360	San Diego	183
Honolulu	630-720	San Francisco	270
Houston	270	San Jose	365-400
Indianapolis	210-270	Santa Antonio	150-210
Kansas City, MO	300-365	Seattle	No report
Miami	180-365	St. Paul	270-360
Las Vegas	No report	Tampa	365
Louisville	No report	Washington, D.C. (Arlington Office)	360-480
Los Angeles	270-360	Wichita, KS	270-330

applicants have lately waited as long as four months. Nevertheless, if you don't get your receipt notice within two months of mailing, we recommend that you follow up with the USCIS Service Center.

Unfortunately, USCIS Service Centers are like walled fortresses. You can't visit them, and it's almost impossible to reach them by phone. (The Service Center's phone lines tend to always be busy, and even if you do get through, USCIS operators provide only the barest computer-generated information.) Your best option is to check the status of your application online, at www.uscis.gov. Click "Immigration Services and Benefits Programs," then "USCIS National Customer Service Center", then "Finding the Status of Your Case", then "Applications for Naturalization (N-400)," then "Case Status Service." You will need the processing number from your USCIS receipt notice. However, if USCIS has failed to send you a receipt notice, you won't get very far with this.

In the end, you may have to resort to old-fashioned letter writing to inquire about a missing receipt notice. Use the sample letter below as your guide. Always prominently include your A-number (from your green card) since this number is used to track applications before USCIS assigns them a processing number.

⚠ **The USCIS address in the sample letter—the California Service Center—is provided only by way of example and may not be the one for you.** When modifying the sample letter, use the address of the USCIS Service Center to which you originally mailed your citizenship application.

Include copies of your certified mail receipt and your cashed check (and any other proof that your application was filed) along with your letter. Copy both sides of the check—USCIS stamps a number on the back of the check that's used to trace your application. If you don't get a reply within four weeks, write another, similar letter. Keep writing every two weeks until you get an answer.

Start with polite, short letters and get more insistent as time goes on. Be careful, however, and never insult or threaten a government official. If your letter is interpreted as a threat, your citizenship application will be denied and you may be subject to criminal prosecution.

Sample Letter About Delayed Receipt Notice

344 Eucalyptus Drive
Brentwood, CA 90000
(310) 555-1212
July 16, 200x

USCIS/California Service Center
P.O. Box 10400
Laguna Niguel, CA 92607-0400

RE: N-400 Application for Naturalization
A-Number: A12345678

Dear Sir/Madam:

I filed an application for naturalization on May 1, 200x. It has been more than two months, but I have not received a receipt notice or any other communication from you. I did receive the U.S. Postal Service's certified mail receipt, indicating that my application arrived safely in your office. A copy of that receipt is enclosed. I am concerned, however, that you do not yet appear to have deposited the check that I included with the application.

Please advise me of the status of my application at the above address or phone number. I look forward to your response.

Very truly yours,
Lilka Sobeska
Lilka Sobeska

Enclosure: Copy of Certified Mail Receipt

If your letters do not produce results, consult an attorney (Chapter 10 has tips on finding a good one) or call a U.S. Congressperson's office for help, as described below in Section E.

Eventually, you will get a receipt notice from the USCIS Service Center, whether in response to your first inquiry or in the normal course of processing. Sometime after that—the exact timing remains mysterious—your case will be transferred to your local USCIS office.

b. Incomplete or Lost Portions of Your Application

If you receive a USCIS request for more documentation—such as photos or a missing document—gather whatever was asked for and get it in the mail as soon as possible. Use the same precautions detailed in Section B1, above—include the notification form as a cover sheet—and make a copy for yourself.

What should you do if you're asked for something that you know you've already sent? This is surprisingly common—in fact, an investigative report by *The Oregonian* newspaper found that, "with 25 million case files in storage, the INS [as the USCIS was then known] misplaces tens of thousands of files each year—80,000 in 1998 alone—and leaves immigrants to resubmit applications and pay fees all over again." (From "INS Bureaucracy, Blundering Create 'The Agency From Hell,'" by Brent Walth and Kim Christensen, *The Oregonian*, Monday, December 11, 2000.) If USCIS requests something inexpensive or easy to produce, don't waste time arguing—even if you have photocopies proving that you already sent the item. Assume it has been lost and send another one.

Lost checks or money orders are a different matter. Do not send USCIS another check or money order until you find out what happened to the first payment. If you sent a check and haven't received information about it with your monthly bank statement, ask your bank to determine whether the check has been cashed. If it has been cashed, get the check and send USCIS a copy of both sides, so that USCIS officials can see their own stamp and processing number on the back. If the check hasn't been cashed, send a new check, but make sure to stop payment on the old check first. (Of course, USCIS has been known to relocate lost checks even after new checks have been sent, then attempt to cash the old ones and demand yet another set of checks from applicants when the old checks bounce. If avoiding delays is extremely important to you, go ahead and give USCIS an opportunity to double-charge you, by not stopping payment on the first check—but we think this is a case where it's worth arguing it out with USCIS.)

If you sent a money order and kept the receipt with the tracer number, call the company that issued the money order to find out whether it has been cashed. Ask the company to send you a copy of the cashed money order to prove to USCIS that it did indeed receive your money. If you can't get a copy of the cashed money order, send USCIS a copy of your receipt and an explanation. Hopefully, USCIS will stop bugging you for the money.

Some applicants receive USCIS requests for things that don't exist—proof of having paid child support, for example, even though the applicant has no children. This usually results from a processing error—for example, the USCIS officer issued a form letter and forgot to cross off an item, or a USCIS officer didn't have an applicant's complete immigration history available. If you receive one of these requests, write a polite letter explaining why it is impossible to comply with this request.

c. Important Information on Your Receipt Notice

Carefully examine your receipt notice from the USCIS Service Center. It contains some important pieces of information, including an estimate of when you'll attend your interview and your file's application number.

The estimate—in the main body of the notice—is a guess as to how long it will take for USCIS to schedule an interview with you. In the sample notice in this chapter, you'll see that one California USCIS office had an estimated waiting period of 460 days—well over a year! The estimate not only gives you a rough idea of when you'll attend your interview, but also a sense of when to start inquiring if your interview is delayed.

⚠ **The estimate on your receipt notice is not a guarantee.** Don't be surprised if you must wait longer than the time originally estimated on your receipt notice to get your interview appointment.

Your application number—it's in one of the boxes near the top of the receipt notice—is the number used to identify your application throughout the Service

Preparing for the English Exam

In order to pass the U.S. citizenship test, you will need to demonstrate basic skills in reading, writing, and speaking English. If you're reading this book by yourself, you're already doing quite well. If—like many applicants—someone is assisting you through the process, that's okay, too. Ask your friend to keep reading!

This chapter won't teach you English but it will provide:

- an idea of how much English you'll need to know (Section A)
- a description of the exam you're preparing for (Section B), and
- resources for learning English (Section C).

 If you're older than age 50 or disabled, you may be able to avoid learning English. For details on whether you qualify to have your citizenship interview conducted in your native language, see Chapter 2, Section E.

A. How Much English You'll Need to Know

USCIS does not expect you to sound like a college professor or to win public-speaking awards. The object of testing your English language skills is to determine whether you can have a basic conversation in English—that is, whether you can speak at the same level as "ordinary" U.S. citizens. USCIS is not allowed to impose any "extraordinary or unreasonable condition" on you when testing your English. (See I.N.A. § 312, 8 U.S.C. § 1423.) So, don't worry that the officer will intentionally speak too quickly or use long or obscure words.

That said, we encourage you to put as much effort into learning English as you can. Being comfortable in English will reduce the chances of unpleasant surprises at the interview. For example, many applicants are thrown off when the USCIS interviewer asks a question using different words than they were expecting (such as "Do you have any previous spouses?" instead of "How many times have you been married?"). And some interviewers were simply

born with speaking voices that are unclear, too quick, or otherwise difficult to understand. Speaking English will also help you actively participate in U.S. society.

Should You Submit Your Application Before You Can Speak English?

USCIS doesn't require you to be conversant in English at the time you submit your citizenship application—only that you have learned it by the time your interview rolls around. That gives you the opportunity to take a calculated risk—turn in your citizenship application while your English is still weak, then spend the months leading up to your interview studying intensively. (We discuss study methods in Section C, below.)

If you have the discipline to study diligently, this risk should be manageable. Thanks to USCIS delays, you may have more time before the interview than you expected! But if you are not diligent or if your life is full of unpredictable crises and obligations, don't submit your application until you're comfortable in English. If you submit it without knowledge of English, you will fail the English exam and have to reapply for citizenship.

The exam may have changed by the time you read this. At the time this book went to print, USCIS was in the process of redesigning the citizenship exam questions and procedures. Their stated goal is to make the exam more fair and meaningful. For the latest news on the exam, check the Legal Updates section of Nolo's website (www.nolo.com) and the USCIS website at www.uscis.gov.

B. How USCIS Tests Your English

For some people, the English exam can be one of the most difficult parts of the citizenship process. Others have been speaking English for years, and may not even realize that parts of the exam are happening. During the citizenship interview, you will be tested on your ability to:

- speak English (see Section B1, below)
- read English (see Section B2, below), and
- write in English (see Section B3, below).

1. Testing Your Ability to Speak English

In order to pass the spoken part of the English exam, you must understand what the USCIS interviewing officer says and make yourself understood during the citizenship interview. There is no formal test of your spoken English apart from the requirement that you speak English during the interview.

Much of the interview will involve reviewing your Form N-400, so learning the vocabulary on this form is critical. You may find a number of words on the form difficult to comprehend. Some aren't commonly used. For example, the average American rarely discusses his willingness to "bear arms on behalf of the United States" (translated: "defend the United States by joining the military"). And when was the last time you heard anyone discuss "polygamy," which is the practice of taking several husbands or wives at the same time?

Review the language in Form N-400—with a dictionary in hand—and then have a friend read all the questions aloud to you. The USCIS interviewer probably won't ask you every question on the form—but he or she will ask you a good number of them. Since it's impossible to predict which ones the officer will choose, be prepared for all of them. You'll be much more comfortable at the interview if you prepare!

You don't need to know every word of the English language. During the interview, there may be some words you don't know or recognize. Admitting your lack of knowledge as to a word will not be a deadly strike against you. If you can't comprehend something, say to the interviewer, "I don't know that word, can you repeat what you said in another way?"

You'll impress your interviewer if, instead of answering a question with "yes" or "no" (or nodding your head affirmatively or negatively), you respond in a complete sentence. This may require repeating part of the question back to the interviewer—for example, if he or she asks you "What is your name?," practice answering "My name is Charles Olisadebe" rather than just "Charles Olisadebe." Say your answers clearly and firmly.

Ask an English-speaking friend to rephrase the questions from Form N-400 in different ways. For example, USCIS interviewers often shorten the questions or put them into different words. So, for example, the form reads "If you are now married, give the following information about your spouse; Spouse's Family Name." However, the USCIS interviewer is more likely to ask, "What's your husband's name?"

A tape recorder can be your friend, too. If you need practice with the questions but don't want to impose too much on friends and family, ask one of them to read all the questions on the N-400 application into a tape recorder. Then play the tape back to yourself as many times as you need.

Another, less obvious way in which USCIS tests your English ability is by watching your response to the interviewer's instructions. For example, the officer may say things like, "Follow me," "Please remain standing," "Raise your right hand," "Take a seat," or "Show me any documents that you've brought with you." We know of one case in which the applicant failed to take a seat when asked twice by the officer. He was told to go home. In another case, an applicant failed the interview because she sat down before the officer told her to! The lesson here is to listen very carefully to the interviewer's instructions and, if you really don't understand, to ask the interviewer to rephrase the sentence so you won't be left standing when you should be in your chair.

2. Testing Your Reading of English

In order to test your reading ability, the USCIS officer will give you something to read out loud. If you're clearly doing well, the officer may stop you after one sentence—otherwise you may have to read two or three sentences. We cannot predict your reading matter, but officers have used:

- passages from one of the Federal Textbooks on Citizenship (Publications M-289 and M-291). (Unfortunately, these aren't widely available, so tracking them down is probably not worth your effort.)
- the list of 100 U.S. history and government questions
- material from the applicant's citizenship file, and
- N-400 applications.

A USCIS officer may also combine your reading exam with your U.S. history and government exam—asking that you read and answer a few questions out loud. In general, it's better to focus on learning to read English than on trying to predict what you'll be asked to read.

As you learn English, however, remember that reading out loud is a separate skill than reading quietly to yourself. Some people can understand words on a page without understanding how the sentence flows or how the words are pronounced. So, practice reading out loud—not only will it help you on this portion of the exam, but you'll find that it improves your ability to remember English words. Be sure to pause just a little after the end of every sentence, so that it doesn't sound like you're running all the words together. Ask a friend to listen and correct your pronunciation while you read your Form N-400 or a newspaper out loud.

3. Testing Your Ability to Write English

To test your ability to write English, the USCIS interviewer will ask you to write down two or three sentences that he or she dictates (says out loud). These sentences are, for the most part, not difficult. Usually they come from the INS's list, reproduced at the end of this section. Some officers use vocabulary from the list but come up with sentences that are different.

Spelling and punctuation—things like periods and commas—are important, but getting the right mean-ing is the key to success. If the USCIS officer can figure out what you're trying to write—that is, it's understandable to the average person—you'll pass. Still, your chances are better if you spell everything perfectly.

EXAMPLE 1: The USCIS officer asks Benjiro to write "The sky is blue." He writes "The sky iz blu." He may pass the writing portion of the exam, because the USCIS officer can understand what he has written. However, some USCIS officers are stricter than others.

EXAMPLE 2: The USCIS officer asks Junko to write "The sky is blue." Junko writes "The sky is blew." She fails the writing portion of the exam, because "blew"—though it's an actual word—has a different meaning than "blue," turning the sentence into nonsense.

C. Study Resources

Children learn languages by listening, but for adults it's not so easy. Fortunately, many communities have a wonderful resource called "adult schools" or "adult education programs," which offer classes in "ESL" (English as a Second Language) and citizenship exam preparation. These programs are held on the campuses of local schools, community centers, or community colleges, usually on evenings or weekends. The class term is typically six weeks to two months long, and the tuition is usually fairly low or even free.

To find an adult school or program near you, ask at your local library, community center, public school district, or community college—you may have a hard time finding them in the local phone book or Yellow Pages. Also ask your friends, immigrant or American, whether they've taken any evening classes nearby. Look for a program that fits your schedule and needs. In California at least, most ESL and citizenship classes are offered through local public school districts, and are free.

If you can't find an adult school near you, your local library or bookstore may have English—

language study tapes or CDs. They're not as effective as studying with a live teacher, but are usually better than trying to learn English from a book.

Often, classroom or other formal study isn't enough when it comes to learning a language. If you've been shy about using your English up until now, it's time to come out of your shell. Practice on your children, the bus driver, and the local store clerk. You'll find that many Americans are eager to help you learn, once they see that you're making an effort. You may find it helpful to listen to talk-radio shows or to watch television. The more you speak and listen, the more you'll remember. ■

Preparing for the U.S. History and Government Exam

In order to become a U.S. citizen, you must pass an exam covering U.S. history and government. This exam is part of your citizenship interview and in most USCIS offices the officer will, somewhere in the course of interviewing you, simply ask you up to 14 questions chosen from a list of 100. (In some USCIS offices, however, the officer will hand you a multiple choice test to complete in writing during your interview.) If you're older than 65 and have been a permanent resident for 20 years or more, you'll be asked only ten questions, chosen from a smaller pool of 25 potential questions.

For the average applicant, the questions should be chosen randomly. However, USCIS officers are supposed to select easier questions if your studying would have been hampered by such factors as advanced age or lack of education. You must answer all but two questions correctly in order to pass this exam. After studying this chapter, you should be able to do just that. In Section A, we give you a strategy for preparing for the exam. In Section B, we help you prepare by reviewing the pool of 100 potential questions and by providing answers. In Section C, we review the smaller list of easier questions for people age 65 or older.

Abraham Lincoln—16th President of the U.S.

💡 **If you're age 65 or older and have had a green card for 20 years, you are allowed to study a shorter list of 25 questions (see Section C).** Even if you qualify for this easier exam, we recommend that you still read Sections A and B, below. The background information will be useful as you study, and there will be a great deal of overlap in the questions.

⚠️ **The exam may have changed by the time you read this.** At the time this book went to print, USCIS was in the process of redesigning the citizenship exam questions and procedures. Their stated goal is to make the exam more fair and meaningful. For the latest news on the exam, check the Legal Updates section of Nolo's website (www.nolo.com) and the USCIS website at www.uscis.gov.

A. Your Exam Preparation Strategy

This may be the only exam you take where you receive all the possible questions and answers ahead of time. But having the answers doesn't mean you are guaranteed to pass. Like any exam, if you fail to prepare, you'll flunk. In this section, we'll suggest some preparation strategies.

You could pass the citizenship exam by simply memorizing the answers to all of the questions. That may work for some applicants—though probably not if they wait until the night before the interview to attempt it—but generally, relying solely on memorization makes your task harder, not easier. For example, consider the question "What are the three branches of our government?" If you don't have any idea what the words "Legislative, Executive, and Judicial" mean, you may run into trouble answering this question at your exam. For that reason, it's best to understand at least a little bit about the background and meaning of all 100 questions, and not just memorize the answers.

That said, we're not advocating that you immerse yourself in all 200-plus years of American history. After all, the USCIS officer expects you to give him or her only the answer that appears on the official USCIS list—in the same or similar words, with no added information. Instead, we recommend a combination of memorization and background study.

First, develop some understanding of the background behind each question and answer, and then launch into memorizing the answers on the USCIS list.

> **EXAMPLE:** During her citizenship exam, Matilde was asked, "Who was Martin Luther King, Jr.?" Matilde responded, "I have a dream," quoting from one of Martin Luther King's speeches. Matilde was working on her Ph.D. dissertation in modern U.S. history at a prestigious university and she knew quite a bit about Martin Luther King, Jr. But the answer that the officer was looking for was the one on the list: "A civil rights leader." The officer counted Matilde's answer as wrong.

You'll see that some of the 100 questions are difficult and some are surprisingly easy. Memorizing the 13 original U.S. colonies is tough, but describing the colors of the flag—red, white, and blue—is not. USCIS officers are not supposed to just throw all the hardest questions at you, no matter how cranky they may be feeling that day. In fact, if you are elderly or have a limited education, they're supposed to limit their questions to the easier ones. In all likelihood, you will get a mix of easy and difficult questions in your interview.

Even though you probably won't get all the hard questions, should you still do your best to memorize every one of them? Keep in mind that you will have only eight to 14 questions in which to prove yourself. If the officer asks you the few questions that you decided not to learn (or you happen to forget a few answers on top of the few you avoided), you will fail the exam.

 USCIS's list of 100 questions is a superficial history lesson focusing on basic, not controversial facts. Don't expect to find out much about free speech, civil rights, or other important issues. If you're interested in learning more about what really happened during the two centuries of American history, we recommend easy-to-understand history texts such as *Don't Know Much About History: Everything You Need to Know About American History but Never Learned*, by Kenneth C. Davis (Avon), and *A People's History of the United States: 1492 to Present*, by Howard Zinn (Harper Perennial).

B. Learning the Answers to the 100 Questions

In this section, we've taken the 100 questions on the official USCIS list and rearranged them into categories. Then we've written a paragraph or two to summarize the questions and provide some background for them to make sense. At the end of this section, we give you the 100 questions followed by the answer, so that you'll have a chance to test yourself.

 We've presented the 100 questions in a logical flow based on subject matter. USCIS does not organize the questions in this manner; the agency scrambles the questions randomly. In Appendix B, we've included the official list of questions as presented by USCIS.

If you won't be interviewing in English, get translations of the questions. Applicants who, because of age or disability (see Chapter 7), are eligible to do the USCIS interview in their native language should obtain translations of the 100 history and government questions. If you speak Spanish, Tagalog, Chinese, or Vietnamese, you can find translations of a substantial number of the questions and answers at the USCIS website (www.uscis.gov). On the left side of the home page, click "Immigration Services and Benefit Programs," then click "Naturalization," then click "Guide to Naturalization" and look for your language. You will need Adobe Acrobat in order to download this guide. The questions are printed near the back of the guide. For questions that are not translated or for other languages, you will have to have a friend translate the questions and answers for you.

We've grouped the questions and answers into seven categories:
- the U.S. flag and what it stands for (Section B1)
- U.S. independence and Revolutionary War history (Section B2)
- the U.S. Constitution (Section B3)
- the U.S. federal government today (Section B4)
- your state and local government (Section B5)
- recent U.S. history (Section B6), and
- becoming a U.S. citizen (Section B7).

United States Flag

The American flag is an important symbol. That's why our national song (or "national anthem") was written about it. The title of the our national anthem is "The Star-Spangled Banner," composed by Francis Scott Key. The title is a poetic name for "the flag with stars all over it" (which would not have sounded as nice). Spanish speakers won't have much trouble remembering the word "banner," because it's related to the Spanish word for flag, *"bandera."*

Congratulations—you've now learned enough to answer 14 of the questions on the citizenship exam.

To test yourself in the exam questions covering the U.S. flag and what it stands for, go to the end of this section. (Section B.)

1. The U.S. Flag and What It Stands For

You have no doubt seen the red, white, and blue American flag, shown above.

If the illustration were in color, you would see that the 13 stripes are red and white. They represent the original 13 states that formed the United States when it was founded in 1776. At that time, however, they were not called "states," but "colonies." You'll recognize their names as present-day U.S. states nonetheless: Connecticut, New Hampshire, New York, New Jersey, Massachusetts, Pennsylvania, Delaware, Virginia, North Carolina, South Carolina, Georgia, Rhode Island, and Maryland. Locate these on the map below. With your pencil, put a star on each of the 13 original colonies.

The 50 white stars on the flag represent the 50 states in the United States today, also shown on our map.

The United States is sometimes referred to as the "union." That means the voluntary joining of the various states, each of which also has its own government. So when you are asked how many states are in the union, it simply means in the United States. You won't have to memorize the names of all 50 states, but you will have to know the 49th and 50th states to join the union: Alaska and Hawaii. That's easy to remember, because they are the only ones whose land is not connected to the rest of the United States.

2. U.S. Independence and Early History

Before Europeans landed in America, the land was populated by tribes of native people now often referred to as Native Americans. (Through much of American history, they have been referred to as "Indians" because the early explorers mistakenly believed they had landed in India). Europeans became interested in America in the 1400s and 1500s, and attempted various explorations and settlements. However, the most famous settlement in U.S. history was that of the Pilgrims, who arrived on a boat called the *Mayflower* (in 1620, but you won't be asked for this date). They were originally from England, all members of a religious sect. They believed that the Church of England was harassing them for their religious views, so they left in search of a safer environment—that's why USCIS says they came to America for "religious freedom."

If you have children in school, you've probably seen pictures of the Pilgrims, with the American Indians helping them learn things like how to plant corn. The Pilgrims and the Indians held a great harvest feast together, which later became the model for the holiday called Thanksgiving. The Pilgrims are sometimes also referred to as the Colonists, since they were among the first people to set up colonies in America.

The United States

Now we'll fast-forward about a hundred years.

By the mid-1700s, the American colonies were mostly under the protection of England, which imposed high taxes and exerted control in return. The colonists were unhappy with this. After small-scale battles and angry negotiations and proclamations between the colonists and England, the Revolutionary War broke out in 1775. George Washington was appointed commander-in-chief of the military (the first one ever). One of the famous statements in favor of American freedom during this time period came from Patrick Henry, an outspoken lawyer and states-man, who said, "Give me liberty or give me death."

On July 4, 1776, the colonists announced in the Declaration of Independence that they considered themselves free from all English control. The main author was Thomas Jefferson. One of his arguments for why England should grant independence to the colonies was "that all men are created equal."

If you'd like to see the full text of the Declaration of Independence: Ask at your local law library or go to the website of the National Archives (www.nara .gov). Click "Exhibit Hall," then click "Charters of Freedom," then click "Declaration of Independence."

In recognition of this important declaration, July 4th is now celebrated with fireworks and parties as Independence Day.

Time to fast-forward again, to the 1860s. During the presidency of Abraham Lincoln, the United States went through one of its most difficult periods: the Civil War. This war was fought between the United States' northern and southern states. One of the issues was whether the slavery of Africans should continue. During the third year of the war, President Lincoln issued the "Emancipation Proclamation," declaring that all the slaves in the rebellious southern states were now free.

To test yourself in the exam questions covering U.S. independence and early history, go to the end of this section.

3. The U.S. Constitution

Now that the American colonies had their freedom from England, it was time to think about getting organized as a country. A group of men representing the various colonies met in Philadelphia and drafted the Constitution of the United States, which they finished writing in the year 1787.

If you want to read the full text of the Constitution: Ask at your local library or go to www.nara.gov online. Click "Exhibit Hall," then click "Charters of Freedom," then "Constitution of the United States."

According to the USCIS list of questions, the Constitution is the "supreme law of the land"—meaning that it sets out the basic governmental structure and fundamental guidelines that govern all other laws and acts of government in the United States. The introduction to the Constitution is called the Preamble.

Although you don't have to learn the Preamble to the Constitution, it provides an important message for all U.S. citizens. Here's what it says:

> We the People of the United States, in Order to form a more perfect Union, establish Justice, insure domestic Tranquility, provide for the common defense, promote the general Welfare, and secure the Blessings of Liberty to ourselves and our Posterity, do ordain and establish this Constitution for the United States of America.

One of the most important subjects covered by the Constitution is the structure and function of the U.S. government. Because so many of the questions on the citizenship exam concern governmental structure, we've reserved this for a separate discussion. See Section 4, below.

After the Constitution was sent to the states for approval, many protested that it did not say enough about protecting the rights of individual people. Since the Constitution can be changed, through a process called amendment, the first U.S. Congress wrote the first ten amendments to the Constitution, which are called the Bill of Rights.

The Bill of Rights guarantees rights to both citizens and noncitizens of the United States. The First Amendment is particularly important. Here is what it says:

> Congress shall make no law respecting an establishment of religion, or prohibiting the free exercise thereof; or abridging the freedom of speech, or of the press; or the right of the people peaceably to assemble, and to petition the Government for a redress of grievances.

The U.S. Constitution

In other words, people are guaranteed rights to freedom of religion, freedom of speech, a free press, freedom of peaceful assembly (to gather as a group), and freedom to ask the government to redress grievances (fix things that it has done wrong).

The other amendments include other rights and freedoms. One of the exam questions asks you to name three rights or freedoms from the Bill of Rights (the first ten amendments). You can choose from the following list, which we'll copy here exactly as it appears on the USCIS list of answers. You can, if you wish, put these into your own words.

Freedoms Established in the Bill of Rights

- *the right of freedom of speech, press, religion, peaceable assembly, and requesting change of government*
- *the right to bear arms (the right to have weapons or own a gun, though subject to certain regulations)*
- *the government may not quarter, or house, soldiers in the people's homes during peacetime without the people's consent.*
- *protects people against excessive or unreasonable fines or cruel and unusual punishment, and*
- *the people have rights other than those mentioned in the Constitution. Any power not given to the federal government by the Constitution is a power of either the state or the people.*

In the years since the Constitution and Bill of Rights were written, other changes, or amendments, have been added to the Constitution. Today there are a total of 27 amendments.

A stray question from the past. Although it doesn't appear on the current list of 100 questions, some USCIS officers still ask the following question: "Name one amendment that guarantees or addresses voting rights." You can answer either the 15th, 19th, or 24th Amendment.

 To test yourself in the exam questions covering the U.S. Constitution, go to the end of this section.

4. The U.S. Federal Government Today

Many questions on the U.S. citizenship exam ask about the U.S. federal, or national, government. Once you understand the government's basic structure, these questions are not as hard as they look. In any case, this information will be important once you become a citizen because it will help you understand what the federal government is doing.

After you are a citizen—assuming you're of voting age (the minimum age is 18)—you'll have a chance to cast your vote for many of the political figures described in this section. At some point, you may also want to affiliate with a political party. The two main political parties in the United States are the Democratic and Republican parties. We won't try to describe the differences in philosophy between the two parties. You'll develop your own sense of this by following the news and the words of various politicians. USCIS won't ask you to describe the parties' philosophies or differences.

The U.S. is said to have a "republican" form of government. This use of the word republican doesn't mean to imply that the government is always run by the Republican Party. In this context, the word republican means that the federal government won't extend its powers into matters that are the concern of individual U.S. states. In other words, the states keep some sovereignty or power over the people living within them, and that way, the people gain some protection from centralized U.S. government control.

The federal government is divided into three branches: the executive, legislative, and judicial branches. The three branches share power among themselves. Look at the diagram below.

Three Branches of Government

The executive branch is the one associated with the White House. In fact, the White House is the president's official home and office. The next time you're in Washington, D.C., you can visit the White House—its address is 1600 Pennsylvania Avenue, NW. The executive branch includes the president, the president's cabinet (special advisors in different subject areas, such as the secretary of defense or of the Treasury), and departments led by the cabinet members. The president's duties include leading the country, serving as commander-in-chief of the U.S. military, signing bills passed by Congress into law (discussed below), and much more.

In order to run for president, a person must:
- be a natural born citizen of the United States
- be at least 35 years old by the time he or she will serve as president, and
- have lived in the United States for at least 14 years of his or her life.

The president is elected by the Electoral College, a group of people who represent all U.S. citizens. A presidential election is held every four years, always in the month of November. The new president is "inaugurated," a ceremony in which he or she is sworn into office, in January. A president can serve only for a total of two terms (or eight years).

The first person elected as president was George Washington. He is now called the "father of our country." When this book went to print, the current president was George W. Bush.

We also elect a vice president along with the president. The vice president will step into the president's position if the president dies. If both of them should die, then the speaker of the House of Representatives, (explained below) becomes president. When this book went to print, the current vice president was Richard B. Cheney, commonly referred to as Dick Cheney.

The legislative branch—made up of the U.S. Congress—sits in the U.S. Capitol Building. Congress has two parts: the Senate and the House of Representatives. The members of Congress are elected directly by the U.S. voters—or, as USCIS says, "the people." Congress makes laws that apply to the whole United States. Your state and local government also have elected groups that can make state and local laws. Only the U.S. Congress can declare war, even though the president is the commander-in-chief of the military.

Senators are elected every six years, and every state elects two senators. That means there are a total of 100 senators in Congress. Members of the House of Representatives are elected every two years. The number of representatives per state depends on how many people live in that state. At this time, there are a total of 435 representatives.

There is no limit on the number of times a senator or representative can be reelected—some Congresspeople have served for most of their adult lives; others may serve only one term. You'll need to figure out who the current senators from your state are for the citizenship exam. To find out, look in the federal government pages of your local phone book or go to www.senate.gov.

The third branch of the U.S. federal government is the judiciary, made up of the Supreme Court and other federal courts. The Supreme Court interprets laws. It's the last possible court of appeal for people suing each other or suing the government. As USCIS says, it's the "highest court in the United States." The Supreme Court makes decisions on the few cases that it chooses to accept, and all Americans must follow the law as the court interprets it.

The Supreme Court is the only branch of our government that isn't elected; its justices are

Overcoming Disability When Applying for Citizenship

If you have a physical or mental disability that makes applying for U.S. citizenship very difficult, don't give up. USCIS must make allowances and arrangements for people with disabilities—a responsibility that they have been paying increasing attention to in recent years. USCIS offers the following types of assistance:

- If at any point in the process you need help from a guardian or family member, USCIS may allow this person to do so, as your "designated representative" (see Section A, below)
- If you can meet the basic requirements, but need a little help at the interview or swearing-in (oath) ceremony, USCIS can provide accommodations (see Section B, below)
- If your physical or mental condition makes it impossible to learn English and/or U.S. history and government, USCIS can waive these exam requirements (see Section C, below)
- For a person whose condition is so severe that he or she can neither understand nor repeat the oath of allegiance, which is the final step toward making him or her citizen, USCIS can waive the oath requirement (see Section D, below).

You may have a disability that requires both accommodations and an exam waiver. That's fine, you can ask for both. But before we go any further, understand that nothing is automatic. Even if you have been declared disabled by a doctor, the Social Security Administration, or some other authority, USCIS will want to make its own decision. USCIS is not concerned whether you can work or do the other things usually evaluated in a disability exam; the agency's main concern is whether your disability interferes with your ability to complete the citizenship application requirements.

If you are uncomfortable dealing with the procedures described in this chapter on your own, hire an immigration attorney. You may not need to pay full price—a number of nonprofits serving immigrants and refugees have attorneys or highly qualified paralegals who help people with disabilities apply for U.S. citizenship. For more on how to find helpful nonprofits, see Chapter 10.

A. How to Become the Applicant's Designated Representative

This section is for people trying to help a disabled person who may not be able to make it through the naturalization process on his or her own. Your help is not only allowed, but welcomed, so long as you have been appointed the applicant's "designated representative." Depending on the level of the applicant's disability, you, as the designated representative, may be allowed to help with various tasks, including filling in the applicant's Form N-400, accompanying him or her to the naturalization interview, interpreting for him or her, sometimes even answering questions on his or her behalf, and more. Allowing you to assist in these ways not only helps the applicant, but it helps USCIS, whose officers don't want to waste time or mistreat an applicant simply because they didn't understand his or her special needs.

Only one person can act as the applicant's designated representative at a time, so your first task is to make sure that you're the right person for the job. USCIS requires that the designated representative be one of the following types of caretakers, in this order of priority:

- legal guardian or surrogate
- U.S. citizen spouse

George Washington

- U.S. citizen parent
- U.S. citizen adult son or daughter who acts as the applicant's primary caretaker, or
- U.S. citizen adult brother or sister who acts as the applicant's primary caretaker.

 More than one person may be able to help, without being a designated representative. For example, if the applicant has a legal guardian who needs to speak for him at the interview, but the applicant's brother is the best one at administering regularly needed injections, the applicant could have the legal guardian appointed designated representative, but ask that the brother also be allowed to attend the interview, as a reasonable accommodation. (See Section B, below, for more on requesting accommodations.)

In order to have yourself appointed as designated representative, you'll need to ask USCIS for this, preferably in a letter accompanying the applicant's N-400, or as a paragraph in the cover letter. (There's no need to ask before submitting the N-400—USCIS won't mind if you fill out the form and the applicant signs it, but you should enter your name in the preparer's box.) However, if you come into the picture after the N-400 has been filed, don't hesitate to send your letter separately (remembering to mention the applicant's A-number in your letter) or even arrive at the applicant's interview and hand the letter to the person at the appointment desk. In addition to making your request and stating your relationship to the applicant, your letter should state that, to the best of your knowledge and belief, no other person has been granted legal guardianship or authority over the affairs of the applicant. Along with your letter, you'll need to provide proof that your relationship to the applicant qualifies you to be a designated representative, as follows:

- If you're the applicant's **legal guardian or surrogate**, include a copy of the court order or evidence from another state authority granting you guardianship or custody. Make sure the order is from the same state in which the applicant is applying for citizenship.
- If you're the applicant's U.S. citizen **spouse**, include a copy of proof of your citizenship status (such as a birth certificate, passport, naturalization certificate, or other official document), a copy of your marriage certificate, and a sworn statement that you're still married.
- If you're the applicant's U.S. citizen **parent**, include a copy of proof of your citizenship status (such as a birth certificate, passport, naturalization certificate, or other official document) and a copy of your child's birth certificate.
- If you're the applicant's U.S. citizen **adult son or daughter**, include a copy of proof of your citizenship status (such as a birth certificate, passport, naturalization certificate, or other official document), a copy of your birth or adoption certificate, and evidence that you have primary custodial responsibility for the applicant, such as an executed power of attorney, or tax returns reflecting that the applicant has been declared a dependent in your household.
- If you're the applicant's U.S. citizen **brother or sister**, include a copy of proof of your citizenship status (such as a birth certificate, passport, naturalization certificate, or other official document), proof that you have the same parents (such as copies of both your birth certificates), and evidence that you have primary custodial responsibility for the applicant, such as an executed power of attorney, or tax returns reflecting that the applicant has been declared a dependent in your household.

If you submit your letter by mail and hear nothing back from USCIS, it's safe to assume that they've either accepted your request to act as designated representative, or that they'll make the final decision at the applicant's interview. Go ahead and accompany the applicant to the interview, if that was part of your request.

 Bring complete copies of your request, as well as original documents, to the interview. USCIS may want to review your request at that time, and your mailed documents may have gotten separated from the applicant's file. Also, USCIS likes to view original versions of documents such as court orders and marriage certificates to be sure that they're the real thing.

B. Accommodating Your Disability

In a normal USCIS interview, you must get to the USCIS office, wait an hour or more for your interview, make your way into the USCIS officer's cubicle or space, sit by his or her desk, raise your hand to take an oath, answer questions, and generally cope with a stressful situation. Any of these tasks, which might seem simple to another person, can seem like giant challenges to someone with physical or mental disabilities.

Fortunately, you can ask for accommodations in advance. If these accommodations are reasonable, and you can prove your need for them (particularly with reports from your doctor), USCIS will make an effort to grant them.

1. What You Can Ask For

Although you know best what you might need in the way of help, we include some examples below of the type of accommodations others might reasonably request. In general, the accommodations that USCIS will arrange usually have to do with the physical setting of the interview—where it's held, how quickly you're called in, whether your wheelchair will fit, whether you can bring a caregiver or guardian, whether someone will show you the way if you're blind (or you can bring your guide dog), whether someone will interpret for you if you're deaf, and more.

EXAMPLE 1: Dante's entire right side is paralyzed. He gets around using a motorized wheelchair and advises USCIS that he will be arriving in it. (Federal buildings are required by law to be wheelchair accessible, but unfortunately, the law and reality don't always match up.) Since Dante fatigues easily, he requests that USCIS interview him as soon as possible after he arrives. He explains that he will not be able to raise his right hand when swearing to tell the truth at the beginning of the interview. Under these circumstances, USCIS will allow him to take the oath using his left hand. Because he has difficulty making himself understood, Dante asks permission for a close friend to accompany him—someone who is accustomed to his mode of speech and can repeat his words to the USCIS officer.

EXAMPLE 2: Athena is severely developmentally disabled and hard of hearing. She was sexually abused as a child and now refuses to talk when any man speaks to her. She (or a guardian acting for her) requests that USCIS provide a female officer who is comfortable speaking loudly and clearly. In addition, Athena requests that USCIS allow her mother to accompany her into the interview to help Athena and the officer understand each other's words and to maintain Athena's comfort. (Athena separately requests waivers of the exam requirements, as covered in Section B, below.)

EXAMPLE 3: Kim has an advanced kidney ailment, and is confined to a hospital bed, and his long-term prognosis is not good. Kim asks USCIS to send an officer to interview him in his hospital room. (USCIS can also send someone to swear Kim in if he passes.) In addition, since Kim is afraid he won't survive until the regularly scheduled interview date and wants very badly to become a U.S. citizen, he requests an expedited (speeded up) interview date—and assuming he passes, requests that the USCIS officer swear him in as a citizen at the same time. (Note: USCIS usually grants these expedited interviews only in life or death situations.)

For various reasons, USCIS has been seeing more requests for accommodations recently, so don't worry that your situation will seem unusual. If you truly need assistance, don't be shy about making your request.

2. Requesting Accommodations

In order to alert USCIS that you need accommodations, check the "yes" box on Part 3, Question I, of the citizenship application form (Form N-400). Below that, you are given a few options, or yu can specifically explain what accommodations you'll need in the blank lines by the fourth box. If this isn't enough space, attach a more complete explanation on a separate piece of paper and in your cover letter. Be as specific as you can in your request. For example, instead of saying "I need a friend with me because I am sick," say "I need a friend to accompany me into the interview in case I have a seizure and need an injection administered quickly."

Regardless of the information provided on the application form, it's a good idea to repeat your accommodations request in your cover letter and to include a doctor's letter to your application packet.

Ask your doctor to write a letter—there's no special form to use—explaining your condition in medical terms and confirming the assistance you will need at the interview and swearing-in ceremony. (Although doctor's letters are not required, they're very helpful in convincing USCIS that you need certain accommodations. You could also simply use copies of test results.) Note: If your doctor is already separately filling out an exam waiver request for you (discussed in the next section), he or she won't need to separately discuss your medical condition in this letter.

If you're asking to be interviewed soon after arrival at the USCIS office, alert a USCIS officer in person. Most people, upon arriving for their interview, are told to put their interview notice in a basket. This would result in your being interviewed in the same order as everyone else, usually after a long wait. Tell the USCIS officer in charge of the intake desk you're asking for a "special accommodation interview." Give the officer your interview notice, along with a copy of an explanatory letter from your doctor or your Form N-648 (if you filed one—this is the form requesting waivers of the exam requirements, discussed in Section C2, below). Don't sit down until you're sure the officer understands your request.

If USCIS refuses to make the accommodations that you requested, talk to a lawyer, a nonprofit organization serving immigrants and refugees, or a disability advocate. Hopefully, a third party will be able to help resolve any USCIS misunderstandings.

House Calls: When to Ask

It is unusual for USCIS to visit someone at their home or hospital. The agency—already backed up with applicants—is afraid that if one person receives a home visit, everyone who is in less than great shape will want one too.

Nevertheless, if you really can't leave your home or your hospital bed, USCIS can arrange to come to you for every element of the citizenship application process. It has the power to send a fingerprinting specialist to take your fingerprints, and to send a USCIS officer to conduct your interview and to swear you in for citizenship. (The interview and the swearing-in can sometimes be done by the same officer on the same day.)

Unfortunately, in some districts, USCIS is not very responsive—for example, consider the 87-year-old bedridden resident of a nursing home who waited two years for an interview and eventually had to file a lawsuit to get action on her request.

To request home services, follow the procedures described in this chapter. After you make your request, USCIS may take the unusual step of calling you or your family on the phone and asking for more details about your illness and your needs.

If USCIS seems inattentive to your requests—for example, if you receive a normal fingerprint appointment notice—write a letter reminding the agency of the situation and repeating your request. Some USCIS regions have a special staff person dedicated to helping people with disabilities. You may need to ask a friend or relative to go to the local USCIS office and ask who that person is. When making the inquiry, have your friend or relative bring a complete copy of your citizenship application and your receipt notice. Local nonprofits serving immigrants and refugees may also provide you with this information.

C. Obtaining a Disability-Based Waiver of the Exam Requirements

Many medical conditions make it difficult to learn English and/or the necessary U.S. history and government information. Besides permanent conditions—for example, developmental disability, deafness and blindness—a severe illness can bring on pain and decreased functioning that interfere with your ability to learn. In addition, prescription medications may impair your concentration and memory. Some conditions may confine you at home, making it impossible to attend classes and prepare for the exams. Psychological conditions can have as serious an impact as physical ones. In particular, it's not uncommon for refugees to have posttraumatic stress disorder (PTSD) and to therefore experience problems with concentration and memory.

If you have such a disability, you can request a waiver of the English requirement, the U.S. history and government requirement, or both. You cannot request the exam waiver(s) by yourself; your doctor must prepare a detailed form that explains your situation to USCIS. Not every medical problem qualifies you for a waiver, however. That's why it's important for you to review this chapter carefully and work closely with your doctor to prepare your waiver request convincingly.

⚠ **The disability waiver** excuses you from the citizenship exams, but not from other U.S. citizenship requirements discussed in Chapter 2. For example, you will still need to fulfill location, physical presence, green card, and moral character requirements.

You will not find out whether USCIS will grant your disability waiver until your interview. (It's rare for them to even look at your file until that date). However, the N-648 is supposed to be the first thing they look at during the interview. Nevertheless, you might want to prepare for the exams to the extent possible. If you already speak English, or if your N-648 isn't quite good enough and will need to be redone anyway, some officers will ask you U.S. history and government questions despite your waiver request. They're probably not doing it to make your life difficult—they're just hoping that they can grant you citizenship without having to make a decision on the waiver. If the officer can get you to answer six questions correctly (and they'll always choose the easiest questions), everyone will win. You'll be approved for citizenship, and the officer won't have to deal with the waiver application. If this process causes you too much stress, however, you can protest and ask the officer to follow normal procedures.

1. Qualifying Disabilities

To qualify for a disability waiver, your condition must, at a minimum, be "medically determinable." That means that your doctor must have diagnosed it using medically accepted clinical and laboratory techniques. The tests must show anatomical, physiological, or psychological abnormalities. Also, your condition must not be temporary—in fact, it must be expected to last for at least 12 months. And, it must not be the result of illegal drug use.

⚠ **If your doctor believes your condition comes from illegal drug use, don't ask for an exam waiver.** Alerting USCIS to your drug use can result in your being denied citizenship and being placed in deportation proceedings.

All of the medical conditions mentioned above—deafness, blindness, developmental disabilities, severe illness or injury (physical or psychological), memory, and concentration problems—might qualify a person for a waiver of the English and/or U.S. history and government exams. A combination of such medical conditions might also qualify you, even if each one taken alone wouldn't be severe enough to require a waiver. Other conditions not included in our list might also qualify—for example, depression may qualify, though this is an area of ongoing USCIS controversy. You'll have to prove that the depression truly impairs your functioning to the point where you can't learn the material on the tests.

Letter to Doctor Performing Exam for Disability Waiver

Dear Physician:

Your patient plans to submit an application for U.S. citizenship to U.S. Citizenship and Immigration Services (USCIS). Part of the application process normally involves taking exams covering the English language (in writing and orally) and U.S. history and government (orally). However, your patient feels that his or her physical or psychological condition makes it unduly difficult to prepare for or pass these exams. Your patient will be asking for a waiver of one or both of these exams. In support of this waiver request, the patient asks that you assess his or her disability and fill out government Form N-648.

This letter is to give you an introduction, or perhaps a reminder, of what USCIS needs to see on Form N-648 in order to consider or grant the waiver. In particular, three key things must emerge from your statements on the form—or the waiver will be denied, even if, in your professional opinion, it should have been granted. These three critical things include:

1. a full explanation of your patient's condition(s), physical or mental, including its severity or DSM code

2. an explanation of how this condition(s) affects the patient's ability to study, learn, or remember the exam material, and

3. your opinion on whether a waiver of the exam requirements is appropriate.

Please give special attention to the second item on this list, since it's the one that most often causes USCIS to reject a doctor's disability waiver recommendation. USCIS feels that many doctors don't answer the question, "Why should having this condition excuse this person from taking these exams?"

Here are examples, straight from U.S. government memos, of the types of physician's statements that would lead to a denial or an approval of the very same patient's request:

WAIVER DENIED:

The patient suffers from Down's Syndrome. He should be exempted from the English language and U.S. civics requirements for citizenship.

WAIVER GRANTED:

The patient suffers from Down's Syndrome. He was tested with Wechsler Adult Intelligence Scale and was found to be moderately retarded with an IQ of 50 (tested on June 1, 1995). The patient's mental retardation is a global impairment, which affects cognition, language, and motor skills. Because of the patient's global impairment, he cannot learn new skills and is not capable of reasoning. His memory is deficient, and he is capable of performing only simple daily activities. Because of the patient's mental disability, he is incapable of learning a new language (even basic words of a new language) and U.S. history and civics.

Letter to Doctor Performing Exam for Disability Waiver (Continued)

The more you can do to tie the patient's condition to an inability to study, learn, or memorize words or concepts, the better. Also, you'll be reducing the chances that USCIS will request follow-up information from you!

A few other points to consider:

- Because there are two separate exams, one covering English and one covering U.S. civics, please specify whether the patient is unable to learn one or both of these subjects.

- If you believe the patient's impairment is due to illegal drug use, please stop now and tell the patient you can't fill out this form. Submitting a form with this information could cause your patient to be deported from the United States.

- If you believe the patient's medical condition will not last at least twelve months, please stop now and tell the patient you can't fill out this form. Temporary disabilities will not qualify applicants for the waiver.

- Avoid referring to the patient as illiterate, lacking in formal education, or being of advanced age if you can point to a separate or more fundamental medical reason that he or she can't learn—otherwise USCIS may deny the waiver, believing that illiteracy, age, etc., is the only problem.

- Although old age alone is not sufficient to qualify a person for a disability waiver, diseases caused by old age, such as Alzheimer's, Parkinson's, or senile dementia, are often sufficient.

- You don't need to attach medical records, though they can be helpful, and USCIS reserves the right to request them later.

- USCIS has been complaining that it can't read doctors' handwriting, and it has been rejecting waiver requests as a result. Please print or type legibly! Return the form directly to the patient, unsealed.

Thank you very much for your attention to this letter and for assisting your patient to become a U.S. citizen.

USCIS does not grant the disability waiver automatically for any particular illnesses and the agency does not maintain a list of medical conditions recognized as worthy of waivers. USCIS knows that every person's medical history and life circumstances are unique. Factors such as age, the severity of the medical condition, its combination with other conditions or illnesses, and the type of medication prescribed can make a huge difference in a person's ability to study or learn. And USCIS is well aware that modern training techniques can help some people overcome certain disabilities—for example, a blind or deaf person might be taught English and eventually be able to study for the U.S. history and government exam.

For these reasons, USCIS relies heavily on your doctor to tell them what you can and can't do. And that's why you will need to work closely with your doctor to make sure your doctor understands your situation and presents it completely and accurately.

> ⚠ **USCIS can reject your doctor's recommendation.** If your doctor doesn't give a good explanation of why your condition impedes you from learning the necessary material, your waiver request will be rejected. We advise you on how to get what you need from your doctor in Section B2, below.

2. Requesting Disability-Based Waivers

To request a disability-based waiver, first check the "yes" box in Part 3, Question H, of Form N-400. Then schedule an appointment with your doctor, osteopath, or clinical psychologist. Explain to the appointment desk that you'll need sufficient time— your appointment will resemble a full physical. Your doctor will be examining you in preparation for filling out Form N-648, Medical Certification for Disability Exceptions.

> ⚠ **Don't ask your doctor to prepare Form N-648 more than six months before you submit it to USCIS.** Otherwise, you might have to get your doctor to redo the form. Once it's submitted, however, it doesn't expire.

Before you go to your doctor's office, copy or print out Form N-648. On Part I of the form, fill out your name, other identifying information, and permission for the doctor to release information. If your disability prevents you from writing or signing your own name (for example, because your hands don't work, or because of cognitive difficulties), you can have someone else fill in most of the information for you—except for your signature. For the signature, you have two choices. You can either mark an "X" in place of your signature, or your legal guardian can sign for you. (After the signature, guardians should put in parentheses "signed by [*guardian's name*], designated representative".)

Take the form to your appointment. Your request on Form N-400 and the doctor's report on Form N-648 are all you'll need to request this waiver.

> Form N-648 is included in Appendix C and is available from USCIS by phone at 800-870-3676. You can also download it from the USCIS website (www.uscis.gov).

> 📋 Include Form N-648 with the application packet that you submit to USCIS.

You should use your own doctor for this exam— USCIS doesn't provide a list of doctors for disability exams. However, your doctor must be a U.S.-licensed physician, osteopath, or clinical psychologist. Any doctor you normally see—either your primary care (or family) doctor or a specialist—can fill out Form N-648, so long as he or she has access to the appropriate medical records and test results.

> ⚠ **Don't go to a special doctor just because you hear that he or she is "easy" about giving out disability waivers.** USCIS quickly picks up on patterns of abuse, and if the agency sees many waivers from the same doctor, it will consider your case more suspiciously.

If your doctor hasn't done disability waiver evaluations before, he or she will need your help. So, don't just hand the doctor Form N-648 and say, "Please fill it out."

Most doctors are accustomed to having their instructions followed, so they often believe that they can just write "patient has X condition, is disabled, and merits a waiver of the citizenship exam requirements" and be done with the matter. They're wrong. USCIS will not be convinced by this type of statement and will not grant a disability waiver unless the doctor has stated a *connection* between your illness and your inability to take the exam.

The best way to explain all of this is to copy the letter above and hand it to your doctor at your appointment. (Read the letter yourself, too, so as to better understand the process.)

If you picked up this book after submitting your citizenship application to USCIS, but now realize you need a disability waiver, it's not too late. You can ask your doctor to prepare a Form N-648 and submit it at your interview.

The "six months" rule still applies, however—the doctor's signature on the form can't be more than six months old when you submit it. Since you can't be sure when your interview will be scheduled, timing your doctor's signature can be a bit tricky. Explain the situation to the person making appointments at your doctor's office, and make sure that the doctor can schedule you for an appointment as soon as you receive your interview notice (you'll have about a two-week window). Alternately, find out when USCIS "normally" calls people for interviews in your area and schedule a medical appointment close to that time—recognizing, of course, that the interview could occur earlier or later than the "normal" date.

If you've already submitted your N-648, but your condition has since gotten significantly worse, bring an updated N-648 to your interview. This will, of course, require attending another doctor's appointment, but it will make your waiver case stronger.

D. Requesting a Waiver of the Oath of Allegiance Requirement

The last step in becoming a U.S. citizen is to attend a ceremony in which you take an oath, swearing allegiance to the United States. Despite their

disabilities, many applicants successfully attend the ceremony and take the oath. However, for some, particularly those with severe developmental or cognitive difficulties, understanding or repeating the Oath of Allegiance will be impossible. Although the former INS refused citizenship to many applicants who couldn't take the oath, a law passed in 2000 fixed the problem by providing a waiver of the oath requirement. The waiver applies to people who are "unable to understand, or to communicate an understanding of [the oath's] meaning because of a physical or developmental disability or mental impairment." (See I.N.A. § 337(a), 8 U.S.C. 1448(a).)

If you are the naturalization applicant, and you are reading and understanding this paragraph, you don't need this waiver. It's also not meant for people who would find it physically very difficult to attend the ceremony—USCIS prefers to find a way to accommodate such people, including visiting them at home if absolutely necessary. The oath waiver is most appropriate for people who are virtually beyond communication, or who must depend on others to do their thinking for them. Normally ,such people have a friend or family member act as their representative during the naturalization interview. For example, I once met an applicant who was both severely mentally retarded and deaf, and who had been unable to learn any sort of sign language other than pressing her mother's hand. She is a classic example of someone who would qualify for a waiver under the new law.

Unfortunately, the oath waiver isn't automatic. The applicant (or whoever is preparing the application for him or her) must separately request the waiver. Moreover, USCIS has not created any formal way to make this request. As mentioned earlier, USCIS suggests that you (presumably, the applicant's representative) write a note under Part 3, Question I, of Form N-400, or write a separate statement explaining the situation. If USCIS needs more information before the interview, it will send you a written request. In addition, you'll need to obtain a separate written evaluation from the applicant's doctor (medical doctor, osteopath, or clinical psychologist) supporting the oath waiver request. The evaluation must be written by the doctor who has had the longest relationship with the applicant, or who is most familiar with his or her medical history. Here's what the doctor should put into the evaluation:

- an explanation of the applicant's condition and disability, in terms that can be easily understood by the applicant's representative and the USCIS officer

- a thorough statement of why and how the applicant's disability makes him or her unable to understand or communicate an understanding of what the oath means

- an indication of how likely it is that in the near future, the applicant will be able to communicate or show an understanding of the oath's meaning, and

- the doctor's signature and state license number.

At the applicant's naturalization interview, a USCIS officer will decide whether to grant the oath waiver. The interviewing officer will not only review the written materials you have submitted, but will also attempt to communicate with the applicant him or herself. In particular, the officer will want to discover whether the applicant understands that he or she is:

- becoming a U.S. citizen

- giving up allegiance to his or her home country, and

- personally and voluntarily agreeing to this change.

The officer is allowed to try all sorts of things in attempting to communicate with the applicant. For example, the officer may use the applicant's family members as interpreters, asking them to convey the above three concepts in a way the applicant can understand. The officer may also ask the applicant to give "yes" or "no" responses to simplified questions about these concepts. If the only way the applicant can communicate is through physical motions or signals, that's okay, these will be relied on.

If it turns out that the applicant can understand, at some basic level, the idea that he or she is becoming a U.S. citizen, the waiver may be denied—but don't worry, this is good news in its own way. It means that the applicant can go forward to the oath ceremony, and, probably with the help of his or her representative and other accommodations, take the oath to become a U.S. citizen. If the waiver is granted, that's also good—the applicant's citizenship can be granted right away. Although applicants who are granted the waiver need not attend the oath ceremony, USCIS will allow them or their designated representatives to participate if they so desire. ■

The Interview

Your appointment notice—when you finally receive it—will tell you where and when to present yourself for your citizenship interview. An example is provided below. After you receive this notice, you have only one major hurdle left to citizenship—a successful interview.

In this chapter, we'll help you prepare for your interview by discussing:

- what to bring, what to wear, and what to do before your interview (see Section A)
- what to expect and how to handle yourself at the interview (see Section B), and
- how to deal with difficult interviews and unpleasant officers (see Section C).

If your interview appointment arrives and you aren't ready—that is, you haven't learned as much English as you thought you would, or you are having trouble remembering the exam questions and answers—we recommend that you attend anyway. For one thing, the interview might be easier than you think. Remember, the USCIS officer is supposed to take into account any factors related to your education or age that would make the interview difficult for you. As we'll discuss in Section C below, you'll get a second chance if you fail the exam portion of

the first interview, so, in that case, consider this first interview as a practice round.

If, however, you are afraid to attend the interview because you now realize you are ineligible for citizenship or are putting your green card at risk by continuing with your application, reschedule your interview. (In your request letter, you'll have to simply say that circumstances beyond your control require you to miss the scheduled interview.) Then consult with a lawyer immediately. If the situation is serious enough, the lawyer may recommend that you withdraw your application to remove it from USCIS's attention.

A. Final Preparation

The key to a successful interview is preparation. Hopefully, you've been studying English and U.S. history during the months leading up to the interview. Now, you'll need to:

- review your application
- assemble the documents you'll bring with you
- decide what to wear, and
- make sure you know where you're going.

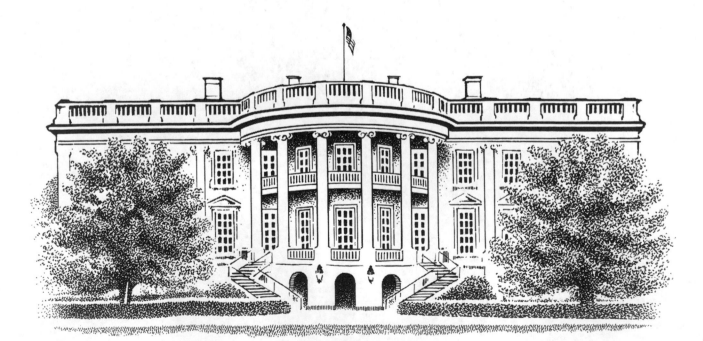

White House—Washington, D.C.

U.S. Department of Justice
Immigration and Naturalization Service

Notice of Action

THE UNITED STATES OF AMERICA

Request That Applicant Appear For Naturalization Initial Interview		NOTICE DATE May 10, 2001
CASE TYPE N400 Application For Naturalization		**INS A#** A 023 456 789
APPLICATION NUMBER WSC*000513770	**RECEIVED DATE** July 25, 2000 **PRIORITY DATE** July 25, 2000	**PAGE** 1 of 1

APPLICANT NAME AND MAILING ADDRESS	
WOLFGANG KOHL 950 PARKER STREET BERKELEY, CA 94610	**Please come to:** USINS OAKLAND CUSA 1301 CLAY ST ROOM 380N MAIN ROOM OAKLAND CA 94612 **On (Date):** Wednesday, August 22, 2001 **At (Time):** 08:20 AM

You are hereby notified to appear for an interview on your Application for Naturalization at the date, time, and place indicated above. **Waiting room capacity is limited. Please do not arrive any earlier than 30 minutes before your scheduled appointment time.** The proceeding will take about two hours. If for any reason you cannot keep this appointment, return this letter immediately with your explanation and a request for a new appointment; otherwise, no further action will be taken on your application.

If you are applying for citizenship for yourself, you will be tested on your knowledge of the government and history of the United States. You will also be tested on reading, writing, and speaking English, unless on the day you filed your application, you have been living in the United States for a total of at least 20 years as a lawful permanent resident and are over 50 years old, or you have been living in the United States for a total of 15 years as a lawful permanent resident and are over 55 years old, or unless you have a medically determinable disability (you must have filed form N648 Medical Certification for Disability Exception, with your N400 Application for Naturalization).

You MUST BRING the following with you to the interview:

- This letter.
- Your Alien Registration Card (green card).
- Any evidence of Selective Service Registration.
- Your passport and/or any other documents you used in connection with any entries into the United States.
- Those items noted below which are applicable to you:

If applying for NATURALIZATION AS THE SPOUSE of a United States Citizen;

- Your marriage certificate.
- Proof of death or divorce for each prior marriage of yourself or spouse.
- Your spouse's birth or naturalization certificate or certificate of citizenship.

If applying for NATURALIZATION as a member of the United States Armed Forces;

- Your discharge certificate, or form DD 214.

If copies of a document were submitted as evidence with your N400 application, the originals of those documents should be brought to the interview.

PLEASE keep this appointment, even if you do not have all the items indicated above.

If you have any questions or comments regarding this notice or the status of your case, please contact our office at the below address or customer service number. You will be notified separately about any other cases you may have filed.

INS Office Address:
US IMMIGRATION AND NATURALIZATION SERVICE
P.O BOX 10400 CALIFORNIA SERVICE CENTER
LAGUNA NIGUEL, CA 92607-

INS Customer Service Number:
(949) 831-8427

Form I 797 (Rev. 09/07/93)N

How to Reschedule an Interview

If it's truly impossible to make the scheduled appointment, ask for a new date. But we recommend that you try your hardest to make the initial appointment. If you reschedule, you could wait a long time for a new date—possibly many months. If you must reschedule, either go to the office where the interview was scheduled and explain the situation, or write the office a letter. You can use the form letter, below, as a guide. (Don't send the letter to the same address that you first sent your application—that's a USCIS Service Center, and once it has transferred your file to the local USCIS office, it has no power over your case.)

In order to qualify for a new appointment, you'll need to show that you are prevented from attending for reasons beyond your control. "I'm not ready" is not an acceptable excuse. (If you're not ready, we recommend that you attend anyway; see below.)

If you fail to appear at your initial interview and take no other action, USCIS will not reschedule your interview—it will simply close your file.

[*Your address and the date*]

U.S. Citizenship and Immigration Services
Citizenship Unit
[*Address from which the interview notice came*]

RE: [*Your full name and A-number*]; Request for Reschedule

Dear Sir/Madam:

I am unable to attend the citizenship interview that you set for [*date*]. The reason is that [*explain your reason*]. Please reschedule me for a later date. I can be reached at the address above, or by telephone at [*your number*].

Thank you for your attention to this matter.

Very truly yours,
[*sign your name*]
[*type your name*]

---

1. Review Your Application and Note Changes

You may be surprised at how much of your interview is spent going over your written application, particularly Form N-400. The USCIS officer uses the simple inquiries on your form such as "Your current legal name" and "What is your current marital status?" to test your English and to confirm that the information you have given is correct. Before the interview, go over your copy of Form N-400 carefully. Then, simulate the interview at home. Have a friend ask you each one of the questions.

Be on the lookout for any mistakes or changes to the information on the form. The officer at your interview may ask near the beginning, "Are there any changes to your application?" Be prepared to provide corrections—most changes are not a problem. If, for example, you have had another child, be prepared with the child's exact name and a copy of the birth certificate. If you've taken a trip outside the United States, memorize or write down the exact dates and other information that the N-400 asks for regarding trips (and, of course, make sure that none of those trips broke the continuity of your U.S. stay; see Chapter 2, Section B2). If you've changed jobs, it would be helpful to have a business card handy showing your new employer's name and address.

 If you bring written material to your interview, be prepared to share it with the USCIS officer. An officer may ask to see any personal notes you've brought to avoid suspicion that you've got the answers to the U.S. history and government exam.

Two particular changes to your Form N-400 could have a serious impact on your citizenship chances:

- If you've recently been divorced from the person who sponsored you for a green card, see Chapter 1, Section A.
- If you've recently been arrested or done anything else that would cause you to change your answer on the questions in Part 5 of the Form N-400 to "yes," see an immigration attorney immediately.

If either of the above are true, it may not only affect your eligibility for citizenship, but your right to remain in the United States.

2. What to Bring

Assemble the items on the list below. The USCIS officer may not ask for all of them, but it's better to be over-prepared. Also take a look at the list of items requested by USCIS in your interview notice. Most of this list is "boilerplate"—in other words, USCIS includes it on everyone's letter, even if items on it don't apply to you. Occasionally, however, USCIS will identify something particular to your case that you must bring.

You will see items on our list that USCIS doesn't request. Bring those items anyway—the USCIS officer often asks for items without warning you before the interview.

Bring the following to your interview:

- green card
- photo identification, such as a driver's license
- passport and any travel documents that USCIS has issued to you, such as a reentry permit for a trip of more than one year, and
- copies of your tax returns for the last three years (to show that you've paid taxes).

If you meet any of the following conditions, bring the items listed below:

- If you are a male and were required to register with the Selective Service, bring proof that you did so.
- If you're applying as a member of the military, bring your discharge certificate or your form DD 214 Record of Separation.
- If you have young children who are in someone else's care, bring proof that you have continuously paid child support (such as cancelled checks, bank records of your payments, and a copy of any court or government orders showing what you owe).
- If you are married to a U.S. citizen and applying after only three years, bring:
  - your marriage certificate
  - evidence that your spouse has been a U.S. citizen for all of the three years, such as a copy of his or her birth or naturalization certificate or U.S. passport
  - proof that any of your and/or your spouse's prior marriages were legally ended, such as death or divorce certificates, and
  - proof that you are still living together, such as rent receipts, joint credit card statements, and other documents showing that you share your home and finances.

If you qualify for and requested a waiver of the English language requirements, you'll need an interpreter. Ask the USCIS office whether you can bring your own interpreter (allowed in some, but not all, districts) or whether USCIS will hire an interpreter. (See 8 C.F.R. § 312.4.) USCIS often uses AT&T telephone interpreters for citizenship interviews. The AT&T interpreters will be on speakerphone and a little difficult to hear, so if you have a choice, you might want to bring an interpreter. You don't necessarily have to hire a professional—a friend or relative who is older than 18 and fluent in both English and your native language will do. But, if USCIS decides that your interpreter isn't good enough for the job, it can refuse to use that person and reschedule your interview.

⚠ Unless you are disabled or need an interpreter and have arranged for this in advance, USCIS will not allow friends or family members at your interview. Any friends or family who accompany you will be required to sit in the waiting room—and USCIS discourages this as well. See Chapter 7 regarding accommodations for the disabled.

3. What to Wear—And What to Leave at Home

It's improper for the USCIS officer's decision about citizenship to be affected by your appearance, but it's also hard to believe that it's not a factor—at least at some level. Although we don't want to limit your ability to express your personal style, we recommend that you dress neatly, professionally, and conservatively—in short, look the way you might if going for an important job interview.

In any case, avoid wearing T-shirts or jewelry that might make the officer wonder about your lifestyle or morals. We've known people who attended their USCIS interview wearing a T-shirt that said "S—happens!" or a necklace with a gold marijuana leaf hanging from it. Those style decisions are likely to distract the interviewer and lead to unwanted personal questions.

![warning icon] **Remember the metal detector.** When you go into a federal building, you'll be subject to a security search. Don't carry anything that resembles a weapon, or you'll have to check it with the security guard. (Of course, if it *is* a weapon, you'll be arrested.) Don't suffer the same result as the author of this book, who lost her favorite Swiss Army knife when the door guards checked it in and then accidentally gave it to another visitor.

4. Know Where You're Going

Why is that buses run late and parking spots are hardest to find on days when you're desperate to get somewhere? Whatever the reason, make sure you know how to get to the USCIS office listed on the letter and leave plenty of extra time to get there. It's better to spend some extra time in the waiting room than to arrive at the last minute in a panic, or worse, to miss your interview.

Also, keep in mind that the address on your appointment letter may not be the central USCIS office that you're accustomed to visiting. In some regions, USCIS has arranged for extra offices to handle citizenship interviews—for example, in the San Francisco Bay Area, some people are sent to the USCIS's San Francisco District office, while many others are sent to an office in Oakland that handles only citizenship interviews.

B. The Interview

When you get to the USCIS office, the usual procedure is for you to place your interview notice in a box and wait for your name to be called. You may have to wait a very long time, since USCIS often schedules many people for the same block of time.

When it's your turn, a USCIS officer will call you in to the inner office, and very quickly—usually within 20 minutes—conduct the interview. In this section, we discuss what the officer will say and do during those 20 minutes (Section B1) and the best ways for you to respond (Section B2).

 If you're disabled and asked for an immediate interview, don't put your notice in the box. Find a USCIS officer and hand him or her your appointment notice personally, and explain you have a disability and are requesting an immediate interview.

1. A Sample Interview

A single USCIS officer will usually bring you to his or her desk to interview you. Don't sit down when you get there—the officer will probably want you to remain standing until he or she tells you it's time to sit down. (As we explained in Chapter 5, your ability to follow instructions is important in proving that you speak English.) If the officer does not tell you his or her name, ask for it, and write it down or do your best to remember it (USCIS officers don't give out business cards). If anything goes wrong and you later need to consult with a lawyer, it will help if you can then tell your lawyer the name of the officer. Experienced immigration lawyers often know the personalities of the various USCIS officers, and that information may assist in preparing your case.

First, the interviewing officer will ask you to stand up, raise your right hand, and swear to tell the truth. After that, you'll sit down and the officer will proceed with three tasks:

- verifying the information on your Form N-400
- determining whether you speak, read, and write English, and
- testing you on U.S. history and government.

The tasks will flow together—that is, the officer won't tell you "this is step one," etc. To see how this works, let's look at the script of a typical interview—one in which the applicant did a good job of handling herself. Because the applicant speaks English well and has a college education, the USCIS officer gave her more difficult questions than would be given to someone with less ability.

USCIS: *Right this way, please. Remain standing. Now raise your right hand. Do you swear that during today's interview you'll tell me the truth, the whole truth, and nothing but the truth?*
Applicant: Yes.

USCIS: *You may sit down. May I see your green card and photo identification?*
Applicant: Yes, here they are.

USCIS: *Okay, what is your full name?*
Applicant: My name is Xena Nassopoulous.

USCIS: *I see here that you want to change your last name to Nassbaum, is that right?*
Applicant: Yes, I'm married, and my husband and I want to invent a last name by combining our two names.

USCIS: *All right, that's fine, your name will be changed at the swearing-in, if you're approved today.*

USCIS: *What is your address?*
Applicant: I live at 459 Gooseberry Drive, in Jay, Vermont.

USCIS: *When and where were you born?*
Applicant: I was born in Greece on July 12, 1972.

USCIS: *You say on your application that you've taken only two trips outside the United States since you became a permanent resident in 1994. Is that true?*
Applicant: Yes, I just took two trips home to Greece.

USCIS: *Are you sure? What about short trips to Mexico or Canada?*
Applicant: We live near the Canadian border, so we sometimes go visit there for a day. But we've never spent a night there.

USCIS: *What is your husband's name?*

Applicant: His name is Ernest Birnbaum.

USCIS: *Are there any changes to the rest of the personal information on your application?*
Applicant: Yes, my husband and I had a daughter last year, named Artemis. Here is a copy of her birth certificate.

USCIS: *Thank you.* [Officer writes the information from the birth certificate onto the application.]

USCIS: *Have you ever failed to file your federal income taxes?*
Applicant: I'm sorry, could you say that in another way? I didn't quite understand it.

USCIS: *Have you ever failed to send the IRS an annual tax form and any payments owing?*
Applicant: No, that is, I've paid taxes every year since I've been here.

USCIS: *Did you bring copies of your tax returns today?*
Applicant: Yes, here they are.

USCIS: *Your application form says that you are a member of Amnesty International. Are you involved in any other groups or organizations?*
Applicant: Not formally. I attend religious services with my husband sometimes, and I contribute to some charities, but I'm not really a member of anything else.

USCIS: *Have you ever been a member of the Communist Party?*
Applicant: No.

USCIS: [Reviews the rest of the questions on Part 10 of the N-400; Xena answers "no" to all of them. The USCIS officer opens the results of her fingerprint check with the FBI and confirms that Xena has no record of criminal or USCIS violations.]

USCIS: *Now I'll ask you a few questions about U.S. history and government. What do the stripes on the U.S. flag mean?*
Applicant: They represent the thirteen original states. [*Correct.*]

USCIS: Can you name the thirteen original states?

Applicant: Connecticut, New Hampshire, New York, Massachusetts, Pennsylvania, Delaware, Virginia, North Carolina, South Carolina, Georgia, Rhode Island, and … and … oh dear, I can never remember the last one. [*Incorrect: Xena forgot Maryland.*]

USCIS: *What is the name of the ship that brought the Pilgrims to America?*

Applicant: The *Mayflower*. [*Correct.*]

USCIS: *Which President freed the slaves?*

Applicant: Abraham Lincoln. [*Correct.*]

USCIS: *What is the Constitution?*

Applicant: The supreme law of the land. [*Correct.*]

USCIS: *Name one right guaranteed by the First Amendment.*

Applicant: Freedom of the press. [*Correct.*]

USCIS: *Who is the governor of our state, Vermont?*

Applicant: Jim Douglas. [*Correct.*]

USCIS: *Okay, you've answered six correctly, that's enough. Now take this pencil and write the sentence, "She is my daughter, and he is my son."* [Xena writes the sentence correctly.]

USCIS: *Please read this passage of text.* [Xena reads the passage correctly.]

USCIS: *Do you believe in the U.S. Constitution?*

Applicant: Uh, huh.

USCIS: *Please state "Yes" or "No" clearly.*

Applicant: I meant, yes.

USCIS: *Are you willing to take the Oath of Allegiance?*

Applicant: Yes.

USCIS: *If the law requires it, will you fight and defend the United States, or assist those who do?*

Applicant: Yes.

USCIS: *That's all for today, I'm going to approve your application. Please sign here, and take this sheet explaining when you'll be called for the swearing-in ceremony.*

Applicant: Thank you!

USCIS: *Congratulations, and good-bye.*

2. Interview Tips

For you, the interview may be one of the most important events of your life. But keep in mind that, to the USCIS officer who is at work, you're just one person in a long day full of people. That doesn't mean the officer doesn't care about you—but in order to maintain efficiency, the officer will appreciate it if you're prepared, organized, and professional. Wait for the officer's questions and answer them as briefly as you can while still using full sentences.

If you don't understand a question, ask the officer to rephrase it. Rather than guessing at what the officer is saying—which could get you into trouble—simply say, "I'm sorry, could you repeat that using different words?" In fact, USCIS has instructed officers "to repeat and rephrase questions until the officer is satisfied that the applicant either fully understands the question or does not understand English."

a. Avoid Putting on an Act

Some immigrants cynically conclude that they can win the officer's favor through tactics like personal compliments or pro-American statements. Telling the officer, "My, that's a lovely outfit you're wearing today" is unnecessary, and could seem like an effort at distraction. One applicant showed up for his USCIS interview wearing a tie covered with U.S. flags, and peppered the interview with comments about America's greatness. (The interviewing officer obviously felt that the applicant was pushing this too far.) USCIS certainly wants you to act courteously and be supportive of the United States, but self-serving speeches are a waste of the officer's time and an insult to his or her intelligence.

b. Honesty Is the Best Policy

One of the worst things you can do at your interview is to lie. If you're caught—and USCIS has a surprising number of ways at catching people in lies—the effect on your application may be devastating—far worse than if you had told the truth. Even if you're caught years later, your citizenship can be taken away at that time.

On the other hand, don't view the USCIS office as a confession booth. Only answer what you are asked, and avoid volunteering information unless it is needed to better understand the information provided on the application.

c. Present Yourself Confidently

In some cultures, it is impolite to look someone in the eyes when you speak. That's not the case in the United States, where looking away or at the floor are often perceived as a sign of deception. At your interview, look straight at the officer's eyes when the two of you speak. (If you find this difficult, try looking at the officer's forehead or nose.) Speak confidently and, if possible, try to relax. Think positive! The USCIS officers are usually pleased to meet someone like yourself who has prepared the paperwork carefully and studied hard.

C. If the Interview Goes Badly

Although a good number of USCIS officers are helpful and interested in seeing you become a citizen, you may run into one whose manner is rude or hostile. First, remember that it's probably not personal. Some USCIS officers become jaded and cynical after years of investigating fraudulent citizenship claims.

Second, try not to get angry. Remain respectful and answer honestly if you don't know or remember something. You might encounter an officer who makes irrelevant or unfounded accusations, acts in a discriminatory manner based on your race or gender, becomes uncontrollably angry, or persists with a line of questions or statements that is completely inappropriate.

Another problem is when the USCIS officer does something that deviates from normal procedures. For example, if you realize that one of the U.S. government questions the officer asked you is not from the list of 100 questions—for example, he or she asked you the name of a U.S. president's wife— that's a violation of procedure. If any of these things happens, politely ask to see a supervisor before continuing with the interview. Explain the situation to the supervisor and ask him or her to intervene or reschedule you with a different officer.

If you deal with an irate officer who demands information or documents that you don't have on hand, ask to either reschedule the interview or to be allowed to submit supplemental documents by mail. The latter approach may avoid having an angry officer making a final decision on the spot. (Hopefully by the time the officer receives your follow-up materials, he or she will have cooled down.)

If you believe that a USCIS officer behaved improperly, write down as many details as you can remember of the interview, while it's fresh in your mind. Then consider consulting an attorney about your experience, to learn what you can do to improve USCIS's reaction to your application.

Even if you don't speak to or hire a lawyer, you can write a letter to the USCIS office. USCIS supervisors assume that officers act appropriately unless you tell them otherwise, so alert the supervisor to any inappropriate behavior and ask that the supervisor consider the officer's conduct when making his or her final review of your case.

> **EXAMPLE:** At Johan's interview, the USCIS officer barrages him with personal questions, such as why he got divorced, what he did wrong to drive his wife away, why people of his religion always have so many children, and finally, why he isn't paying child support. Although Johan explains that the court did not require him to pay child support and his wife makes a better income than he does, the officer denies his application on moral character grounds. Johan writes a letter asking the supervisor to consider the officer's hostile and discriminatory attitude and overturn the denial.

You have the right to file a formal complaint against a USCIS employee. In an attempt to improve its image, USCIS has established a procedure for filing complaints. Filing a complaint will not hurt your case—USCIS will not retaliate, and the office you complain to is well-removed from your file, in Washington, DC. To file a complaint, use Form I-847 (included in Appendix C). Send it to the Director, Office of Internal Audit, U.S. Citizenship and Immigration Services, 425 I St. NW, Room 3260, Washington, DC 20536.

Form I-847 is available as a tear-out in Appendix C and can be downloaded from the USCIS website (www.uscis.gov).

D. Approval or Denial: What's Next?

If all goes well at your interview, the officer will tell you that you've been approved and may hand you a piece of paper with information about your swearing-in ceremony. In some areas, you have a choice between going to a court run or a USCIS-run ceremony, and the officer will show you the schedule and ask you to choose a date. (Remember to choose a court ceremony if you're requesting that your name be changed.) (Most USCIS offices notify you about the swearing-in ceremony by mail.) In any case, you're one or two months away from citizenship.

If the interview goes badly, the officer may deny your citizenship application on the spot. Again, you should receive a piece of paper explaining the reasons—see the sample below. If the basis for denial was that you failed the English or U.S. history and government exam, you'll automatically get a second-chance interview. If there is some other problem regarding your case, the officer may give you a chance to provide follow-up documents rather than deny your citizenship. In some cases, the office may need to think about your case before making a decision.

If the officer doesn't make a decision on your case at your interview, you are supposed to receive a decision within 120 days of your interview. (See I.N.A. § 366(b), 8 U.S.C. § 1447(b).) However, as with all USCIS responses, you may have to wait longer than expected. If the officer requested more documents, the time period for the decision may get dragged further into the future.

Security checks may also add to the time that you wait. The USCIS may run your name and fingerprints through a security check not just one time, but once when you file your application, again before your interview, and often a third time before your swearing-in ceremony.

If you've waited well past 120 days and have an urgent need for citizenship, you may want to consult with an attorney, who can file an action in federal court. The court can either decide your case on its own or send it back to USCIS for an immediate decision.

If you aren't scheduled for a follow-up interview, you will get your approval or denial by mail. If you are approved, see Chapter 11 for details on the swearing-in ceremony and your new rights as a citizen. If you are denied citizenship, see Chapter 9 for information on how to appeal the decision.

The Alamo—San Antonio, Texas

Sample Interview Decision

U.S. Department of Homeland Security
San Francisco, CA 94111

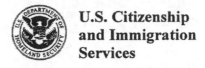

**U.S. Citizenship
and Immigration
Services**

A12345678

On **December 11, 2004**   you were interview by CIS Officer Nelson

☑ You passed the tests of English and U.S. history and government.
☐ You passed the test of U.S. history and government and the English language requirement was waived.
☐ The Service has accepted your request for a Disability Exception. You are exempted from the requirement to demonstrate English language ability and/or knowledge of U.S. history and government.
☐ You will be given another opportunity to be tested on your ability to _____speak / _____read / _____ / write English.
☐ You will be given another opportunity to be tested on your knowledge of U.S. history and government.
☑ Please follow the instructions on the Form N-14.
☑ INS will send you a written decision about your application.
☐ You did not pass the second and final test of your _____ English ability / _____ knowledge of U.S. history and government. You will not be rescheduled for another interview for this N-400. INS will send you a written decision about your application.
☐ Your application is pending completion of background checks. You will be notified when the checks are completed.

A)   _____ **Congratulations! Your application has been recommended for approval.**
At this time, it appears that you have established your eligibility for naturalization. If final approval is granted, you will be notified when and where to report for the Oath Ceremony.

B)   ___✗___ **A decision cannot yet be made about your application.**

   It is very important that you:

✓ Notify INS if you change your address.
✓ Come to any scheduled interview.
✓ Submit all requested documents.
✓ Send any questions about this application in writing to the named above. Include your full name, A-number, and a copy of this paper.
✓ Go to any oath ceremony that you are scheduled to attend.
✓ Notify INS as soon as possible in writing if you cannot come to any scheduled interview or oath ceremony. Include a copy of this paper and a copy of the scheduling notice.

www.dhs.gov

Denials, Appeals, and Repeat Interviews

I f USCIS does not grant your U.S. citizenship at your first interview, don't despair. It happens to many people—and many of them are later approved.

If USCIS is giving you some sort of a last chance, you can still turn things around. For example,

- If the officer delayed making a decision until you provide additional documents, complying with the officer's request will give you a good shot at gaining approval. In Section B, we'll give you advice on preparing and submitting these documents.
- If you failed the English or U.S. history and government exam, you'll get one chance at a repeat interview. (See Section A.)

If you are issued a final denial, USCIS will tell you its reason, either during your citizenship interview or in a subsequent letter. In Section C, we'll help you determine the appropriate next step, based on USCIS's reasoning and other factors. That step may be to appeal, as described in Sections D and E; or it may be to submit a new application for citizenship, as described in Section F.

A. Retaking the Exams

If you failed your first interview because you lacked sufficient English language skills, couldn't answer enough U.S. history and government questions, or both, it's time for intensive study. USCIS automatically gives you a second chance at the exam(s)—but you won't have much time to prepare. You could be scheduled for your second interview anytime between 60 to 90 days after your first one. (See 8 C.F.R. § 312.5(a).) So, if you didn't attend a preparatory course, you should quickly enroll in one now—see Chapter 5, Section C, for advice on finding a good one.

At your second interview, you will probably meet with a different officer, who will concentrate on the exam and not repeat the rest of the interview. Your meeting shouldn't last more than a few minutes.

If you don't pass on the second try, that's it—your citizenship application will be denied. But don't sit around moping. File an appeal or get a new citizen-ship application into the mail while the process is still fresh in your mind. (See Sections E and F, below, to help you choose between these procedural options.)

B. Providing More Documents

The USCIS interviewer may need additional docu-mentation before making a decision about your application. In that case, the officer will give you a written request describing the documents needed— for example, a copy of your recent tax returns, or proof of your dates of travel outside the United States. See the sample form below, from the San Francisco USCIS office.

Normally you'll send these documents by mail. However, if the USCIS officer wants an opportunity to discuss the documents with you, you will be asked to bring them to another interview. In general, however, USCIS prefers not to interview applicants a second time.

Being asked for more documents can be seen as a good sign—it means that the officer believes there are good reasons to pursue your case further. Now you must do your best to swing things in your favor.

1. To Provide or Not to Provide?

Don't automatically provide requested documents until you have closely reviewed the request and de-cided that the situation doesn't call for an attorney's help. If you are convinced that the document will help your quest for citizenship, go ahead and send it in. For example, if the document is one that you knew you should have brought to your interview, but forgot—such as a letter from your church exempting you from the Oath of Allegiance—that's easy, and you can take care of it on your own.

Similarly, if the document is one that the officer has clearly described, such as your certificate of divorce from your first husband or a police certificate showing that you haven't been arrested, obtaining it should be within your power (unless, of course, no such document exists).

MAIL DOCUMENTS/INFORMATION TO:

US. Department of Justice
Immigration and Naturalization Service

630 Sansome Street, Room 237/CB
San Francisco, CA 94111

File No: A

Officer:

Date: January 15, 2003

Examination of your application (N400) shows that additional information, documents or forms are needed before your application can be acted upon. Please **RETURN THIS LETTER WITH REQUESTED INFORMATION and/or DOCUMENTATION by:**

Failure to do so may result in the denial of your application.

☐ A **court** certified complaint, disposition, sentence, and proof of fulfillment of sentence (i.e. completion of probation, completion of community service, completion of term of imprisonment) for **any and all your arrests** even if expunged. If no record is available, submit a certified letter from the **court** <u>stating there is no record,</u> **No photocopy.**

☐ A Police clearance from all cities you have resided since _____. (Documentation must be original and/or certified by the police)

☐ Proof of child support (e.g. copy of canceled checks, DA letter, notarized letter from child's other parent) for your children:
_____

☐ Two copies of the birth and baptismal certificates for all children (with translations, if applicable).

☐ Marriage certificate from all marriages <u>and/or</u> petition *and* final divorce decree from former spouse(s).

☐ Copy of rent agreement, deed, insurance binder, utility bills, bank/credit statements, other specified evidence of marital union:
_____. *Submit* _____ *of these.*

☐ Copy of first two pages of income tax returns (forms 1040 & 540) <u>and</u> W-2's for you and your spouse for tax year(s)
_____.

☐ A more **detailed** Form N-648 or letter from your medical doctor/psychiatrist to support your disability exception claim.

☐ Letter from Welfare Department/Social Security agency regarding eligibility, attached.

☐ List of all trips from _____ to _____ **AND** copies of <u>all</u> pages of your passports and/or travel documents.

☐ Proof of registration with the Selective Service or affidavit in regards to why you did not register for the Selective Service.

☐ Copy of the front *and* back of your Alien Registration Card.

☐ Other:

Please notify this office of any address changes before the final decision in your case.
Due to heavy work loads, please allow a minimum of three months past the due date noted above for a response.

Form N-14 (Rev. 9/16/97) N

However, you should think twice about your next step if:

- you don't understand the reason for the request, or
- the request implies that the officer has serious doubts about your eligibility for naturalization or even for a green card.

If you can't understand why the officer requested a specific document, you should not furnish the document until your attorney has reviewed the request. You may make a serious error furnishing a document affecting your right to stay in the United States—for example, providing a certificate from your home country saying that you were convicted of child abuse will get you a quick denial and a plane ticket home. The same is true for requests that cast doubts on your right to citizenship. For example, if you were divorced from the spouse through whom you got your green card, brought documents to prove that the marriage was bona fide, but are now being asked for more such documents, you may have a problem. The USCIS officer may believe that you've committed marriage fraud. Instead of just putting some more documents in the mail and hoping for the best, consult an attorney to get to the root of what's bothering USCIS.

Of course, if you just ignore the officer's request for documents, your citizenship application will be denied automatically.

2. Preparing Documents

The USCIS officer may give you an exact description of the documents he or she wants to see—such as a letter from the IRS saying you owe no taxes—or the officer may leave the exact choice of documents to your imagination. If, for example, the officer requests "documents to prove your good moral character for the last five years," you'll have to decide what documents will serve this purpose. (In Chapter 2, Section D, we describe suitable documents concerning good moral character.)

After you've gathered the necessary documents, put them together in an orderly manner. Each document must be readable and contain your name or other identifying information. If there are any items that belong in a series, such as your paychecks over the last six months, put them in chronological (date) order. If you don't believe the officer can tell from looking at a document what it is or why it's important, add a Post-It note or a cover letter. For example, if the officer asked for evidence that you returned to the United States before August 2002 and you include photos of yourself at a July 4th barbecue in Cincinnati, make sure the photos are dated and that you are clearly recognizable in them.

The first item in your document packet should be a copy of USCIS's written request for documents. A separate cover letter is not usually necessary, though adding one would be helpful if the documents are not self-explanatory. (A cover letter, if you include it, should go second in the packet.) Then add copies of the documents themselves—remember, send originals only if you don't need them back … ever. Make a copy of everything for your records.

Empire State Building—New York, New York

3. Documents by Mail

You'll find the mailing address to which you'll need to send the documents on the USCIS officer's written request. (It will be the same office as where you had your interview, not the office to which you originally submitted your Form N-400 citizenship application.) Always add the officer's name to the letter—or, if you weren't given his or her name, include your A-number in the letter—so that your letter will be put on the correct officer's desk. Use certified mail with a return receipt requested. Certified mail is especially important at this stage, since delays are common and you may need evidence of the date when you submitted your documents in order to follow up with USCIS. Or, for potentially faster service, use an overnight courier service such as Federal Express or DHL—unless the USCIS address is at a post office box, in which case these services cannot deliver.

4. The Decision

Sometimes the USCIS officer will make a decision within a few weeks of your sending in your documents—other times it could be months. If three or more months pass and you haven't heard from USCIS, write an inquiry letter, and send it to the same officer and address to which you sent your documents.

After the USCIS officer decides, you will be notified by mail. If the decision is favorable, congratulations—you can move on to Chapter 11, which describes your swearing-in ceremony and your new rights as a citizen. If the decision is negative, see Sections E and F, below, to help you decide whether to appeal or start over and file a new application.

C. Choosing to Appeal or Reapply

If your citizenship application is denied, you will receive a written explanation from USCIS as to why, along with information on how to file an administrative appeal.

You should seek legal assistance if:

- the reason for denial is confusing

- the reason for denial is difficult for you to overcome on your own, or
- USCIS has indicated that it will refer you to Immigration Court for deportation proceedings.

In these instances, the stakes are too high for self-help efforts. Consult an attorney.

If, however, you believe that with a minimum of time and effort you can win your case—for example, you suddenly discover a document that could prove your foreign trip lasted less than a year—then continue reading.

Before filing an appeal, you'll need to consider two things:

- whether you have any basis on which to appeal (see Section C1, below), and
- whether filing an appeal is any better than starting over and reapplying (see Section C2, below).

1. Determining Whether You Have a Basis for Appeal

Before filing an appeal, you need to determine whether you have a basis for appealing the decision—that is, you must be able to demonstrate that a mistake was made and that you are eligible for citizenship. Keep in mind that appeals are appropriate *only* when you believe that the USCIS officer who interviewed you made a mistake or acted inappropriately. For example, if the officer confused your belief in "communes" with a belief in "communism," an appeal is a fine way to ask that the error be corrected. However, if your denial resulted from your own actions, reapplying is more appropriate (after correcting the problem).

EXAMPLE 1: During her citizenship interview, Olga told the USCIS officer that, during a period of unemployment, she had regularly eaten dinner at a church soup kitchen. The officer took this as a sign of bad moral character and denied Olga's application. However, since Olga was not at fault in being unemployed, and eating at a soup kitchen is perfectly legal, the officer's decision was wrong. Olga should appeal the denial.

EXAMPLE 2: When preparing his application, Fyodor included the proper dates of travel on his form, but he miscalculated when adding up the time spent abroad. At the interview, the officer determined that Fyodor had actually spent more than one year outside the U.S. and had therefore broken the continuity of his U.S. stay. Fyodor was ineligible for citizenship and had no basis on which to appeal. (Chapter 2 explains how to deal with such problems in order to reapply.) If the USCIS officer believed that Fyodor had lied on his application, or was deliberately concealing information, Fyodor would need an attorney's help before reapplying.

As noted, you can appeal only if you can demonstrate that the officer was wrong or made a mistake when denying your citizenship application. Therefore, if you didn't study for the U.S. history and government exams before your first two interviews, you shouldn't look at an appeal as your third chance. Similarly, if you aren't eligible for citizenship and didn't realize this at the time you submitted your application, an appeal is not the way to cure the problem.

If you don't have strong grounds for an appeal and you're not sure whether you would prevail, the wisest course is to file a new application for citizenship, as described in Section F, below.

2. Appeal or New Application?

As mentioned above, an appeal is not your only option. You can, if you wish, skip the appeal and reapply by submitting a new N-400 application (see Section F, below).

For many people, the most important factor to consider when making this decision is the length of time each option will take. There's no blanket rule regarding which will take less time—an appeal or a new application—because the answer will differ depending on the USCIS district in which you live. In some USCIS districts, applicants rarely file appeals because USCIS consistently takes longer to act on

them than it does to call applicants in for a new interview.

You can find out about USCIS's timing on your own by doing a little legwork. Talk to the staff at local nonprofits serving immigrants and refugees, or visit your local USCIS office and ask in person. If you determine that you'll wait longer for your appeal interview than for a new interview (after reapplying), it's probably better to reapply. This may not be the case, however, if you're one of those people who want a long time to pass before the interview—for example, to get the maximum time to learn English or to make sure that ten years have passed since their involvement in the Communist Party.

Another factor to consider is cost. You'll pay less for filing an appeal (currently $195) than for filing a new citizenship application ($310, including fingerprints).

A final factor in deciding whether to appeal or reapply is your relationship with USCIS. If you file a new N-400 application, the dynamics between you and USCIS will change. You're no longer trying to prove that USCIS was wrong, and USCIS is no longer trying to prove you shouldn't be a citizen. By reapplying, you'll start over with a different interviewer and an application specially tailored to deal with the problems that previously sank your application. (You won't, however, be able to hide the previous citizenship application from the new interviewing officer.) For information on reapplying, see Section F, below.

D. How to Appeal

If you choose to go the administrative appeal route, you must act quickly. Your appeal notice is due at USCIS within 30 days of the date your citizenship was denied. (The date you were denied is shown on your written denial notice.) Some applicants receive this notice in person, on the day they were interviewed, while others receive it by mail from USCIS. If you receive your notice by mail, your appeal notice must be sent with 33 days of the date on the USCIS letter, because USCIS presumes that you received its letter within three days after mailing.

In order to persuade a second (or third) USCIS officer to view your case positively, we recommend that you include a standard appeal form and an accompanying sworn statement and supporting documents.

The necessary and recommended paperwork for filing an administrative appeal includes:

- Form N-336, Request for a Hearing on a Decision in Naturalization Proceedings Under Section 336 of the Act (see line-by-line instructions in Section D1, below)
- fee (currently $250, but check for changes on the USCIS website, www.uscis.gov. Click "Immigration Forms, Fees and Fingerprints," then click "Forms and Fees," then scroll down the chart to the line showing Form N-336 —the current fee will be listed on this chart.) Send a personal check or money order made out to USCIS—do not send cash
- documents to overcome the basis for the denial (see Section D2, below), and
- your sworn statement to overcome the basis for the denial (see Section D3, below).

You'll also need to choose whether or not to appear in person, as described in Section D4, below.

 If someone else pays by check for you, make sure that your name and A-number appear on the line at the lower left of the check. That way if the check gets separated from your application, USCIS will be able to trace it, and you won't have to pay twice.

1. Completing Form N-336

Form N-336—a one-page form—is the only form you'll need to fill out for your appeal. As with all USCIS forms, it's best to type the information. If that's not possible, write clearly, using black ink.

Form N-336, pictured below, is available as a tear-out in Appendix C. You can also get it from USCIS by calling 800-870-3676, or by visiting a local USCIS office or the USCIS website (www.uscis.gov; you have a choice of printing the form out or downloading it and filling it out on your computer).

OMB No. 1615-0050; Exp. 7-31-05

U.S. Department of Homeland Security
Bureau of Citizenship and Immigration Services

N-336, Request for a Hearing on a Decision in Naturalization Proceedings Under Section 336 of the Act

Decision: ☐ Grant ☐ Denial	Fee:
1. In the Matter of: (Name of Naturalization Applicant)	File Number: **A-**

2. I am filing a request for hearing on the decision dated:

3. Please check the one block which applies:

a. ☐ I am *not submitting* a separate brief, statement or evidence.

b. ☐ I *am submitting* a separate brief, statement and/or evidence with this form.

c. ☐ I need _____ days to submit a brief, statement and/or evidence to the CIS. (May be granted only for good cause shown. Explain in a separate letter.)

g request

When completing Form N-336, follow the line-by-line instructions below. Although the form is easy to complete, we recommend that you make a copy before entering information. That way you can use one as a draft and one as a final version.

Box above Question 1: This section is for USCIS—don't write anything here.

Question 1: Enter your full name, exactly as you entered it on your Form N-400. (The exception would be if your name has changed since then, for example through marriage or divorce. In such a case, you should attach a document that explains this, such as a marriage or divorce certificate.)

Question 2: Enter the date your citizenship application was denied. If the date was more than 30 days ago (or 33 days if the decision was mailed to you) you can stop now, because you've already lost your chance to appeal. (See the paragraph at the opening of this Section D, above.) Your only option is to reapply for citizenship, as described in Section F, below.

Question 3: This question asks whether you'll be turning in this form by itself or will be adding a "separate brief, statement and/or evidence." (A brief is a legal memo explaining how the law supports your case.) Chances are good that you'll need to submit some sort of evidence or statement to support your appeal, as discussed in Section D2, below. If at all possible, get the evidence ready in time to submit it with this form, and check the second box.

If you need more time, check the third box and indicate how much time you'll need. Thirty days is the standard—if you ask for more, USCIS will want a solid explanation (such as "I am asking the Internal Revenue Service for a tax transcript, but am told that its turnaround time is six weeks"). Attach a statement (with your name and A-number at the top) explaining why you need the amount of time you've requested.

Question 4: Enter your name, address, signature, and the date.

Question 5: If you can adequately explain in these few lines your reason why you believe USCIS made the wrong decision, do so. If, as is more likely, you can't fit your argument into this space, write "please see attached statement," and follow the instructions in Subsection D2, below.

2. Preparing Supporting Documents

As you may have noticed, USCIS officers love documents. A convincing document in your file gives the USCIS officer an outside authority on which to base decisions, and a defense against doubting supervisors. Unless the basis of your appeal involves something that can't be proven on paper—such as your English ability—assemble documents that will prove your point.

To organize your ideas for documents, get a piece of scratch paper and write down every document you've thought of that might help your case. For example, let's take an applicant named Sara, who is trying to convince the USCIS officer that her marriage to the spouse who got her a green card was not a sham. Sara might write up the following list of potential supporting documents:

Sara's List of Possible Documents

- ☐ my sworn statement
- ☐ photos of me and my husband on summer vacation in Mexico
- ☐ letters from friends addressed to both of us
- ☐ sworn statement by neighbors saying that they saw us sharing the house, taking out the garbage, barbecuing together, etc.
- ☐ copies of records from meetings with marriage counselor
- ☐ copies of bills and receipts sent to our address in both our names, and
- ☐ medical records from fertility specialist showing that we were both tested to find out why I hadn't gotten pregnant yet.

⚠ The above list doesn't include videotapes. The USCIS officers rarely have a time or place to view videotapes, so there's no point in sending them.

After you've made your own list, put check marks next to the five or six strongest, most convincing items. The idea is to give enough information to be convincing, but to avoid burying USCIS in a mountain of paperwork.

Looking at Sara's list above, which entries strike you as the most convincing? We believe the strongest document is the last one—medical records from the fertility specialist. This document is almost enough by itself, because it is from an independent, outside source; it was created for a separate purpose, not just for sending to USCIS; and it shows that Sara and her husband were attempting to have children together—a classic sign of a real marriage. The records from the counselor are also excellent evidence, for similar reasons.

All of the other entries on Sara's list are good ideas, however. Given the strength of the other documents this applicant will obtain, she might choose to drop the idea of bothering the neighbors for sworn statements.

You aren't limited in the type or number of documents you can present during your appeal. If there were gaps in your previous documents or other evidence, you now have an opportunity to fill them.

Think creatively about what documents will most convincingly show that USCIS got its facts wrong. Letters or records from official, trustworthy sources such as doctors, government officials, or schools are the best. See, for example, the list of documents included in the Sample Statement in Support of Appeal in Section D3, below. This person was able to show that, although USCIS may not have believed that his trips to Canada lasted fewer than 24 hours, he had independent confirmation from his credit card company, a hotel, and a kennel—none of whom would be expected to lie for him. He also included a sworn statement from a friend. The friend's statement is weaker evidence, but when added to the rest, it persuasively rounds out the picture.

If you use letters or sworn statements from friends and relatives, make sure they include as much detail as possible and are signed. For example, having your husband say in a letter that, "I swear that my wife has never abused drugs," is not strong evidence by itself. However, he will provide a more convincing statement if he writes, "I swear that my wife has never abused drugs—in fact, she's so opposed to unnatural chemical substances that I have to beg her to take an aspirin when she has the flu."

In Chapter 2, we provide a sample letter by a friend or relative. This sample was written for someone attempting to prove her good moral character for her original application—and such an issue might also come up on appeal. The sample shows an appropriate letter format and level of detail. To make the letter more legally convincing, the writer can turn it into a sworn statement by adding the following language at the bottom:

> I swear, under penalty of perjury, that the contents of the foregoing statement are true and correct to the best of my knowledge.

(See Section D3, for a full sample of a sworn statement, which can be tailored for use by a friend or relative.)

It's always a good idea to start with your own sworn statement, explaining the situation and giving an overview of the documents you're presenting. We'll discuss how to prepare a sworn statement in Section D3.

3. Preparing a Sworn Statement

Form N-336 provides only a few lines in which to explain the basis for your appeal. It's possible your case is so simple that it could be explained within these few lines—but it's not likely. Avoid summarizing your reasoning into something cursory like, "I deserve citizenship and my case should be approved." Instead, use a separate page or two in which to fully explain why USCIS was wrong and you truly deserve U.S. citizenship. Write your statement in plain English and avoid legal-sounding language.

In addition, you can use this statement as a way to summarize and explain the documents that you've enclosed in support of your appeal. Look at the sample statement below for ideas on formatting and the appropriate level of detail, then write your own.

You might be wondering why, if USCIS already doubts your right to citizenship, would it take your word on appeal and grant you citizenship? Obviously,

Sample Statement in Support of Appeal

876 48th Street, Apartment 9A
Detroit, MI 48207

March 7, 2003

U.S. Citizenship and Immigration Services
Detroit District Office
333 Mt. Eliot
Detroit, MI 48207

RE: Citizenship Appeal
    A#87654321

Dear Sir/Madam:

I am requesting an appeal of my citizenship application because the USCIS officer who heard my case made a mistake. I explained during the interview that I had not entered my trips to Canada on the N-400 application form because none of my trips were for longer than 24 hours. The officer assumed that I was lying and denied the application.

I do not understand why the officer believed that I was lying. My USCIS file shows I have always been truthful in my dealings with USCIS and other government officials and I am telling the truth in this instance. Though it may seem unlikely that I would never stay in Canada for more than 24 hours, the fact of the matter is that I drive up there only for the purpose of meeting an old friend for dinner at our favorite restaurant. I stay the night at a hotel afterwards and return the next morning. Also, I hate to stay away too long, since my dog, Richie, suffers greatly during my absences and the kennel is expensive.

In fact, I can prove that my trips to Canada were short ones. Enclosed please find the following:

- credit card bills showing purchases of gas and other items north and south of the Canadian border before, during, and after each of my brief trips

- a letter from the friend with whom I have dinner confirming our regular meetings

- a letter from the hotel where I always stay showing the dates of all my stays over the past five years and confirming that I've never stayed for more than one night, and

- a sworn statement from the kennel that boards my dog, Richie, while I'm away, confirming that, on all the dates of my Canadian trips, I picked up Richie within 26 hours (the two extra hours represent the time it takes to get from the Canadian border to the kennel).

Thank you for this opportunity to clarify matters and to show my eligibility for U.S. citizenship.

Ercan Bensusan
Ercan Bensusan

if you've lied to USCIS or another government official in the past, USCIS will look skeptically at your sworn statement. But it is not always possible for an applicant to come up with a document that covers every relevant life issue, and USCIS knows it. The USCIS officer will carefully consider your sworn statement—check it for detail, completeness and internal logic—and then potentially give it great weight in deciding on your case.

4. Deciding Whether to Appear Personally

The appeal form provides a section in which you can request a personal meeting with the officer deciding your appeal. If you feel you can best explain your reasons for citizenship in person, or if it's impossible to prove your qualifications without being there (for example, if the issue is whether you speak English), make this request. If, however, the matter is something that you think can be resolved on paper, or if you're extremely shy about defending your case in front of another USCIS officer, don't request a personal interview. The appeals officer can review your file based on the paperwork in your file and on any additional written explanation or documents that you submit for the appeal.

5. Submitting Your Appeal; Attending Your Interview

Submit your appeal by mail, to the USCIS office at which you had your interview. The address will be shown on your denial notice. As always, protect your packet from loss by keeping a copy for your records and by sending it certified mail with a return receipt requested.

If you request an interview, the agency has 180 days to call you in. (Don't panic if more time passes, however—USCIS often fails to meet its scheduling obligations.) Be sure to bring copies of all your appeal materials as well as all the documents you brought to your original USCIS interview.

There's not much difference between your original interview and an appeal. When you appeal, you

return to the USCIS office and meet with a different USCIS officer—one who may be higher-ranking or of equal rank to the one who originally denied your application.

Look again at Chapter 8 for tips on getting through a USCIS interview. The appeal proceedings are usually as informal as your initial interview. The officer may conduct the whole interview over, as if the first one never happened. Or the officer may simply focus on the problem area. Be prepared to make a brief statement about why you should not have been denied citizenship.

6. Your Decision

USCIS may tell you its decision on your appeal at the end of the interview, if you attend one, or it may send you a decision by mail. (See the sample decision below.) If you're waiting for a decision by mail, we can't predict how long you'll wait—it varies by local district offices.

If you win your appeal and USCIS approves you for U.S. citizenship, see Chapter 11 for information on the swearing-in ceremony and your new rights as a citizen. If USCIS still refuses to grant you U.S. citizenship, see Section E, below.

E. What to Do If You Lose the Appeal

If your citizenship appeal is denied for a reason that clearly doesn't affect your eligibility to remain in the United States with a green card—for example, failing the English exam—the easiest thing to do is fix the problem and submit a new citizenship application (see Section F), or simply decide to do nothing for now. Presuming you don't do anything to endanger your green card status (such as getting arrested or abandoning your U.S. residence), you are allowed to live in the United States permanently, without ever becoming a U.S. citizen.

If, however, your case is denied for a reason that does affect your right to remain in the United States—for example, because you committed a crime, abandoned your U.S. residence, or smuggled aliens—seek skilled legal help immediately. Depending on the basis for the denial, you could be put into deportation proceedings and lose your green card altogether. The attorney may also be able to help you file an appeal in federal court. For information on finding a good attorney, see Chapter 10.

F. Reapplying for Citizenship

If you've decided to skip the appeal and reapply for citizenship, or if your appeal was denied but you still feel sure you qualify for citizenship, go back to Chapter 3 and start fresh—but use the lessons you learned during this application process. Examine USCIS's written reasons for your denial and make sure that your next application corrects the problem. While you're at it, review your USCIS interview in your mind. Was there anything about your application that bothered the USCIS officer? If, for example, an officer had trouble reading your handwriting, it would probably be worth typing the application this time around.

Some applicants wonder whether they should wait a while to reapply, to give their case a "rest."

Given the many months or years you'll wait for your interview and the strong likelihood that your case will be interviewed by a different USCIS officer, there is no advantage to waiting. The only reasons to wait are:

- you need extra time to prepare for the exams, or
- you were denied for a time-sensitive reason, such as failure to complete probation or failure to show a sufficient number of years with good moral character.

In these cases, you should not reapply until the appropriate length of time has passed.

In terms of procedures, your new application won't be treated any differently than your previous application. You will wait the same length of time and will be randomly assigned a USCIS officer for your interview. On the other hand, your old file will not be forgotten. The USCIS officer will have a chance to review your old citizenship application before making a decision concerning the new one. So don't view your new application as an opportunity to hide past problems with your application.

There is no limit on how many times you can reapply for citizenship—but we sincerely hope that you won't have to put this rule to the test!

Ellis Island—Immigration Station, 1892–1954

U.S. Department of Justice
Immigration and Naturalization Service

San Francisco District Office
630 Sansome Street,, Citizenship Branch
San Francisco, Ca. 94111

EUGENIA KAIRYS   Refer to File Number
111 OAK ROAD, APT. 2   A 12 395 678/CB
BERKELEY, CA 94710

                                                    OCT -9 2004

N-336 HEARING DECISION

On July 21, 2004, your application for naturalization was denied. You have filed timely a "Request for Hearing on a Decision [in] Naturalization Proceedings," Form N-336, under Section 336 of the Immigration & Nationality Act.

Your application was denied because *you failed to demonstrate ability to speak and understand the English language sufficiently to answer the questions in your interview and on your application, and you failed to establish that you were exempt from this requirement.*

On October 02, 2004, you appeared for a Review Hearing. You submitted a Form N-648, Medical Certification For Disability Exceptions and your English and civics requirements were waived. It is determined that you have sufficiently overcome the reasons for the denial of your application for naturalization, and your application is now GRANTED.   You will become a citizen upon taking the Oath of Allegiance to the United States, and you will receive an appointment notice by mail scheduling you for the oath-taking ceremony.

ORDER: It is hereby ordered that your application for naturalization be
              granted and that you be scheduled for an oath-taking
              ceremony.

David N. Still
District Director

cc: Attorney Ilona Bray

Some research inquiries are quite safe—for instance, if we've cited a section of the law and you want to read the exact language or see whether that section has changed, there's no magic in looking up the law and reading it. But in general, be cautious when researching. If possible, look at several sources to confirm your findings.

Immigration laws are federal, meaning they are written by the U.S. Congress and do not vary from one state to another (though procedures and priorities for carrying out the laws may vary among USCIS offices in different cities or states). Below we give you a rundown on the most accessible research tools—and not coincidentally, the ones that immigration lawyers most often use.

Law libraries aren't just for lawyers. Many law libraries, particularly those connected with public law schools, are state-funded. These libraries must make federal statutes and regulations available to the public. Don't be shy about using such libraries as a resource. (This is not the case with all law school libraries—private law school libraries are not always open to the public.)

1. The Federal Code

Federal immigration law is located in Title 8 of the United States Code. The U.S. Code consists of federal laws passed by Congress and applicable throughout the United States. Below we explain how to locate the text of these laws.

a. Searching on the Internet

The easiest way to access the U.S. Code is via the Internet. For example, you can review the code at Nolo's website (www.nolo.com). On the home page, click "U.S. Laws and Regulations." If you already know the title (which is 8) and section, you can enter them and pull up the text immediately. If you don't have the section number, you can search using relevant terms.

When doing word-based searches, avoid common terms. Words such as "immigration," "citizenship," or "naturalization" will bring up thousands of results. Try to think of narrower or unusual combinations of terms for your search, such as "good moral character" or "continuous residence." (And make sure to use the proper legal term, not Nolo's substitute for it—we always alert you to the legal term at the opening of the section that discusses the concept.)

b. Using Law Libraries

Any law library (such as the one at your local courthouse or law school) should have a complete set of the U.S. Code (traditionally abbreviated as U.S.C. or U.S.C.A.). The library may also have a separate volume containing exactly the same material, but called the Immigration and Nationality Act, or I.N.A.

Unfortunately, the two sets of laws are numbered a bit differently, and not all volumes of the I.N.A. cross-reference to the U.S. Code and vice versa. For this reason, when code citations are mentioned in this book, we include both the U.S.C. and I.N.A. numbers.

2. USCIS and State Department Regulations and Guidance

Another important source of immigration law is the Code of Federal Regulations, or C.F.R. Federal regulations are written by the agencies responsible for carrying out federal law. The regulations are meant to explain in greater detail just how the federal agency is going to carry out the law. You'll find the USCIS regulations at Title 8 of the C.F.R. The USCIS regulations are helpful, but certainly don't have all the answers. Again, the easiest way to access these rules is via the Internet. Visit Nolo's Legal Research Center (www.nolo.com). On the home page, click "U.S. Laws and Regulations." Scroll down to "Code of Federal Regulations." If you already know the title (which is 8) and section, you can enter them and pull up the text immediately. If you don't have the section number, you can search by terms. If you don't have access to the Internet, your local law library will also have print copies of the C.F.R.s.

3. Information on the Internet

If you have Internet access, familiarize yourself with the USCIS website (www.uscis.gov), where you can obtain information on various immigration benefits and applications (including citizenship through naturalization), downloads of most immigration forms, and current fees.

On the Internet you'll also find sites provided by immigration lawyers as well as immigrants. The quality of these sites varies widely, so we don't attempt to review all of them here. Many of the lawyers' sites are blatant attempts to bring in business by providing a little information. That said, a couple of lawyer sites that contain useful information include:

- www.shusterman.com (by Los Angeles-based attorney Carl Shusterman, with daily news of immigration law changes and current processing times at the USCIS Service Centers)
- www.cyrusmehta.com (by the New York-based firm of Cyrus D. Mehta and Associates, PLLC, and including overviews on immigration law matters, recent news articles, and visa priority dates.)
- www.visalaw.com (by the firm of Siskind, Susser, Haas & Devine, and including regular updates on immigration law matters), and
- www.ilw.com (a privately run website called the "immigration portal," which includes various chat room opportunities).

Sites created by immigrants offering immigration information and experiences, although well-meaning, are not always reliable when it comes to legal or procedural facts.

4. Court Decisions

Immigrants who have been denied citizenship may appeal these decisions to the federal courts. The courts' decisions in these cases are supposed to govern the future behavior of USCIS. Hopefully, you will never have to argue with a USCIS official that your case should (or should not) fit within a particular court decision. For one thing, the officials are not likely to listen until they get a specific directive from their superiors or until the court decision is incorporated into the USCIS regulations (the C.F.R.). For another thing, such discussions probably mean that your case has become complicated enough to need a lawyer. For these reasons, we do not attempt to teach you how to research federal court decisions here. For more information on performing that type of research, read *Legal Research: How to Find & Understand the Law,* by Stephen Elias and Susan Levenkind (Nolo).

5. Legal Publications

We recommend two legal publications used by immigration lawyers:

- *Interpreter Releases,* a weekly update published by Federal Publications Inc. (a West Group company), and
- *Immigration Law and Procedure,* a multi-volume, continually updated loose-leaf set by Charles Gordon, Stanley Mailman, and Stephen Yale-Loehr (LEXIS Publishing).

You should be able to find both at your local law library. Both are very well indexed. They are written for lawyers, so you'll have to wade through some technical terminology.

Internet Resources

This list summarizes the useful Internet sites that have been mentioned in this book.

- U.S. Citizenship and Immigration Services (USCIS) (www.uscis.gov)
- Attorney Carl Shusterman (www.shusterman.com)
- Siskind, Susser, Haas & Devine (www.visalaw.com)
- The Immigration Portal (www.ilw.com)
- Lists of overseas embassies in the U.S (www.embassy.org or www.embpage.org)

After You Are Approved

If you have been approved for U.S. citizenship, congratulations! This chapter will guide you through the final phases of the citizenship process and help you claim some of the rights that are now owed to you. (For a review of those rights, see Chapter 1.) We'll discuss:

- the swearing-in ceremony—what to bring and what will happen (Section A)
- how to prove your citizenship (Section B)
- how to register to vote (Section C)
- how your children can become citizens automatically (Section D), and
- how you can help certain family members to immigrate (Section E).

A. The Swearing-In Ceremony

You are not a citizen until you attend a swearing-in (or "oath") ceremony. Either at your USCIS interview or soon after, you will receive a written notice (Form N-445) telling you the date and time at which the ceremony will be held. See the sample notice from the Oakland USCIS office, below. USCIS usually holds such ceremonies twice a month.

Since you do not become a citizen until the ceremony, you must continue to maintain your eligibility for citizenship. In fact, you will be asked before the ceremony to sign a paper assuring USCIS that you are still eligible for citizenship. Now is not the time to jeopardize your chances for citizenship by getting arrested or by suddenly divorcing the person through whom you obtained your green card.

If you won't be able to make the appointment for the swearing-in ceremony, return the notice to USCIS along with a letter explaining why you're unable to attend and asking the agency to reschedule you. Make a copy of both items for yourself before mailing them. Send the request by certified mail to the USCIS office where you had your interview—you'll find the address on the swearing-in notice. The USCIS office will reschedule you and send you a new Form N-445 appointment notice to tell you when your swearing-in ceremony will be. We recommend trying to make the appointment, however, because rescheduling always seems to produce delays.

1. What to Bring

As you can see from the sample appointment notice, USCIS asks you to bring a variety of things to your swearing-in ceremony, including:

- **The swearing-in notice, with the back side of the notice filled in.** You're expected to fill this in just before you go to your swearing-in ceremony. Take a look at the questions you'll be asked on the sample—questions about whether you've recently married, divorced, traveled outside the United States, and more. These questions are designed to make sure that nothing has changed since your citizenship interview—most importantly, that you still have the same name and are still eligible for U.S. citizenship. If your answer to any of the questions impacts your citizenship eligibility (see Chapter 2) or if you aren't sure, consult a lawyer.
- **Your green card ("Alien Registration Card").** To avoid any fraudulent uses of your green card, you must return it to USCIS at the swearing-in ceremony. You won't need it once you're a citizen. If you've lost it, expect some heavy questioning.
- **Your Reentry Permit or Refugee Travel Document.** If you have either of these documents, bring them so that USCIS can review your travel history and verify your continued eligibility for citizenship.
- **Any immigration documents you have.** Bring your passport with any U.S. visas you might once have obtained, as well as any other important INS or USCIS approvals or permits (such as old Employment Authorization Documents). Although USCIS isn't likely to examine these documents, there's a chance you may be asked to show them or give them back.
- **Other.** The items listed above are things that everyone will be asked to bring, if they have them. If USCIS wants you to bring anything additional, it will mention it in this Other category.

☐ Reentry Permit   ☐ I-551/I-1⌐   ☐ 316(a)   ☐ 319(a)   ☐ 50.⌐ /5/15   ☐ I-215 in file

U.S. Department of Justice   OMB No. 1115-0062
Immigration and Naturalization Service   Notice of Naturalization Oath Ceremony

1301 Clay Street, Room 380-N
Oakland CA 94612-5217

RECEIVED SEP 0 5 2001
RECEIVE— SE. 2001

AR#:   A071 123 456/SC

Date: September 4, 2003

ILONA BRAY, ATTORNEY
950 PARKER STREET
BERKELEY, CA 94710

cc: NGUYEN VU

You are hereby notified to appear for a Naturalization Oath Ceremony on: **TUESDAY, SEPTEMBER 9, 2003**

at: **The Nob Hill Masonic Center**

Masonic Auditorium, First Floor

1111 California Street at Taylor Street

San Francisco CA 94108

USE MUNI'S LINE 1, CALIFORNIA STREET OR POWELL STREET CABLE CAR, AND CONNECTIONS TO BAY AREA TRANSIT. PARKING AT $9 IN THE CENTER IS LIMITED; TAKE THE ELEVATOR TO LEVEL 1.
LOBBY DOORS OPEN AT 7:15AM

Please report promptly at   **12:45**   **P.M.,**   **TABLE:**   **2**

Allow a minimum of four (4) hours for the processing and the Oath Ceremony.

You must bring the following with you:

☒ This letter, WITH ALL OF THE QUESTIONS ON THE OTHER SIDE ANSWERED IN INK OR ON A TYPEWRITER.
☒ Alien Registration Card.
☒ Reentry Permit, or Refugee Travel Document
☒ Any Immigration documents you may have.
☐ If the naturalization application is on behalf of your child (children), bring your child (children).
☐ Other

Proper attire should be worn.

If you cannot come to this ceremony, return this notice immediately and state why you cannot appear. In such case, you will be sent another notice of ceremony at a later date. You must appear at an oath ceremony to complete the naturalization process.

(SEE OTHER SIDE)

Form N-445 (Rev. 01/08/92)

A071 948 293

In connection with your application for naturalization, please answer each of the questions by checking "Yes" or "No". You should answer these questions the day you are to appear for the citizenship oath ceremony. These questions refer to actions since the date you were first interviewed on you Application for Naturalization. They do not refer to anything that happened before that interview.

After you have answered every question, sign your name and fill in the date and place of signing, and provide your current address.

You must bring this completed questionnaire with you to the oath ceremony, as well as the documents indicated on the front, and give them to the Immigration employee at the oath ceremony. You may be questioned further on your answers at that time.

AFTER the date you were first interviewed on your Application for Naturalization, Form N-400:

ANSWERS

1. Have you married, or been widowed, separated, or divorced? (If "Yes" Please bring documented proof of marriage, death, separation or divorce.)

1. ☐ Yes   ☐ No

2. Have you traveled outside the United States?

2. ☐ Yes   ☐ No

3. Have you knowingly committed any crime or offense, for which you have not been arrested; or have you been arrested, cited, charged, indicted, convicted, fined, or imprisoned for breaking or violating any law or ordinance, including traffic violations?

3. ☐ Yes   ☐ No

4. Have you joined any organization, including the Communist Party, or become associated or connected therewith in any way?

4. ☐ Yes   ☐ No

5. Have you claimed exemption from military service?

5. ☐ Yes   ☐ No

6. Has there been any change in your willingness to bear arms on behalf of the United States; to perform non-combatant service in the armed forces of the United States; to perform work of national importance under civilian direction, if the law requires it?

6. ☐ Yes   ☐ No

7. Have you practiced polygamy; received income from illegal gambling; been a prostitute, procured anyone for prostitution or been involved in any other unlawful commercialized vice; encourage or helped any alien to enter the United States illegally; illicitly trafficked in drugs or marihuana; given any false testimony to obtain immigration benefits; or been a habitual drunkard.

7. ☐ Yes   ☐ No

I certify that each of the answers shown above were made by me or at my direction, and that they are true and correct.

Signed at _____   ,On _____
         City and State   Date

_____   _____
         Full Signature   Full Address and ZIP Code

The USCIS notice advises you to wear "proper attire." This doesn't mean you have to go out and buy a suit—just avoid bare feet and disrespectful clothing.

The USCIS materials sent to you will explain whether you can bring family members to the ceremony. This will depend in part on the size of the hall where the ceremony is to be held. Unfortunately, not all halls are large enough for everyone in one's family to attend. If USCIS permits your family members to watch the proceedings, they won't be allowed to sit with you—family members are the "audience" and are usually asked to sit in the balcony or in the seats to the rear of the hall. With over a thousand or more new citizens often sworn in at a single ceremony, space can be tight. You may need to arrive early to assure your family members of getting a seat.

2. What to Expect

The swearing-in is a group ceremony, which will probably last two to three hours.

When you first arrive, a USCIS officer or a volunteer will point you to an area where you'll turn in your appointment notice and meet briefly with an officer. Usually this will be at a series of tables divided alphabetically, to correspond with the letters of your last name (surname). You'll need to know the English alphabet to figure out which table to go to—you may, for example, see signs saying "A-F," "G-L," "M-R," and S-Z." Go to the table whose letters include the first letter of your last name. For example, if your last name is Yang, then you would go to the S-Z table.

The USCIS officer at the table will review your appointment notice, including the portion on the back that you filled in. He or she may ask to see other immigration documents. Assuming everything is acceptable, you will hand in your green card and receive any additional citizenship information. Then you'll proceed into the main hall for the ceremony.

The ceremony is meant to be a celebration—there may be speeches, television cameras, and more.

You'll hear various people's ideas of what it means to be a U.S. citizen. The ceremony is often held in a courtroom, with a judge presiding. (Of course, if you are sworn in by a USCIS officer, rather than a judge, it's just as valid.)

The crucial moment is when you raise your hand and repeat, together with the group, the Oath of Allegiance making you a U.S. citizen. (For information on how members of certain religious groups and conscientious objectors to military service can modify the oath to match their beliefs, see Chapter 2, Section G.) You've seen the oath elsewhere in this book, but here it is once more:

The Oath of Allegiance

I hereby declare, on oath,

that I absolutely and entirely renounce and abjure all allegiance and fidelity to any foreign prince, potentate, state or sovereignty, of whom or which I have heretofore been a subject or citizen;

that I will support and defend the Constitution and the laws of the United States against all enemies, foreign and domestic;

that I will bear true faith and allegiance to the same;

that I will bear arms on behalf of the United States when required by the law; and

that I take this obligation freely, without any mental reservation or purpose of evasion, so help me God.

B. How to Prove Your Citizenship

At the end of your swearing-in ceremony, the judge or USCIS officer will call you up to receive your Naturalization Certificate—a document that looks like a college diploma and is more suitable for framing than for carrying around. You may be asked to sign it in front of a USCIS or court official (if you're changing your name, don't forget to use the new one).

Before you hang your certificate on the wall, however, make photocopies in case you want to help other family members immigrate. (You'll need to send the copies to USCIS with the visa petitions you submit for them.) Yes, we know it says on the certificate that copying it is illegal—but USCIS does not object to making copies for purposes of an immigration application. It *is* illegal to forge additional copies of the certificate for other people to use.

⚠ Check your Naturalization Certificate for errors. Even before you leave the ceremony hall, take a close look at your name and the other information on your certificate. If anything is wrong, look around for the Resolution Table or a USCIS officer who can help you. USCIS may be able to fix your certificate that same day. If you don't notice the error until you've gone home, go to your local USCIS office within five days, if possible—that's the time window within which USCIS is usually willing to fix any mistakes that are its fault, for free. After that you'll have to file Form N-565, and pay a fee.

Your U.S. passport is a more useful form of proof of citizenship status. If you are asked, at the swearing-in ceremony, whether you want to fill out a passport application, we recommend that you do so. You'll need a passport in order to travel and return to the United States, and it's convenient for showing to employers and the like. If you don't apply for a passport at the ceremony, you can obtain one later through the U.S. State Department (a different agency from the one that runs USCIS). For contact information, look in the blue, federal government pages of your phone book or check online (www.state.gov).

C. Registering to Vote

After you have been sworn in as a citizen, you are eligible to vote in U.S. elections—national and local. We recommend taking advantage of this right even if you distrust politicians, feel that you don't understand the issues, or are unsure of the English language.

There are ways of dealing with voting barriers. Community and ethnic organizations often hold seminars in other languages to help educate foreign-born voters. Organizations or newspapers that you trust will analyze the issues and recommend ways to vote. And when you do go to vote, remember that you don't have to vote on every single item; you can choose to punch your ballot slip—or click the computer screen—only for those candidates or issues of importance to you.

To sign up to vote, contact your local Registrar of Voters (you have to be on the Registrar's list in advance of the next election if you want to vote in it). Elections are commonly held on the Tuesday on or after the second day of November.

You can find the Registrar's phone number in the blue or white pages of your local phone book, usually under the city or county section. If this doesn't work, look for voter registration forms at local government offices—for example, departments of motor vehicles, post offices, fire stations, and city halls.

D. Citizenship for Your Children

If you give birth to a child in the United States (including Guam, the Northern Mariana Islands, Puerto Rico, and the Virgin Islands), that child is a U.S. citizen. Of course, that was true even before you became a citizen. However, by becoming a citizen you have gained some important new rights, including the ability to pass citizenship automatically to:

- certain of your existing children born outside the United States (see Section 1), and
- your future children born outside the United States (see Section 2).

If, after reading the sections below, you don't see a way for your child to become a citizen automatically, don't give up—see an attorney. There are ways that children can become citizens that we don't describe here, because they are obscure and rarely used. Act quickly—certain opportunities available to your child may run out after he or she turns 18.

⚠ **Do not use the information in this chapter to analyze the citizenship rights of anyone other than your own child or the child of someone just becoming a citizen.** The laws have changed over the years, but the older laws remain in force for certain children, depending on when they were born, when their parents became citizens and more. For more information, see Nolo's Legal Encyclopedia (www.nolo.com). Click "Immigration and Green Cards," then click "U.S. Citizenship," then click "U.S. Citizenship by Birth or Through Parents."

1. Citizenship for Existing Children

Certain children can become citizens automatically through their citizen parents under a legal concept called "derivation." The Child Citizenship Act of 2000 provides that your children will become U.S. citizens the moment that all of the following become true:

- the child has lawful permanent residence (a green card) and got that permanent residence before he or she was age 18
- the child is living in the United States
- the child is living under your legal and physical custody, and
- you become a citizen before your child turns 18.

It doesn't matter when your child was born or whether the other parent is a U.S. citizen.

Adopted children are included among those who can derive citizenship under this provision. The child must have either been adopted as an orphan or been adopted before the age of 16 and have lived with you (an adopting parent), in your legal custody, for at least two years.

Although derivation of citizenship is "automatic," there is a down side to this. It means that no one will actually check to see whether your children are citizens—and therefore no one will give you any proof of their new status as citizens. To resolve this, apply for Certificates of Citizenship for your children using Form N-600. You can obtain this form by calling USCIS at 800-870-3676, or online (www.uscis.gov).

An alternative is for your child to apply for a U.S. passport, but because derivation is a complicated matter, the passport can be harder to get (and to renew). You should definitely apply for a passport for your child at some point, but see if you can get a Certificate of Citizenship as well. For information on obtaining U.S. passports, contact the State Department (www.state.gov).

2. Citizenship for Future Foreign-Born Children

If, in the future, one of your children is born outside the United States, that child may acquire U.S. citizenship, depending on whether your child's other parent is also a U.S. citizen (covered in Subsection a, below), and if not, whether you, the citizen parent, are the child's mother or the father (discussed in Subsection b, below). (In addition, it's possible that the child will gain citizenship in the country of birth—but that depends on the laws of that country; not all countries grant citizenship based on birth.)

a. If Both Parents Are U.S. Citizens

If both you and your child's other parent are U.S. citizens, your foreign-born child will acquire citizenship if:

- you and your child's other parent are married to one another, and
- either you or your spouse have lived in the United States before the birth date.

There is no time minimum on how long you or your spouse lived in the United States, but it needs to have been your primary home at some point— not just a temporary tourist destination. However, since you probably had to live in the United States for a time before you became a citizen, you have likely satisfied this requirement already.

If the two of you are not married when your child is born, and you are the father concerned with getting citizenship for your child, the same requirements as above apply—but you'll need to take an added step: Legitimate the child before his or her 18th birthday.

"Legitimation" is a legal term meaning that you accept the child as being yours under the laws of the country where you live. This may be as simple as putting your name on the child's birth certificate. If you're not sure what the local procedure is, an alternative is to acknowledge your paternity in writing under oath (again, before the child is 18). In addition, you'll need to sign a statement that you will provide financial support for the child until he or she reaches age 18. If you're overseas, the local U.S. consulate may be able to help you with this paperwork. If not, you may need the help of an experienced immigration attorney.

If the two of you are not married and you are the child's mother, and if the father refuses to admit that he's the father, then the residence requirements become a bit more strict: You must have lived in the United States for at least a full year before the child is born in order for the child to acquire citizenship. Again, however, since you probably already lived in the United States for that amount of time in order to become a citizen, this probably won't be a problem.

b. If Only One Parent Is a Citizen

If your child's other parent is not a U.S. citizen and you want the child to acquire your U.S. citizenship when born overseas, it is still possible. However, the requirements are slightly stiffer than if both parents had been U.S. citizens. If you're the mother and a U.S. citizen, you'll need to have been physically present in the United States or its outlying possessions for at least five years before the child's birth. At least two of those five years must have been after you reached age 14. It doesn't matter if you weren't a citizen during the entire five years.

If you are the child's father and a U.S. citizen, and you are married to the mother, then the same requirement described just above applies: You'll need to have been physically present in the United States or its outlying possessions for at least five years before the birth. At least two of those years must have been after you had reached age 14. Again, it doesn't matter if you weren't a citizen during the entire five years.

However, if you are the child's father and you aren't married to the mother, you'll also need to legitimate the child before his or her 18th birthday.

(See Subsection a, above, for more about legitimation.) In addition, you'll need to sign a statement that you will provide financial support for the child until he or she reaches age 18. If you're overseas, the local U.S. consulate may be able to help you with this paperwork. If not, you may need the help of an experienced immigration attorney.

c. Obtaining Proof of Your Child's Citizenship

Although your child's citizenship acquisition is, in theory, automatic, you'll still want to be able to prove it. If you're overseas, ask your local U.S. consulate for a document called an FS-240, or Report of Birth Abroad of a Citizen of the United States of America. If you happen to have returned to the United States, you can apply to USCIS for a Certificate of Citizenship. This is done using Form N-600, which you can order from USCIS at 800-870-3676 or obtain online at www.uscis.gov.

Another alternative is to ask the U.S. State Department to give your child a U.S. passport. This may prove difficult, since State Department officials are less familiar with the details of the immigration laws than USCIS officials. In any case, you should definitely apply for a passport for your child at some point, and see if you can get a Certificate of Citizenship as well.

E. Helping Other Family Members Immigrate

Your ability to help your foreign-born family members immigrate to the United States improves dramatically after you become a U.S. citizen. While you had a green card, your rights were quite limited. You could sponsor (file a visa petition for) only your spouse and unmarried children—no one else. In fact, you may have filed visa petitions for these family members and still be waiting for them to immigrate. Spouses and unmarried children of permanent residents, as well as various other family members, are called "preference relatives." That means that Congress has set annual limits on the number of visas available to them. Because the demand for these visas always exceeds the supply, preference relatives end up on waiting lists that last many years before they can immigrate to the United States.

But now that you're a citizen, the situation improves for:

- family members for whom you may have already started the immigration process, including your spouse and unmarried children, who will be able to immigrate faster (see Section 1), and

- other family members—including your parents, married children, brothers, and sisters—for whom you now can start the immigration process (see Section 2).

1. Helping Your Foreign-Born Spouse and Children

Once you're a citizen, your spouse and your unmarried children who are younger than age 21 turn from preference relatives into "immediate relatives"—relatives who can apply for lawful permanent residence right away, with no annual limits and no waiting lists to delay their progress. You can either start the immigration process for them now or, if you've already started it by filing an initial visa petition for them, have them continue the process at a faster pace.

Unfortunately, even immediate relatives must go through a lot of application paperwork before they can get their green cards—the application process often takes a year or more to complete. You can't avoid the paperwork. But at least you'll know that their cases are progressing.

If you have unmarried children who are already older than 21 (in visa preference category "2B"), your citizenship turns them into what are called "first preference relatives." This is not as beneficial as being an immediate relative—it means that they are subject to the annual limits on the number of visas and will have to wait for an available visa before they can continue with their immigration process. However, they are fairly high on the priority list. Their wait will average about two years (though longer if they're coming from Mexico or the Philippines)—normally a huge improvement over when

you were a permanent resident, at which time they were in a lower category called "2B" and their wait for a visa averaged nine years. (In the rare cases where this conversion is not an improvement, your child can elect to remain in category 2B, assuming you filed a visa petition for him or her while you were still a permanent resident. This option is mainly used by children from the Philippines, where the first preference category tends to be more backlogged than category 2B.)

If you've already filed a visa petition to start the immigration process for your spouse or children (Form I-130), but they're still on the waiting list for a visa or green card, you don't have to restart the process from the beginning, but can advance them forward. In other words, you don't have to file a new visa petition, and they don't have to lose their place in line. If they have become immediate relatives, they can jump straight to the head of the line and continue with the final stages of their applications for green cards. If they're your children older than 21, they can go from the 2B waiting list to the first preference waiting list with full credit for the years they have already waited. (In technical terms, they can use the same "priority date" as they had before.) In either case, the procedure is to send a copy of your citizenship certificate and a letter explaining the situation to whichever office is currently handling your family members' files.

A further benefit to your citizenship is that as soon as your children become lawful permanent residents, they may also become instant citizens—so long as they're younger than age 18 when you become a citizen and they're living in the United States in your legal and physical custody. (For more information, see Section D, above, concerning derivation of citizenship.)

2. Helping Other Family Members

Becoming a citizen allows you to start the immigration process for certain family members other than your spouse and unmarried children. These include your parents, married children, and brothers and sisters. (Unfortunately, it doesn't include family members such as grandparents, aunts, uncles, cousins, nieces, and nephews.) Not all of your eligible family members will become immediate relatives, however; some of them will have to wait many years before having the opportunity to immigrate through you.

Your parents benefit the most. They become your immediate relatives and can apply to immigrate to the United States right away. (As described earlier, however, even immediate relatives must get through the paperwork of immigrating, which tends to take at least a year to complete.)

Your married children as well as your brothers and sisters benefit, because you can now file visa petitions starting the immigration process for them. However, they will be considered your preference relatives, meaning that your visa petition won't get them a visa or green card anytime soon. First, they'll be put on a waiting list and subject to an annual limit on the number of visas that are given out. Your married children will fall into the third preference category, your brothers and sisters into the fourth preference category. Both are fairly low on the priority list and are likely to wait many years before becoming eligible to immigrate to the United States.

See the chart below, "Bringing the Family Over," for a summary of who you can help immigrate and how long they are likely to wait. Unfortunately, these estimates of waiting times are inexact—they merely show how long the wait was for people who are finally receiving visas now. Because the length of the wait depends on supply and demand, it is unpredictable and could be far different—probably longer—by the time your relatives apply. The waits rarely get shorter.

Note also that the length of time your family member waits can be affected by which country he or she is coming from. For countries that have large numbers of visa applicants, the wait gets longer, because the laws contain per-country limits. As a result, the State Department usually creates a separate (and longer) waiting list for Mexico, the Philippines, and sometimes India.

A full discussion of the rules and procedures for assisting family members to immigrate is beyond the scope of this book. For more information on immigrating spouses, see *Fiancé and Marriage Visas: A Couple's Guide to U.S. Immigration*, by Ilona Bray (Nolo). For information on immigrating other family members, see *How to Get a Green Card*, by Loida Nicolas Lewis and Len T. Madlansacay (Nolo), or *U.S. Immigration Made Easy*, by Laurence A. Canter and Martha S. Siegel (Nolo). Family members who are either living in the United States illegally, have lived here illegally in the past, or have ever been in deportation proceedings will probably need the help of an experienced immigration lawyer.

Bringing the Family Over		
Relationship to U.S. Citizen	**Category Name**	**Average Length of Wait**
Husband or wife	Immediate relative	No wait other than application processing time
Unmarried child younger than 21	Immediate relative	No wait other than application processing time
Parent	Immediate relative	No wait other than application processing time
Unmarried child older than 21	Family first preference	Four years from most countries, 14 years if the child is from the Philippines, and ten years if the child is from Mexico
Married child	Family third preference	Seven years from most countries, 14 years if the child is from the Philippines, and nine years if the child is from Mexico
Brother or sister	Family fourth preference	Fourteen years from most countries, 22 years if they're from the Philippines, and 12 years if they're from Mexico

USCIS District Office and Suboffice Addresses

NOTE: The below list contains the street addresses (not mailing addresses) of USCIS District Offices and Suboffices or Satellite Offices (which perform most of the same functions as District Offices) serving your state. You can visit these offices in person for USCIS forms and information.

You may see an address listed below your state's name that is in another state—that means that it's the closest USCIS District Office to you, and also serves your state. For more information on USCIS office locations or contact information, see the USCIS website at www.uscis.gov.

ALABAMA
USCIS Atlanta District Office
Martin Luther King, Jr., Federal Building
77 Forsyth Street SW
Atlanta, GA 30303

ALASKA
USCIS Anchorage District Office
620 East 10th Avenue, Suite 102
Anchorage, AK 99501

ARIZONA
USCIS Tucson Suboffice
6431 South Country Club Road
Tucson, AZ 85706-5907

USCIS Phoenix District Office
2035 North Central Avenue
Phoenix, AZ 85004

ARKANSAS
USCIS New Orleans District Office
701 Loyola Avenue
New Orleans, LA 70113

USCIS Fort Smith Suboffice
4991 Old Greenwood Road
Fort Smith, AR 72903

CALIFORNIA
USCIS Fresno Suboffice
1177 Fulton Mall
Fresno, CA 93721

USCIS Los Angeles District Office
300 North Los Angeles Street, Room 1001
Los Angeles, CA 90012

USCIS Sacramento Suboffice
650 Capitol Mall
Sacramento, CA 95814

USCIS San Diego District Office
880 Front Street, Suite 1234
San Diego, CA 92101

USCIS San Francisco District Office
444 Washington Street
San Francisco, CA 94111

USCIS San Jose Suboffice
1887 Monterey Road
San Jose, CA 95112

USCIS Santa Ana Suboffice
34 Civic Center Plaza
Federal Building
Santa Ana, CA 92701

COLORADO
USCIS Denver District Office
4730 Paris Street
Denver, CO 80239

CONNECTICUT
USCIS Boston District Office
John F. Kennedy Federal Building
Government Center
Boston, MA 02203

USCIS Hartford Suboffice
450 Main Street, 4th Floor
Hartford, CT 06103-3060

DELAWARE
USCIS Philadelphia District Office
1600 Callowhill Street
Philadelphia, PA 19130

USCIS Dover Satellite Office
1305 McD Drive
Dover, DE 19901

DISTRICT OF COLUMBIA
USCIS Washington District Office
4420 N. Fairfax Drive
Arlington, VA 22203

FLORIDA
USCIS Miami District Office
7880 Biscayne Boulevard
Miami, FL 33138

USCIS Jacksonville Suboffice
4121 Southpoint Boulevard
Jacksonville, FL 32216

USCIS Orlando Suboffice
9403 Tradeport Drive
Orlando, FL 32827

USCIS Tampa Suboffice
5524 West Cypress Street
Tampa, FL 33607-1708

USCIS West Palm Beach Satellite
  Office
326 Fern Street
West Palm Beach, FL 33401

GEORGIA
USCIS Atlanta District Office
Martin Luther King, Jr., Federal
  Building
77 Forsyth Street SW
Atlanta, GA 30303

GUAM
USCIS Honolulu District Office
595 Ala Moana Boulevard
Honolulu, HI 96813

HAWAII
USCIS Honolulu District Office
595 Ala Moana Boulevard
Honolulu, HI 96813

IDAHO
USCIS Helena District Office
2800 Skyway Drive
Helena, MT 59602

USCIS Boise Suboffice
1185 South Vinnell Way
Boise, ID 83709

ILLINOIS
USCIS Chicago District Office
10 West Jackson Boulevard
Chicago, IL 60604

Chicago USCIS Adjudications
  Office
230 S. Dearborn, 23rd floor
Chicago, IL 60604

Chicago USCIS Citizenship Office
539 S. LaSalle
Chicago, IL 60605

INDIANA
USCIS Chicago District Office
10 West Jackson Boulevard
Chicago, IL 60604

USCIS Indianapolis Suboffice
950 N. Meridian St., Room 400
Indianapolis, IN 46204

IOWA
USCIS Omaha District Office
3736 South 132nd Street
Omaha, NE 68144

KANSAS
USCIS Kansas City District Office
9747 Northwest Conant Avenue
Kansas City, MO 64153

USCIS Wichita Satellite Office
271 West 3rd Street North,
  Suite 1050
Wichita, KS 67202-1212

KENTUCKY
USCIS New Orleans District
701 Loyola Avenue
New Orleans, LA 70113

USCIS Louisville Suboffice
Gene Snyder U.S. Courthouse and
  Customhouse, Room 390
601 West Broadway
Louisville, KY 40202

LOUISIANA
USCIS New Orleans District
701 Loyola Avenue
New Orleans, LA 70113

MAINE
USCIS Portland District Office
176 Gannett Drive
South Portland, ME 04106

MARYLAND
USCIS Baltimore District Office
Fallon Federal Building
31 Hopkins Plaza
Baltimore, MD 21201

MASSACHUSETTS
USCIS Boston District Office
John F. Kennedy Federal Building
Government Center
Boston, MA 02203

MICHIGAN
USCIS Detroit District Office
333 Mt. Elliot
Detroit, MI 48207

MINNESOTA
USCIS St. Paul District Office
2901 Metro Drive, Suite 100
Bloomington, MN 55425

MISSISSIPPI
USCIS New Orleans District
701 Loyola Avenue
New Orleans, LA 70113

USCIS Jackson Suboffice
100 West Capitol Street
Jackson, MS 36269

MISSOURI
USCIS Kansas City District
9747 Northwest Conant Avenue
Kansas City, MO 64153

MONTANA
USCIS Helena District Office
2800 Skyway Drive
Helena, MT 59602

NEBRASKA
USCIS Omaha District Office
3736 South 132nd Street
Omaha, NE 68144

NEVADA
USCIS Phoenix District Office
2035 North Central Avenue
Phoenix, AZ 85004

USCIS Las Vegas Suboffice
3373 Pepper Lane
Las Vegas, NV 89120-2739

USCIS Reno Subofficc
1351 Corporate Boulevard
Reno, NV 89502

NEW HAMPSHIRE
USCIS Boston District Office
John F. Kennedy Federal Building
Government Center
Boston, MA 02203

USCIS Manchester Satellite Office
803 Canal Street
Manchester, NH 03101

NEW JERSEY
USCIS Newark District Office
Peter Rodino, Jr., Federal Building
970 Broad Street
Newark, NJ 07102

USCIS Cherry Hill Suboffice
1886 Greentree Road
Cherry Hill, NJ 08003

NEW MEXICO
USCIS El Paso District Office
1545 Hawkins Boulevard, Suite 167
El Paso, TX 79925

USCIS Albuquerque Suboffice
1720 Randolph Road SE
Albuquerque, NM 87106

NEW YORK
USCIS Buffalo District Office
Federal Center
130 Delaware Avenue
Buffalo, NY 14202

USCIS New York City District
Office
26 Federal Plaza
New York City, NY 10278

USCIS Albany Suboffice
1086 Troy-Schenectady Road
Latham, NY 12110

NORTH CAROLINA
USCIS Atlanta District Office
Martin Luther King, Jr., Federal
Building
77 Forsyth Street SW
Atlanta, GA 30303

USCIS Charlotte Suboffice
6130 Tyvola Centre Drive
Charlotte, NC 28217

NORTH DAKOTA
USCIS St. Paul District Office
2901 Metro Drive, Suite 100
Bloomington, MN 55425

OHIO
USCIS Cleveland District Office
A.J.C. Federal Building
1240 East Ninth Street, Room 501
Cleveland, OH 44199

USCIS Cincinnati Suboffice
J.W. Peck Federal Building
550 Main Street, Room 4001
Cincinnati, OH 45202

OKLAHOMA
USCIS Dallas District Office
8101 North Stemmons Freeway
Dallas, TX 75247

USCIS Oklahoma City Suboffice
4400 SW 44th Street
Oklahoma City, OK 73119

OREGON
USCIS Portland, Oregon, District
Office
511 NW Broadway
Portland, OR 97209

PENNSYLVANIA
USCIS Philadelphia District Office
1600 Callowhill Street
Philadelphia, PA 19130

USCIS Pittsburgh Suboffice
1000 Liberty Avenue
Federal Building, Room 314
Pittsburgh, PA 15222-4181

PUERTO RICO
USCIS San Juan District Office
San Patricio Office Center
7 Tabonuco Street, Suite 100
Guaynabo, PR 00968

USCIS Charlotte Amalie Suboffice
Nisky Center, Suite 1A
First Floor South
Charlotte Amalie, St. Thomas
U.S. Virgin Islands 00802

USCIS San Croix Suboffice
Sunny Isle Shopping Center
Christiansted, St. Croix
U.S. Virgin Islands 00820

RHODE ISLAND
USCIS Boston District Office
John F. Kennedy Federal Building
Government Center
Boston, MA 02203

USCIS Providence Suboffice
200 Dyer Street
Providence, RI 02903

SOUTH CAROLINA
USCIS Atlanta District Office
Martin Luther King, Jr., Federal
Building
77 Forsyth Street SW
Atlanta, GA 30303

USCIS Charleston Satellite Office
170 Meeting Street, Fifth Floor
Charleston, SC 29401

SOUTH DAKOTA
USCIS St. Paul District Office
2901 Metro Drive, Suite 100
Bloomington, MN 55425

TENNESSEE
USCIS New Orleans District Office
701 Loyola Avenue
New Orleans, LA 70113

USCIS Memphis Suboffice
Suite 100
1341 Sycamore View Road
Memphis, TN 38134

TEXAS
USCIS Dallas District Office
8101 North Stemmons Freeway
Dallas, TX 75247

USCIS El Paso District Office
1545 Hawkins Boulevard, Suite 167
El Paso, TX 79925

USCIS Harlingen District Office
1717 Zoy Street
Harlingen, TX 78552

USCIS Houston District Office
126 Northpoint
Houston, TX 77060

USCIS San Antonio District Office
8940 Fourwinds Drive
San Antonio, TX 78239

UTAH
USCIS Denver District Office
4730 Paris Street
Denver, CO 80239

USCIS Salt Lake City Suboffice
5272 South College Drive, #100
Murray, UT 84123

VERMONT
USCIS Portland District Office
176 Gannett Drive
South Portland, ME 04106

USCIS St. Albans Suboffice
64 Gricebrook Road
St. Albans, VT 05478

VIRGIN ISLANDS
USCIS San Juan District Office
San Patricio Office Center
7 Tabonuco Street, Suite 100
Guaynabo, PR 00968

USCIS Charlotte Amalie Suboffice
Nisky Center, Suite 1A
First Floor South
Charlotte Amalie, St. Thomas
U.S. Virgin Islands 00802

San Croix Suboffice
Sunny Isle Shopping Center
Christiansted, St. Croix
U.S. Virgin Islands 00820

VIRGINIA
USCIS Washington District Office
4420 N. Fairfax Drive
Arlington, VA 22203

USCIS Norfolk Suboffice
5280 Henneman Drive
Norfolk, VA 23513

WASHINGTON
USCIS Seattle District Office
815 Airport Way South
Seattle, WA 98134

USCIS Spokane Suboffice
U.S. Courthouse
920 W. Riverside, Room 691
Spokane, WA 99201

USCIS Yakima Suboffice
415 North 3rd Street
Yakima, WA 98901

WEST VIRGINIA
USCIS Philadelphia District Office
1600 Callowhill Street
Philadelphia, PA 19130

USCIS West Virginia Satellite Office
210 Kanawha Boulevard West
Charleston, WV 25302

USCIS Pittsburgh Suboffice
1000 Liberty Avenue
Federal Building, Room 314
Pittsburgh, PA 15222-4181

WISCONSIN
USCIS Chicago District Office
10 West Jackson Boulevard
Chicago, IL 60604

USCIS Milwaukee Suboffice
310 E. Knapp Street
Milwaukee, WI 53202

WYOMING
USCIS Denver District Office
4730 Paris Street
Denver, CO 80239

100 Sample U.S. History and Government Questions With Answers (USCIS Version)

DEPARTMENT OF JUSTICE
Immigration & Naturalization Service   **100 Typical Questions**

1.   WHAT ARE THE COLORS OF OUR FLAG?

2.   HOW MANY STARS ARE THERE IN OUR FLAG?

3.   WHAT COLOR ARE THE STARS ON OUR FLAG?

4.   WHAT DO THE STARS ON THE FLAG MEAN?

5.   HOW MANY STRIPES ARE THERE IN THE FLAG?

6.   WHAT COLOR ARE THE STRIPES?

7.   WHAT DO THE STRIPES ON THE FLAG MEAN?

8.   HOW MANY STATES ARE THERE IN THE UNION?

9.   WHAT IS THE 4TH OF JULY?

10.   WHAT IS THE DATE OF INDEPENDENCE DAY?

11.   INDEPENDENCE FROM WHOM?

12.   WHAT COUNTRY DID WE FIGHT DURING THE REVOLUTIONARY WAR?

13.   WHO WAS THE FIRST PRESIDENT OF THE UNITED STATES?

14.   WHO IS THE PRESIDENT OF THE UNITED STATES TODAY?

15.   WHO IS THE VICE-PRESIDENT OF THE UNITED STATES TODAY?

16.   WHO ELECTS THE PRESIDENT OF THE UNITED STATES?

17.   WHO BECOMES PRESIDENT OF THE UNITED STATES IF THE PRESIDENT SHOULD DIE?

18.   FOR HOW LONG DO WE ELECT THE PRESIDENT?

19.   WHAT IS THE CONSTITUTION?

20.   CAN THE CONSTITUTION BE CHANGED?

21.   WHAT DO WE CALL A CHANGE TO THE CONSTITUTION?

22.   HOW MANY CHANGES OR AMENDMENTS ARE THERE TO THE CONSTITUTION?

23.   HOW MANY BRANCHES ARE THERE IN OUR GOVERNMENT?

24.   WHAT ARE THE THREE BRANCHES OF OUR GOVERNMENT?

25.   WHAT IS THE LEGISLATIVE BRANCH OF OUR GOVERNMENT?

26.   WHO MAKES THE LAWS IN THE UNITED STATES?

27.   WHAT IS CONGRESS?

28.   WHAT ARE THE DUTIES OF CONGRESS?

29.   WHO ELECTS CONGRESS?

30.   HOW MANY SENATORS ARE THERE IN CONGRESS?

31.   CAN YOU NAME THE TWO SENATORS FROM YOUR STATE?

32.   FOR HOW LONG DO WE ELECT EACH SENATOR?

33.   HOW MANY REPRESENTATIVES ARE THERE IN CONGRESS?

34.   FOR HOW LONG DO WE ELECT THE REPRESENTATIVES?

35.   WHAT IS THE EXECUTIVE BRANCH OF OUR GOVERNMENT?

36.   WHAT IS THE JUDICIARY BRANCH OF OUR GOVERNMENT?

37.   WHAT ARE THE DUTIES OF THE SUPREME COURT?

38.   WHAT IS THE SUPREME LAW OF THE UNITED STATES?

39.   WHAT IS THE BILL OF RIGHTS?

40.   WHAT IS THE CAPITAL OF YOUR STATE?

41.   WHO IS THE CURRENT GOVERNOR OF YOUR STATE?

42.   WHO BECOMES PRESIDENT OF THE U.S.A. IF THE PRESIDENT AND THE VICE-PRESIDENT
      SHOULD DIE?

43.   WHO IS THE CHIEF JUSTICE OF THE SUPREME COURT?

44.   CAN YOU NAME THE THIRTEEN ORIGINAL STATES?

45.   WHO SAID, "GIVE ME LIBERTY OR GIVE ME DEATH"?

46.   WHICH COUNTRIES WERE OUR ENEMIES DURING WORLD WAR II?

47.   WHAT ARE THE 49TH AND 50TH STATES OF THE UNION?

48.   HOW MANY TERMS CAN A PRESIDENT SERVE?

49.   WHO WAS MARTIN LUTHER KING, JR.?

50.   WHO IS THE HEAD OF YOUR LOCAL GOVERNMENT?

51.   ACCORDING TO THE CONSTITUTION, A PERSON MUST MEET CERTAIN REQUIREMENTS IN
      ORDER TO BE ELIGIBLE TO BECOME PRESIDENT. NAME ONE OF THESE REQUIREMENTS.

52. WHY ARE THERE 100 SENATORS IN THE SENATE?

53. WHO SELECTS THE SUPREME COURT JUSTICES?

54. HOW MANY SUPREME COURT JUSTICES ARE THERE?

55. WHY DID THE PILGRIMS COME TO AMERICA?

56. WHAT IS THE HEAD EXECUTIVE OF A STATE GOVERNMENT CALLED?

57. WHAT IS THE HEAD EXECUTIVE OF A CITY GOVERNMENT CALLED?

58. WHAT HOLIDAY WAS CELEBRATED FOR THE FIRST TIME BY THE AMERICAN COLONISTS?

59. WHO WAS THE MAIN WRITER OF THE DECLARATION OF INDEPENDENCE?

60. WHEN WAS THE DECLARATION OF INDEPENDENCE ADOPTED?

61. WHAT IS THE BASIC BELIEF OF THE DECLARATION OF INDEPENDENCE?

62. WHAT IS THE NATIONAL ANTHEM OF THE UNITED STATES?

63. WHO WROTE THE STAR-SPANGLED BANNER?

64. WHERE DOES FREEDOM OF SPEECH COME FROM?

65. WHAT IS THE MINIMUM VOTING AGE IN THE UNITED STATES?

66. WHO SIGNS BILLS INTO LAW?

67. WHAT IS THE HIGHEST COURT IN THE UNTIED STATES?

68. WHO WAS THE PRESIDENT DURING THE CIVIL WAR?

69. WHAT DID THE EMANCIPATION PROCLAMATION DO?

70. WHAT SPECIAL GROUP ADVISES THE PRESIDENT?

71. WHICH PRESIDENT IS CALLED THE "FATHER OF OUR COUNTRY"?

72. WHAT IMMIGRATION AND NATURALIZATION SERVICE FORM IS USED TO APPLY TO BECOME A NATURALIZED CITIZEN?

73. WHO HELPED THE PILGRIMS IN AMERICA?

74. WHAT IS THE NAME OF THE SHIP THAT BROUGHT THE PILGRIMS TO AMERICA?

75. WHAT WERE THE 13 ORIGINAL STATES OF THE UNITED STATES CALLED?

76. NAME 3 RIGHTS OR FREEDOMS GUARANTEED BY THE BILL OF RIGHTS.

77. WHO HAS THE POWER TO DECLARE WAR?

78.   WHAT KIND OF GOVERNMENT DOES THE UNITED STATES HAVE?

79.   WHICH PRESIDENT FREED THE SLAVES?

80.   IN WHAT YEAR WAS THE CONSTITUTION WRITTEN?

81.   WHAT ARE THE FIRST 10 AMENDMENTS TO THE CONSTITUTION CALLED?

82.   NAME ONE PURPOSE OF THE UNITED NATIONS.

83.   WHERE DOES CONGRESS MEET?

84.   WHOSE RIGHTS ARE GUARANTEED BY THE CONSTITUTION AND THE BILL OF RIGHTS?

85.   WHAT IS THE INTRODUCTION TO THE CONSTITUTION CALLED?

86.   NAME ONE BENEFIT OF BEING A CITIZEN OF THE UNITED STATES.

87.   WHAT IS THE MOST IMPORTANT RIGHT GRANTED TO U.S. CITIZENS?

88.   WHAT IS THE UNITED STATES CAPITOL?

89.   WHAT IS THE WHITE HOUSE?

90.   WHERE IS THE WHITE HOUSE LOCATED?

91.   WHAT IS THE NAME OF THE PRESIDENT'S OFFICIAL HOME?

92.   NAME ONE RIGHT GUARANTEED BY THE FIRST AMENDMENT.

93.   WHO IS THE COMMANDER IN CHIEF OF THE U.S. MILITARY?

94.   WHICH PRESIDENT WAS THE FIRST COMMANDER IN CHIEF OF THE U.S. MILITARY?

95.   IN WHAT MONTH DO WE VOTE FOR THE PRESIDENT?

96.   IN WHAT MONTH IS THE NEW PRESIDENT INAUGURATED?

97.   HOW MANY TIMES MAY A SENATOR BE RE-ELECTED?

98.   HOW MANY TIMES MAY A CONGRESSMAN BE RE-ELECTED?

99.   WHAT ARE THE 2 MAJOR POLITICAL PARTIES IN THE U.S. TODAY?

100.   HOW MANY STATES ARE THERE IN THE UNITED STATES?

ANSWER SHEET

1. RED, WHITE, AND BLUE

2. 50

3. WHITE

4. ONE FOR EACH STATE IN THE UNION

5. 13

6. RED AND WHITE

7. THEY REPRESENT THE ORIGINAL 13 STATES

8. 50

9. INDEPENDENCE DAY

10. JULY 4TH

11. ENGLAND

12. ENGLAND

13. GEORGE WASHINGTON

14. GEORGE W. BUSH

15. DICK CHENEY

16. THE ELECTORAL COLLEGE

17. VICE PRESIDENT

18. FOUR YEARS

19. THE SUPREME LAW OF THE LAND

20. YES

21. AMENDMENTS

22. 27

23. 3

24. LEGISLATIVE, EXECUTIVE, AND JUDICIARY

25. CONGRESS

26. CONGRESS

27. THE SENATE AND THE HOUSE OF REPRESENTATIVES

28. TO MAKE LAWS

29. THE PEOPLE

30. 100

31. **(INSERT LOCAL INFORMATION)**

32. 6 YEARS

33. 435

34. 2 YEARS

35. THE PRESIDENT, CABINET, AND DEPARTMENTS UNDER THE CABINET MEMBERS

36. THE SUPREME COURT

37. TO INTERPRET LAWS

38. THE CONSTITUTION

39. THE FIRST 10 AMENDMENTS OF THE CONSTITUTION

40. **(INSERT LOCAL INFORMATION)**

41. **(INSERT LOCAL INFORMATION)**

42. SPEAKER OF THE HOUSE OF REPRESENTATIVES

43. WILLIAM REHNQUIST

44. CONNECTICUT, NEW HAMPSHIRE, NEW YORK, NEW JERSEY, MASSACHUSETTS, PENNSYLVANIA, DELAWARE, VIRGINIA, NORTH CAROLINA, SOUTH CAROLINA, GEORGIA, RHODE ISLAND, AND MARYLAND

45. PATRICK HENRY

46. GERMANY, ITALY, AND JAPAN

47. HAWAII AND ALASKA

48. 2

49. A CIVIL RIGHTS LEADER

50. **(INSERT LOCAL INFORMATION)**

51. MUST BE A NATURAL BORN CITIZEN OF THE UNITED STATES;
MUST BE AT LEAST 35 YEARS OLD BY THE TIME HE/SHE WILL SERVE; MUST HAVE LIVED IN THE UNITED STATES FOR AT LEAST 14 YEARS

52. TWO **(2)** FROM EACH STATE

53. APPOINTED BY THE PRESIDENT

54. NINE **(9)**

55. FOR RELIGIOUS FREEDOM

56 GOVERNOR

57. MAYOR

58. THANKSGIVING

59. THOMAS JEFFERSON

60. JULY 4, 1776

61. THAT ALL MEN ARE CREATED EQUAL

62. THE STAR-SPANGLED BANNER

63. FRANCIS SCOTT KEY

64. THE BILL OF RIGHTS

65. EIGHTEEN (18)

66. THE PRESIDENT

67. THE SUPREME COURT

68. ABRAHAM LINCOLN

69. FREED MANY SLAVES

70. THE CABINET

71. GEORGE WASHINGTON

72. FORM N-400, "APPLICATION TO FILE PETITION FOR NATURALIZATION"

73. THE AMERICAN INDIANS (NATIVE AMERICANS)

74. THE MAYFLOWER

75. COLONIES

76.

(A) THE RIGHT OF FREEDOM OF SPEECH, PRESS, RELIGION, PEACEABLE ASSEMBLY AND REQUESTING CHANGE OF GOVERNMENT.

(B)   THE RIGHT TO BEAR ARMS (THE RIGHT TO HAVE WEAPONS OR OWN A GUN, THOUGH SUBJECT TO CERTAIN REGULATIONS).

(C)   THE GOVERNMENT MAY NOT QUARTER, OR HOUSE, SOLDIERS IN THE PEOPLE'S HOMES DURING PEACETIME WITHOUT THE PEOPLE'S CONSENT.

(D)   THE GOVERNMENT MAY NOT SEARCH OR TAKE A PERSON'S PROPERTY WITHOUT A WARRANT.

(E)   A PERSON MAY NOT BE TRIED TWICE FOR THE SAME CRIME AND DOES NOT HAVE TO TESTIFY AGAINST HIMSELF.

(F)   A PERSON CHARGED WITH A CRIME STILL HAS SOME RIGHTS, SUCH AS THE RIGHT TO A TRIAL AND TO HAVE A LAWYER.

(G)   THE RIGHT TO TRIAL BY JURY IN MOST CASES.

(H)   PROTECTS PEOPLE AGAINST EXCESSIVE OR UNREASONABLE FINES OR CRUEL AND UNUSUAL PUNISHMENT.

(I)   THE PEOPLE HAVE RIGHTS OTHER THAN THOSE MENTIONED IN THE CONSTITUTION. ANY POWER NOT GIVEN TO THE FEDERAL GOVERNMENT BY THE CONSTITUTION IS A POWER OF EITHER THE STATE OR THE PEOPLE.

77.   THE CONGRESS

78.   REPUBLICAN

79.   ABRAHAM LINCOLN

80.   1787

81.   THE BILL OF RIGHTS

82.   FOR COUNTRIES TO DISCUSS AND TRY TO RESOLVE WORLD PROBLEMS; TO PROVIDE ECONOMIC AID TO MANY COUNTRIES.

83.   IN THE CAPITOL IN WASHINGTON, D.C.

84.   EVERYONE (CITIZENS AND NON-CITIZENS LIVING IN THE U.S.)

85.   THE PREAMBLE

86.   OBTAIN FEDERAL GOVERNMENT JOBS; TRAVEL WITH A U.S. PASSPORT; PETITION FOR CLOSE RELATIVES TO COME TO THE U.S. TO LIVE

87.   THE RIGHT TO VOTE

88.   THE PLACE WHERE CONGRESS MEETS

89.   THE PRESIDENT'S OFFICIAL HOME

90.   WASHINGTON, D.C. (1600 PENNSYLVANIA AVENUE, NW)

91.   THE WHITE HOUSE

92.   FREEDOM OF: SPEECH, PRESS, RELIGION, PEACEABLE ASSEMBLY, AND REQUESTING CHANGE OF THE GOVERNMENT

93.   THE PRESIDENT

94.   GEORGE WASHINGTON

95.   NOVEMBER

96.   JANUARY

97.   THERE IS NO LIMIT

98.   THERE IS NO LIMIT

99.   DEMOCRATIC AND REPUBLICAN

100.   (50)

C

Tear-Out Immigration Forms

BIOGRAPHIC INFORMATION

U.S. Department of Justice

Immigration and Naturalization Service

OMB No. 1115-0066

(Family name)	(First name)	(Middle name)	☐ MALE ☐ FEMALE	BIRTHDATE (Mo.-Day-Yr.)	NATIONALITY	FILE NUMBER **A-**

ALL OTHER NAMES USED (Including names by previous marriages)	CITY AND COUNTY OF BIRTH	SOCIAL SECURITY NO. (If any)

	FAMILY NAME	FIRST NAME	DATE, CITY AND COUNTRY OF BIRTH (If known)	CITY AND COUNTRY OF RESIDENCE
FATHER				
MOTHER (Maiden name)				

HUSBAND(If none, so state) OR WIFE	FAMILY NAME (For wife, give maiden name)	FIRST NAME	BIRTHDATE	CITY & COUNTRY OF BIRTH	DATE OF MARRIAGE	PLACE OF MARRIAGE

FORMER HUSBANDS OR WIVES (If none, so state)

FAMILY NAME (For wife, give maiden name)	FIRST NAME	BIRTHDATE	DATE AND PLACE OF MARRIAGE	DATE AND PLACE OF TERMINATION OF MARRIAGE

APPLICANTS RESIDENCE LAST FIVE YEARS. LIST PRESENT ADDRESS FIRST.

STREET AND NUMBER	CITY	PROVINCE OR STATE	COUNTRY	FROM MONTH	FROM YEAR	TO MONTH	TO YEAR
						PRESENT TIME	

APPLICANT'S LAST ADDRESS OUTSIDE THE UNITED STATES OF MORE THAN ONE YEAR.	FROM	TO

APPLICANT'S EMPLOYMENT LAST FIVE YEARS. (IF NONE, SO STATE) LIST PRESENT EMPLOYMENT FIRST.

FULL NAME AND ADDRESS OF EMPLOYER	OCCUPATION (Specify)	FROM MONTH	FROM YEAR	TO MONTH	TO YEAR
				PRESENT TIME	

Show below last occupation abroad if not shown above. (Include all information requested above.)

THIS FORM IS SUBMITTED IN CONNECTION WITH APPLICATION FOR:

☐ NATURALIZATION ☐ OTHER (Specify)

☐ STATUS AS PERMANENT RESIDENT

If serving or ever served in the Armed Forces of the United States, complete the following:

Branch of Service	Rank	Service Number

To Other Agency: Please furnish on the reverse of this form, or by attachment hereto, any derogatory information that may be contained in your records concerning the above person, for use in connection with consideration of above application and return to U.S. Immigration and Naturalization Service.

INS USE (Office of Origin)

Office Code

Type of Case

Date

(OTHER AGENCY)

FOR STATE DEPARTMENT USE

MIL PERS	AIR RESERVE
USAF PERS	ARMY PERS

SEE O.I. 328. 1 FOR MAILING ADDRESS

FORM G-325B
(Rev. 10-1-82)Y

OSI (USAF)	ONI (USN)
MID G-2	PROV. MAR.

(ALL DEFENSE CHECKS)

MAIL TO:

DIRECTOR,
UNITED STATES ARMY INVESTIGATIVE
RECORDS REPOSITORY
ATTN: ICIRR-A
FOR MEADE, MARYLAND 20755
ATTENTION: LIAISON OFFICE
IMMIGRATION AND NATURALIZATION SERVICE

STATE (P.P.)	STATE (S.Y.)	OTHER

SEE O.I. 105.4
FOR MAILING ADDRESS

SY
☐ RSC
☐ RMR
☐ C:Visa
☐ R:Visa
☐ ORM

Date _____   19

Date of entry into service _____

Date of seperation _____

Service number _____

The records of this Department show the following with respect to the subject of your inquiry:

All organizations, clubs or societies in the United States, or in any other country, of which subject was a member at any time, and dates thereof. (If none, show "None".)

_____

_____

_____

All arrests, convictions, disciplinary actions, court martial proceedings, and illegal or immoral conduct in which subject involved, including dates and results thereof. (If none, show "None".)

_____

_____

_____

_____

Details of any oral or written statements, conduct, behavior or associations of the subject which may indicate belief in, advocacy of or preference or sympathy for Communism or any other foreign ideology inconsistent with loyalty to the United States or the form of government of the United States or attachment to the principles of the United States Constitution. (If none, show "None".)

_____

_____

_____

Additional information or references.

_____

_____

I certify that the information here given concerning the person named is correct according to the records of the

_____

(Name of Department or organization)

Official signature _____

By _____

U.S. Department of Justice
Immigration and Naturalization Service

OMB No. 1115 -0191
Report of Complaint - Reporte de Queja

Employee _____   Case No. _____

Station _____   Incident _____

Complainant's Name (Nombre)	Address (Domicilio)	Phone No. (Número de Teléfono) ( )
Age (Edad) Race (Raza)	Sex (Sexo) M ☐ F ☐ Occupation (Ocupación)	

Name of Witness (Nombre de Testigo)	Address (Domicilio)	Phone No. (Número de Teléfono)
		( )
		( )
		( )

Subject of Complaint (Persona de quien se queja)
If unknown, please provide description of the employee (Si usted no lo conoce, describa al empleado)

Name (Nombre)	Description (Descripción)

When did incident occur? (¿Cuándo ocurrió el incidente?)				Location (¿Donde ocurrió el incidente?)
Month (Mes)	Day (Día)	Year (Año)	Time (Hora)	

Details of Complaint (Use additional sheet if necessary)
Detalles de la Queja (Uso papel adicional si es necesario)

I certify that, to the best of my knowledge and belief, all my statements are true, correct and made in good faith. (Yo declaro (certifico), a mi mejor conocimiento, que el testimonio hoy dado por mí, es verdadero, correcto y hecho en buena fe.

_____
Signature of Complainant (Firma)

Time and Date Reported (Fecha y Hora del Reporte)	Location Reported (Lugar donde se hizo el Reporte)	Agency (Agencia)

Printed Name of Supervisor Receiving Complaint
(Nombre en letra de molde del Supervisor Recibiendo Queja)

Signature of Supervisor Receiving Complaint
(Firma del Supervisor Recibiendo Queja)

Form I-847 (07/28/99)Y

Instrucciones Para Llenar el Formulario Sus Denuncias Son Importantes

Llene este formulario en la medida de lo posible y sea lo más específico que pueda en la descripción del incidente que denuncie. Si Usted no sabe el nombre del funcionario al que denuncia ni el de la entidad donde está empleado, describa los rasgos físicos de esa persona (estatura, peso, color de cabello, vellos en la cara) y la ropa que llevaba (por ejemplo, uniforme negro con una insignia en el brazo). Es importante que Usted llene este formulario con letra tan clara y elgible como sea posible.

Usted no se perjudicará por haber presentado esta denuncia válida. Si recibe beneficios en forma lícita del Servicio de Inmigración y Naturalización como, por ejemplo, un permiso de trabajo, no los perderá por llener este formulario.

Una vez llenado este formulario, doblelo a lo largo de las líneas de puntos, ciérrelo y échelo en cualquier buzón de correos de los Estados Unidos.

U.S. DEPARTMENT OF JUSTICE
IMMIGRATION AND NATURALIZATION SERVICE

OFFICIAL BUSINESS
PENALTY FOR PRIVATE USE, $300

BUSINESS REPLY MAIL
FIRST CLASS   PERMIT NO. 13147   WASHINGTON, D.C.

POSTAGE WILL BE PAID BY THE IMMIGRATION AND NATURALIZATION SERVICE

OFFICE OF INTERNAL AUDIT
IMMIGRATION AND NATURALIZATION SERVICE
425 I STREET, N.W.
WASHINGTON, D.C. 20536-0001

Instructions For Filling Out This Form With Your Complaints

Fill out this form describing the incident about which you wish to complain as specifically and completely as possible. If you do not know the names of the officials about whom your are complaining nor the organization they work for, describe the physical characteristics of the person (height, weight, color of hair, any facial hair) and the clothing they were wearing (for example, black uniform with a patch on the arm). It is important that you give as much information as possible, clearly and completely.

There will be no retaliation for submitting a complaint. Submitting this form will have no effect on your case or eligibility for any benefits to which you are entitled under the Immigration and Nationality Act.

After filing out this form, fold along the dotted lines, seal and mail in the postal system of the United States.

Form I-847 (Rev. 07/28/99)Y

U.S. Department of Homeland Security
Bureau of Citizenship and Immigration Services

N-336, Request for a Hearing on a Decision in Naturalization Proceedings Under Section 336 of the Act

Decision: ☐ Grant ☐ Denial	Fee:

1. In the Matter of: (Name of Naturalization Applicant)

File Number:

A-

2. I am filing a request for hearing on the decision dated:

3. Please check the one block which applies:

a. ☐ I am *not submitting* a separate brief, statement or evidence.

b. ☐ I *am submitting* a separate brief, statement and/or evidence with this form.

c. ☐ I need _____ days to submit a brief, statement and/or evidence to the CIS. (May be granted only for good cause shown. Explain in a separate letter.)

4. Person filing request:

Name (Please Type or Print in Black Ink.)

Address (Street Number and Name)   (Apt. Number)

(City)   (State)   (Zip Code)

Signature   Date (mm/dd/yyyy)

☐ I am an attorney or representative and I represent the applicant requesting a hearing on a naturalization proceeding. [You must attach a Notice or Entry or Appearance (Form G-28) if you are an attorney or representative and did not previously submit such a form.]

(Person for whom you are appearing)

5. Briefly state the reason(s) for this request for a hearing:

_____

_____

_____

_____

_____

_____

INSTRUCTIONS

1. Filing. You must file your request for a hearing within 30 calendar days after service of the decision (33 days if your decision was mailed) with the local office of the Bureau of Citizenship and Immigration Services (BCIS) that made the unfavorable decision. (The CIS is comprised of offices of former Immigration and Naturalization Service.) The date of service is normally the date of the decision. Submit an original request only. Additional copies are not required.

2. Fee. You must pay **$250.00** to file this form. This form is to be used to appeal an unfavorable decision for an individual applicant. **The fee will not be refunded, regardless of the action taken in your case. Do not mail cash**. All checks or money orders, whether United States or foreign, must be payable in U.S. currency at a financial institution in the United States. When a check is drawn on the account of a person other than yourself, write your name on the face of the check. If the check is not honored, the CIS will charge you $30.00.

Pay by check or money order in the exact amount. Make the check or money order payable to the **U.S. Department of Homeland Security**; unless:

- If you live in Guam and are filing this form there, make the check or money order payable to the "Treasurer, Guam."

- If you live in the U.S. Virgin Islands and are filing this form there, make the check or money order payable to the "Commissioner of Finance of the Virgin Islands."

When preparing your check or money order, spell out U.S. Department of Homeland Security. Do not use the initials "USDHS" or "DHS."

3. Attorney or Representative. You may, if you wish, be represented, at no expense to the government, by an attorney or other duly authorized representative. If so, that person must submit a Notice of Appearance (Form G-28) with the request for a hearing. Form G-28 can be obtained by calling **1-800-375-5283** or from the CIS internet website at **www.uscis.gov**.

4. Brief. You do not need to submit a brief in support of your request, but you may submit one. You may submit a simple written statement instead of a brief. You may also submit evidence. You must send your request and accompanying fee and documentation to the CIS office which made the unfavorable decision. If you need more than 30 days, you must, within the initial 30 day period, explain why in a separate letter attached to this form. The CIS may grant more time for good cause.

5. Paperwork Reduction Act Notice. A person is not required to respond to a collection of information unless it displays a currently valid OMB control number. This collection of information is estimated to average 10 minutes per response, including the time for reviewing instructions, searching existing data sources, gathering and maintaining the data needed, and completing and reviewing the collection of information. Send comments regarding this burden estimate or any other aspect of this collection of information, including suggestions for reducing this burden, to: Bureau of Citizenship and Immigration Services, HQRFS, 425 I Street N.W., Room 4034, Washington, DC 20529; OMB No.1615-0050. **Do not mail your completed application to this address.**

Instructions

What Is This Form?

This form, the N-400, is an application for United States citizenship (naturalization). For more information about the naturalization process and eligibility requirements, please read *A Guide to Naturalization* (M-476). If you do not already have a copy of the *Guide*, you can get a copy from:

- the INS Web Site (www.ins.usdoj.gov);
- the National Customer Service Center (NCSC) telephone line at 1-800-375-5283 (TTY: 1-800-767-1833); or
- your local INS office.

Who Should Use This Form?

To use this form you must be at least 18 years old. You must also be **ONE** of the following:

(1) A Lawful Permanent Resident for at least 5 years;

(2) A Lawful Permanent Resident for at least 3 years
AND
- you have been married to and living with the same U.S. citizen for the last 3 years,
AND
- your spouse has been a U.S. citizen for the last 3 years;

(3) A person who has served in the U.S. Armed Forces
AND
- you are a Lawful Permanent Resident with at least 3 years of U.S. Armed Forces service **and** you are either on active duty or filing within 6 months of honorable discharge
OR
- you served during a period of recognized hostilities and enlisted or re-enlisted in the United States (you do not need to be a Lawful Permanent Resident);

(4) A member of one of several other groups who are eligible to apply for naturalization (for example, persons who are nationals but not citizens of the United States). For more information about these groups, please see the *Guide*.

Who Should NOT Use This Form?

In certain cases, a person who was born outside of the United States to U.S. citizen parents is already a citizen and does not need to apply for naturalization. To find out more information about this type of citizenship and whether you should file a Form N-600, "Application for Certificate of Citizenship," read the *Guide*.

Other permanent residents under 18 years of age may be eligible for U.S. citizenship if their U.S. citizen parent or parents file a Form N-600 application in their behalf. For more information, see "Frequently Asked Questions" in the *Guide*.

When Am I Eligible To Apply?

You may apply for naturalization when you meet **all** the requirements to become a U.S. citizen. The section of the *Guide* called "Who is Eligible for Naturalization" and the Eligibility Worksheet found in the back of the *Guide* are tools to help you determine whether you are eligible to apply for naturalization. You should complete the Worksheet before filling out this N-400 application.

If you are applying based on 5 years as a Lawful Permanent Resident or based on 3 years as a Lawful Permanent Resident married to a U.S. citizen, you may apply for naturalization up to 90 days before you meet the "continuous residence" requirement. You must meet all other requirements at the time that you file your application with us.

Certain applicants have different English and civics testing requirements based on their age and length of lawful permanent residence **at the time of filing**. If you are over 50 years of age and have lived in the United States as a lawful permanent resident for periods totaling at least 20 years or if you are over 55 years of age and have lived in the United States as a lawful permanent resident for periods totaling at least 15 years, you do not have to take the English test but you do have to take the civics test in the language of your choice.

If you are over 65 years of age and have lived in the United States as a lawful permanent resident for periods totaling at least 20 years, you do not have to take the English test but you do have to take a simpler version of the civics test in the language of your choice.

What Does It Cost To Apply For Naturalization and How Do I Pay?

For information on fees and form of payment, see the *Guide* insert titled "Current Naturalization Fees." Your fee is not refundable, even if you withdraw your application or it is denied.

If you are unable to pay the naturalization application fee, you may apply in writing for a fee waiver. For information about the fee waiver process, call the NCSC telephone line at 1-800-375-5283 (TTY: 1-800-767- 1833) or see the INS Web Site (www.ins.usdoj.gov) section called "Forms and Fees."

What Do I Send With My Application?

All applicants must send certain documents with their application. For information on the documents and other information you must send with your application, see the Document Checklist in the *Guide*.

Where Do I Send My Application?

You must send your N-400 application and supporting documents to an Immigration and Naturalization Service (INS) Service Center. To find the Service Center address you should use, read the section in the *Guide* called "Completing Your Application and Getting Photographed."

Applicants outside the United States who are applying on the basis of their military service should follow the instructions of their designated point of contact at a U.S. military installation.

How Do I Complete This Application?

- Please print clearly or type your answers using CAPITAL letters in each box.

- Use black or blue ink.

- **Write your INS "A"- number on the top right hand corner of each page.** Use your INS "A"- number on your Permanent Resident Card (formerly known as the Alien Registration or "Green" Card). To locate your "A"- number, see the sample Permanent Resident Cards in the *Guide*. The "A" number on your card consists of 7 to 9 numbers, depending on when your record was created. If the "A"- number on your card has fewer than 9 numbers, place enough zeros before the first number to make a *total of 9 numbers* on the application. For example, write card number A1234567 as A001234567, but write card number A12345678 as A012345678.

- If a question does not apply to you, write **N/A** (meaning "Not Applicable") in the space provided.

- If you need extra space to answer any item:
  - Attach a separate sheet of paper (or more sheets if needed);
  - Write your name, your "A"- number, and "N-400" on the top right corner of the sheet; and
  - Write the number of each question for which you are providing additional information.

Step-by-Step Instructions

This form is divided into 14 parts. The information below will help you fill out the form.

Part 1. Your Name *(the Person Applying for Naturalization)*

A. **Your current legal name -** Your current legal name is the name on your birth certificate unless it has been changed after birth by a legal action such as a marriage or court order.

B. **Your name exactly as it appears on your Permanent Resident Card** *(if different from above)*-- Write your name exactly as it appears on your card, even if it is misspelled.

C. **Other names you have used** - If you have used any other names in your life, write them in this section. If you need more space, use a separate sheet of paper.

   If you have NEVER used a different name, write "N/A" in the space for "Family Name *(Last Name)."*

D. **Name change** *(optional)* - A court can allow a change in your name when you are being naturalized. A name change does not become final until a court naturalizes you. For more information regarding a name change, see the *Guide.*

   If you want a court to change your name at a naturalization oath ceremony, check "Yes" and complete this section. If you do not want to change your name, check "No" and go to Part 2.

Part 2. Information About Your Eligibility

Check the box that shows why you are eligible to apply for naturalization. If the basis for your eligibility is not described in one of the first three boxes, check "Other" and briefly write the basis for your application on the lines provided.

Part 3. Information About You

A. **Social Security Number** - Print your Social Security number. If you do not have one, write "N/A" in the space provided.

B. **Date of Birth** - Always use eight numbers to show your date of birth. Write the date in this order: Month, Day, Year. For example, write May 1, 1958 as 05/01/1958.

C. **Date You Became a Permanent Resident -** Write the official date when your lawful permanent residence began, as shown on your Permanent Resident Card. To help locate the date on your card, see the sample Permanent Resident Cards in the *Guide.* Write the date in this order: Month, Day, Year. For example, write August 9, 1988 as 08/09/1988.

D. **Country of Birth** - Write the name of the country where you were born. Write the name of the country even if it no longer exists.

E. **Country of Nationality** - Write the name of the country where you are currently a citizen or national. Write the name of the country even if it no longer exists.

   - If you are stateless, write the name of the country where you were last a citizen or national.

   - If you are a citizen or national of more than one country, write the name of the foreign country that issued your last passport.

F. **Citizenship of Parents** - Check "Yes" if either of your parents is a U.S. citizen. If you answer "Yes," you may already be a citizen. For more information, see "Frequently Asked Questions" in the *Guide.*

G. **Current Marital Status** - Check the marital status you have on the date you are filing this application. If you are currently not married, but had a prior marriage that was annulled (declared by a court to be invalid) check "Other" and explain it.

H. **Request for Disability Waiver** - If you have a medical disability or impairment that you believe qualifies you for a waiver of the tests of English and/or U.S. government and history, check "Yes" and attach a properly completed Form N-648. If you ask for this waiver it does not guarantee that you will be excused from the testing requirements. For more information about this waiver, see the *Guide.*

I. **Request for Disability Accommodations** - We will make every reasonable effort to help applicants with disabilities complete the naturalization process. For example, if you use a wheelchair, we will make sure that you can be fingerprinted and interviewed, and can attend a naturalization ceremony at a location that is wheelchair accessible. If you are deaf or hearing impaired and need a sign language interpreter, we will make arrangements with you to have one at your interview.

If you believe you will need us to modify or change the naturalization process for you, check the box or write in the space the kind of accommodation you need. If you need more space, use a separate sheet of paper. You do not need to send us a Form N-648 to request an accommodation. You only need to send a Form N-648 to request a waiver of the test of English and/or civics.

We consider requests for accommodations on a case-by-case basis. Asking for an accommodation will not affect your eligibility for citizenship.

Part 4. Addresses and Telephone Numbers

A. **Home Address** - Give the address where you now live. Do NOT put post office (P.O.) box numbers here.

B. **Mailing Address** - If your mailing address is the same as your home address, write "same." If your mailing address is different from your home address, write it in this part.

C. **Telephone Numbers (optional)** - If you give us your telephone numbers and e-mail address, we can contact you about your application more quickly. If you are hearing impaired and use a TTY telephone connection, please indicate this by writing "(TTY)" after the telephone number.

Part 5. Information for Criminal Records Search

The Federal Bureau of Investigation (FBI) will use the information in this section, together with your fingerprints, to search for criminal records. Although the results of this search may affect your eligibility, we do NOT make naturalization decisions based on your gender, race, or physical description.

For each item, check the box or boxes that best describes you. The categories are those used by the FBI. Note, you can select one or more.

Part 6. Information About Your Residence and Employment

A. Write every address where you have lived during the last 5 years (including in other countries).

Begin with where you live now. Include the dates you lived in those places. For example, write May 1998 to June 1999 as 05/1998 to 06/1999.

If you need separate sheets of paper to complete section A or B or any other questions on this application, be sure to follow the Instructions in **"How Do I Complete This Application?"** above.

B. List where you have worked (or, if you were a student, the schools you have attended) during the last 5 years. Include military service. If you worked for yourself, write "self employed." Begin with your most recent job. Also, write the dates when you worked or studied in each place.

Part 7. Time Outside the United States *(Including Trips to Canada and Mexico and the Caribbean)*

A. Write the total number of days you spent outside of the United States (including on military service) during the last 5 years. Count the days of every trip that lasted 24 hours or longer.

B. Write the number of trips you have taken outside the United States during the last 5 years. Count every trip that lasted 24 hours or longer.

C. Provide the requested information for every trip that you have taken outside the United States since you became a Lawful Permanent Resident. Begin with your most recent trip.

Part 8. Information About Your Marital History

A. Write the number of times you have been married. Include any annulled marriages. If you were married to the same spouse more than one time, count each time as a separate marriage.

B. If you are now married, provide information about your current spouse.

C. Check the box to indicate whether your current spouse is a U.S. citizen.

D. If your spouse is a citizen through naturalization, give the date and place of naturalization. If your spouse regained U.S. citizenship, write the date and place the citizenship was regained.

E. If your spouse is not a U.S. citizen, complete this section.

F. If you were married before, give information about your former spouse or spouses. In question F.2, check the box showing the immigration status your former spouse had during your marriage. If the spouse was not a U.S. citizen or a Lawful Permanent Resident at that time check "Other" and explain. For question F.5, if your marriage was annulled, check "Other" and explain. If you were married to the same spouse more than one time, write about each marriage separately.

G. For any prior marriages of your current spouse, follow the instructions in section F above.

Note: If you or your present spouse had more than one prior marriage, provide the same information required by section F and section G about every additional marriage on a separate sheet of paper.

Part 9. Information About Your Children

A. Write the total number of sons and daughters you have had. Count **all** of your children, regardless of whether they are:
- alive, missing, or dead;
- born in other countries or in the United States;
- under 18 years old or adults;
- married or unmarried;
- living with you or elsewhere;
- stepsons or stepdaughters or legally adopted; or
- born when you were not married.

B. Write information about all your sons and daughters. In the last column ("Location"), write:
- "with me" - if the son or daughter is currently living with you;
- the street address and state or country where the son or daughter lives - if the son or daughter is NOT currently living with you; or

- "missing" or "dead" - if that son or daughter is missing or dead.

If you need space to list information about additional sons and daughters, attach a separate sheet of paper.

Part 10. Additional Questions

Answer each question by checking "Yes" or "No." If ANY part of a question applies to you, you must answer "Yes." For example, if you were never arrested but *were* once detained by a police officer, check "Yes" to the question "Have you ever been arrested or detained by a law enforcement officer?" and attach a written explanation.

We will use this information to determine your eligibility for citizenship. Answer every question honestly and accurately. If you do not, we may deny your application for lack of good moral character. Answering "Yes" to one of these questions does not always cause an application to be denied. For more information on eligibility, please see the *Guide*.

Part 11. Your Signature

After reading the statement in Part 11, you must sign and date it. You should sign your full name without abbreviating it or using initials. The signature must be legible. Your application may be returned to you if it is not signed.

If you cannot sign your name in English, sign in your native language. If you are unable to write in any language, sign your name with an "X."

NOTE: A designated representative may sign this section on behalf an applicant who qualifies for a waiver of the Oath of Allegiance because of a development or physical impairment (see *Guide* for more information). In such a case the designated representative should write the name of the applicant and then sign his or her own name followed by the words "Designated Representative." The information attested to by the Designated Representative is subject to the same penalties discussed on page 6 of these Instructions.

Part 12. Signature of Person Who Prepared This Application for You

If someone filled out this form for you, he or she must complete this section.

Part 13. Signature at Interview

Do NOT complete this part. You will be asked to complete this part at your interview.

Part 14. Oath of Allegiance

Do NOT complete this part. You will be asked to complete this part at your interview.

If we approve your application, you must take this Oath of Allegiance to become a citizen. In limited cases you can take a modified Oath. The Oath requirement cannot be waived unless you are unable to understand its meaning because of a physical or developmental disability or mental impairment. For more information, see the *Guide*. Your signature on this form only indicates that you have no objections to taking the Oath of Allegiance. **It does not mean that you have taken the Oath or that you are naturalized**. If the INS approves your application for naturalization, you must attend an oath ceremony and take the Oath of Allegiance to the United States.

Penalties

If you knowingly and willfully falsify or conceal a material fact or submit a false document with this request, we will deny your application for naturalization and may deny any other immigration benefit. In addition, you will face severe penalties provided by law and may be subject to a removal proceeding or criminal prosecution.

If we grant you citizenship after you falsify or conceal a material fact or submit a false document with this request, your naturalization may be revoked.

Print clearly or type your answers using CAPITAL letters. Failure to print clearly may delay your application. Use black or blue ink.

Part 1. Your Name *(The Person Applying for Naturalization)*

A. Your current legal name.

Family Name *(Last Name)*

Given Name *(First Name)*

Full Middle Name *(If applicable)*

B. Your name exactly as it appears on your Permanent Resident Card.

Family Name *(Last Name)*

Given Name *(First Name)*

Full Middle Name *(If applicable)*

C. If you have ever used other names, provide them below.

Family Name *(Last Name)*	Given Name *(First Name)*	Middle Name

D. Name change *(optional)*

Please read the Instructions before you decide whether to change your name.

1. Would you like to legally change your name? ☐ Yes ☐ No

2. If "Yes," print the new name you would like to use. Do not use initials or abbreviations when writing your new name.

Family Name *(Last Name)*

Given Name *(First Name)*

Full Middle Name

Write your INS "A"- number here:

A __ __ __ __ __ __ __ __ __

FOR INS USE ONLY

Bar Code	Date Stamp

Remarks

Action

Part 2. Information About Your Eligibility *(Check Only One)*

I am at least 18 years old **AND**

A. ☐ I have been a Lawful Permanent Resident of the United States for at least 5 years.

B. ☐ I have been a Lawful Permanent Resident of the United States for at least 3 years, AND I have been married to and living with the same U.S. citizen for the last 3 years, AND my spouse has been a U.S. citizen for the last 3 years.

C. ☐ I am applying on the basis of qualifying military service.

D. ☐ Other *(Please explain)* _____

Part 3. Information About You

A. Social Security Number

_ _ _ - _ _ - _ _ _ _

B. Date of Birth *(Month/Day/Year)*

_ _ / _ _ / _ _ _ _

C. Date You Became a Permanent Resident *(Month/Day/Year)*

_ _ / _ _ / _ _ _ _

D. Country of Birth

E. Country of Nationality

F. Are either of your parents U.S. citizens? *(if yes, see Instructions)* ☐ Yes ☐ No

G. What is your current marital status? ☐ Single, Never Married ☐ Married ☐ Divorced ☐ Widowed

☐ Marriage Annulled or Other *(Explain)* _____

H. Are you requesting a waiver of the English and/or U.S. History and Government requirements based on a disability or impairment and attaching a Form N-648 with your application? ☐ Yes ☐ No

I. Are you requesting an accommodation to the naturalization process because of a disability or impairment? *(See Instructions for some examples of accommodations.)* ☐ Yes ☐ No

If you answered "Yes", check the box below that applies:

☐ I am deaf or hearing impaired and need a sign language interpreter who uses the following language: _____

☐ I use a wheelchair.

☐ I am blind or sight impaired.

☐ I will need another type of accommodation. Please explain: _____

_____

_____

Part 4. Addresses and Telephone Numbers

A. Home Address - Street Number and Name *(Do NOT write a P.O. Box in this space)*

Apartment Number

City	County	State	ZIP Code	Country

B. Care of

Mailing Address - Street Number and Name *(If different from home address)*

Apartment Number

City	State	ZIP Code	Country

C. Daytime Phone Number *(If any)*

( )

Evening Phone Number *(If any)*

( )

E-mail Address *(If any)*

Part 5. Information for Criminal Records Search

Write your INS "A"- number here:

A _ _ _ _ _ _ _ _ _

Note: The categories below are those required by the FBI. See Instructions for more information.

A. Gender

☐ Male ☐ Female

B. Height

| Feet | Inches |

C. Weight

| Pounds |

D. Are you Hispanic or Latino? ☐ Yes ☐ No

E. Race *(Select one or more.)*

☐ White ☐ Asian ☐ Black or African American ☐ American Indian or Alaskan Native ☐ Native Hawaiian or Other Pacific Islander

F. Hair color

☐ Black ☐ Brown ☐ Blonde ☐ Gray ☐ White ☐ Red ☐ Sandy ☐ Bald (No Hair)

G. Eye color

☐ Brown ☐ Blue ☐ Green ☐ Hazel ☐ Gray ☐ Black ☐ Pink ☐ Maroon ☐ Other

Part 6. Information About Your Residence and Employment

A. Where have you lived during the last 5 years? Begin with where you live now and then list every place you lived for the last 5 years. If you need more space, use a separate sheet of paper.

Street Number and Name, Apartment Number, City, State, Zip Code and Country	Dates *(Month/Year)*	
	From	To
Current Home Address - Same as Part 4.A	_ _ / _ _ _ _	Present
	_ _ / _ _ _ _	_ _ / _ _ _ _
	_ _ / _ _ _ _	_ _ / _ _ _ _
	_ _ / _ _ _ _	_ _ / _ _ _ _
	_ _ / _ _ _ _	_ _ / _ _ _ _

B. Where have you worked (or, if you were a student, what schools did you attend) during the last 5 years? Include military service. Begin with your current or latest employer and then list every place you have worked or studied for the last 5 years. If you need more space, use a separate sheet of paper.

Employer or School Name	Employer or School Address *(Street, City and State)*	Dates *(Month/Year)*		Your Occupation
		From	To	
		_ _ / _ _ _ _	_ _ / _ _ _ _	
		_ _ / _ _ _ _	_ _ / _ _ _ _	
		_ _ / _ _ _ _	_ _ / _ _ _ _	
		_ _ / _ _ _ _	_ _ / _ _ _ _	
		_ _ / _ _ _ _	_ _ / _ _ _ _	

Part 7. Time Outside the United States
(Including Trips to Canada, Mexico, and the Caribbean Islands)

A. How many total days did you spend outside of the United States during the past 5 years? [____] days

B. How many trips of 24 hours or more have you taken outside of the United States during the past 5 years? [____] trips

C. List below all the trips of 24 hours or more that you have taken outside of the United States since becoming a Lawful Permanent Resident. Begin with your most recent trip. If you need more space, use a separate sheet of paper.

Date You Left the United States *(Month/Day/Year)*	Date You Returned to the United States *(Month/Day/Year)*	Did Trip Last 6 Months or More?	Countries to Which You Traveled	Total Days Out of the United States
__ / __ / __ __ __	__ / __ / __ __ __	☐ Yes ☐ No		
__ / __ / __ __ __	__ / __ / __ __ __	☐ Yes ☐ No		
__ / __ / __ __ __	__ / __ / __ __ __	☐ Yes ☐ No		
__ / __ / __ __ __	__ / __ / __ __ __	☐ Yes ☐ No		
__ / __ / __ __ __	__ / __ / __ __ __	☐ Yes ☐ No		
__ / __ / __ __ __	__ / __ / __ __ __	☐ Yes ☐ No		
__ / __ / __ __ __	__ / __ / __ __ __	☐ Yes ☐ No		
__ / __ / __ __ __	__ / __ / __ __ __	☐ Yes ☐ No		
__ / __ / __ __ __	__ / __ / __ __ __	☐ Yes ☐ No		
__ / __ / __ __ __	__ / __ / __ __ __	☐ Yes ☐ No		

Part 8. Information About Your Marital History

A. How many times have you been married (including annulled marriages)? [____] If you have NEVER been married, go to Part 9.

B. If you are now married, give the following information about your spouse:

1. Spouse's Family Name *(Last Name)*   Given Name *(First Name)*   Full Middle Name *(If applicable)*

2. Date of Birth *(Month/Day/Year)*   3. Date of Marriage *(Month/Day/Year)*   4. Spouse's Social Security Number

__ __ / __ __ / __ __ __ __   __ __ / __ __ / __ __ __ __   __ __ __ - __ __ - __ __ __ __

5. Home Address - Street Number and Name   Apartment Number

City   State   ZIP Code

Write your INS "A"- number here:

A __ __ __ __ __ __ __ __ __

C. Is your spouse a U.S. citizen? ☐ Yes ☐ No

D. If your spouse is a U.S. citizen, give the following information:

    1. When did your spouse become a U.S. citizen? ☐ At Birth ☐ Other

      If "Other," give the following information:

    2. Date your spouse became a U.S. citizen

    __ __/__ __/__ __ __ __

    3. Place your spouse became a U.S. citizen *(Please see Instructions)*

                         City and State

E. If your spouse is NOT a U.S. citizen, give the following information :

    1. Spouse's Country of Citizenship

    2. Spouse's INS "A"- Number *(If applicable)*

    A __ __ __ __ __ __ __ __ __

    3. Spouse's Immigration Status

    ☐ Lawful Permanent Resident   ☐ Other _____

F. If you were married before, provide the following information about your prior spouse. If you have more than one previous marriage, use a separate sheet of paper to provide the information requested in questions 1-5 below.

    1. Prior Spouse's Family Name *(Last Name)*   Given Name *(First Name)*   Full Middle Name *(If applicable)*

    2. Prior Spouse's Immigration Status

    ☐ U.S. Citizen

    ☐ Lawful Permanent Resident

    ☐ Other _____

    3. Date of Marriage *(Month/Day/Year)*

    __ __/__ __/__ __ __ __

    5. How Marriage Ended

    ☐ Divorce   ☐ Spouse Died   ☐ Other _____

    4. Date Marriage Ended *(Month/Day/Year)*

    __ __/__ __/__ __ __ __

G. How many times has your current spouse been married (including annulled marriages)? ☐

    If your spouse has EVER been married before, give the following information about **your spouse's** prior marriage.
    If your spouse has more than one previous marriage, use a separate sheet of paper to provide the information requested in questions 1 - 5 below.

    1. Prior Spouse's Family Name *(Last Name)*   Given Name *(First Name)*   Full Middle Name *(If applicable)*

    2. Prior Spouse's Immigration Status

    ☐ U.S. Citizen

    ☐ Lawful Permanent Resident

    ☐ Other _____

    3. Date of Marriage *(Month/Day/Year)*

    __ __/__ __/__ __ __ __

    5. How Marriage Ended

    ☐ Divorce   ☐ Spouse Died   ☐ Other _____

    4. Date Marriage Ended *(Month/Day/Year)*

    __ __/__ __/__ __ __ __

A. How many sons and daughters have you had? For more information on which sons and daughters you should include and how to complete this section, see the Instructions.

B. Provide the following information about all of your sons and daughters. If you need more space, use a separate sheet of paper.

Full Name of Son or Daughter	Date of Birth (Month/Day/Year)	INS "A"- number (if child has one)	Country of Birth	Current Address (Street, City, State & Country)
	_ _ / _ / _ _ _ _	A _ _ _ _ _ _ _ _ _		
	_ _ / _ / _ _ _ _	A _ _ _ _ _ _ _ _ _		
	_ _ / _ / _ _ _ _	A _ _ _ _ _ _ _ _ _		
	_ _ / _ / _ _ _ _	A _ _ _ _ _ _ _ _ _		
	_ _ / _ / _ _ _ _	A _ _ _ _ _ _ _ _ _		
	_ _ / _ / _ _ _ _	A _ _ _ _ _ _ _ _ _		
	_ _ / _ / _ _ _ _	A _ _ _ _ _ _ _ _ _		
	_ _ / _ / _ _ _ _	A _ _ _ _ _ _ _ _ _		

Part 10. Additional Questions

Please answer questions 1 through 14. If you answer "Yes" to any of these questions, include a written explanation with this form. Your written explanation should (1) explain why your answer was "Yes," and (2) provide any additional information that helps to explain your answer.

A. General Questions

1. Have you **EVER** claimed to be a U.S. citizen *(in writing or any other way)*? ☐ Yes ☐ No

2. Have you **EVER** registered to vote in any Federal, state, or local election in the United States? ☐ Yes ☐ No

3. Have you **EVER** voted in any Federal, state, or local election in the United States? ☐ Yes ☐ No

4. Since becoming a Lawful Permanent Resident, have you **EVER** failed to file a required Federal, state, or local tax return? ☐ Yes ☐ No

5. Do you owe any Federal, state, or local taxes that are overdue? ☐ Yes ☐ No

6. Do you have any title of nobility in any foreign country? ☐ Yes ☐ No

7. Have you ever been declared legally incompetent or been confined to a mental institution within the last 5 years? ☐ Yes ☐ No

B. Affiliations

8. a. Have you **EVER** been a member of or associated with any organization, association, fund, foundation, party, club, society, or similar group in the United States or in any other place? ☐ Yes ☐ No

    b. If you answered "Yes," list the name of each group below. If you need more space, attach the names of the other group(s) on a separate sheet of paper.

Name of Group	Name of Group
1.	6.
2.	7.
3.	8.
4.	9.
5.	10.

9. Have you **EVER** been a member of or in any way associated *(either directly or indirectly)* with:

    a. The Communist Party? ☐ Yes ☐ No

    b. Any other totalitarian party? ☐ Yes ☐ No

    c. A terrorist organization? ☐ Yes ☐ No

10. Have you **EVER** advocated *(either directly or indirectly)* the overthrow of any government by force or violence? ☐ Yes ☐ No

11. Have you **EVER** persecuted *(either directly or indirectly)* any person because of race, religion, national origin, membership in a particular social group, or political opinion? ☐ Yes ☐ No

12. Between March 23, 1933, and May 8, 1945, did you work for or associate in any way *(either directly or indirectly)* with:

    a. The Nazi government of Germany? ☐ Yes ☐ No

    b. Any government in any area (1) occupied by, (2) allied with, or (3) established with the help of the Nazi government of Germany? ☐ Yes ☐ No

    c. Any German, Nazi, or S.S. military unit, paramilitary unit, self-defense unit, vigilante unit, citizen unit, police unit, government agency or office, extermination camp, concentration camp, prisoner of war camp, prison, labor camp, or transit camp? ☐ Yes ☐ No

C. Continuous Residence

Since becoming a Lawful Permanent Resident of the United States:

13. Have you **EVER** called yourself a "nonresident" on a Federal, state, or local tax return? ☐ Yes ☐ No

14. Have you **EVER** failed to file a Federal, state, or local tax return because you considered yourself to be a "nonresident"? ☐ Yes ☐ No

D. Good Moral Character

For the purposes of this application, you must answer "Yes" to the following questions, if applicable, even if your records were sealed or otherwise cleared or if anyone, including a judge, law enforcement officer, or attorney, told you that you no longer have a record.

15. Have you **EVER** committed a crime or offense for which you were NOT arrested? ☐ Yes ☐ No

16. Have you **EVER** been arrested, cited, or detained by any law enforcement officer (including INS and military officers) for any reason? ☐ Yes ☐ No

17. Have you **EVER** been charged with committing any crime or offense? ☐ Yes ☐ No

18. Have you **EVER** been convicted of a crime or offense? ☐ Yes ☐ No

19. Have you **EVER** been placed in an alternative sentencing or a rehabilitative program (for example: diversion, deferred prosecution, withheld adjudication, deferred adjudication)? ☐ Yes ☐ No

20. Have you **EVER** received a suspended sentence, been placed on probation, or been paroled? ☐ Yes ☐ No

21. Have you **EVER** been in jail or prison? ☐ Yes ☐ No

If you answered "Yes" to any of questions 15 through 21, complete the following table. If you need more space, use a separate sheet of paper to give the same information.

Why were you arrested, cited, detained, or charged?	Date arrested, cited, detained, or charged *(Month/Day/Year)*	Where were you arrested, cited, detained or charged? *(City, State, Country)*	Outcome or disposition of the arrest, citation, detention or charge *(No charges filed, charges dismissed, jail, probation, etc.)*

Answer questions 22 through 33. If you answer "Yes" to any of these questions, attach (1) your written explanation why your answer was "Yes," and (2) any additional information or documentation that helps explain your answer.

22. Have you **EVER**:

    a. been a habitual drunkard? ☐ Yes ☐ No

    b. been a prostitute, or procured anyone for prostitution? ☐ Yes ☐ No

    c. sold or smuggled controlled substances, illegal drugs or narcotics? ☐ Yes ☐ No

    d. been married to more than one person at the same time? ☐ Yes ☐ No

    e. helped anyone enter or try to enter the United States illegally? ☐ Yes ☐ No

    f. gambled illegally or received income from illegal gambling? ☐ Yes ☐ No

    g. failed to support your dependents or to pay alimony? ☐ Yes ☐ No

23. Have you **EVER** given false or misleading information to any U.S. government official while applying for any immigration benefit or to prevent deportation, exclusion, or removal? ☐ Yes ☐ No

24. Have you **EVER** lied to any U.S. government official to gain entry or admission into the United States? ☐ Yes ☐ No

E. Removal, Exclusion, and Deportation Proceedings

25. Are removal, exclusion, rescission or deportation proceedings pending against you? ☐ Yes ☐ No

26. Have you **EVER** been removed, excluded, or deported from the United States? ☐ Yes ☐ No

27. Have you **EVER** been ordered to be removed, excluded, or deported from the United States? ☐ Yes ☐ No

28. Have you **EVER** applied for any kind of relief from removal, exclusion, or deportation? ☐ Yes ☐ No

F. Military Service

29. Have you **EVER** served in the U.S. Armed Forces? ☐ Yes ☐ No

30. Have you **EVER** left the United States to avoid being drafted into the U.S. Armed Forces? ☐ Yes ☐ No

31. Have you **EVER** applied for any kind of exemption from military service in the U.S. Armed Forces? ☐ Yes ☐ No

32. Have you **EVER** deserted from the U.S. Armed Forces? ☐ Yes ☐ No

G. Selective Service Registration

33. Are you a male who lived in the United States at any time between your 18th and 26th birthdays in any status except as a lawful nonimmigrant? ☐ Yes ☐ No

If you answered "NO", go on to question 34.

If you answered "YES", provide the information below.

If you answered "YES", but you did NOT register with the Selective Service System and are still under 26 years of age, you must register before you apply for naturalization, so that you can complete the information below:

Date Registered (Month/Day/Year) [ ]   Selective Service Number __ __ / __ __ __ __ __ __ / __

If you answered "YES", but you did NOT register with the Selective Service and you are now 26 years old or older, attach a statement explaining why you did not register.

H. Oath Requirements *(See Part 14 for the text of the oath)*

Answer questions 34 through 39. If you answer "No" to any of these questions, attach (1) your written explanation why the answer was "No" and (2) any additional information or documentation that helps to explain your answer.

34. Do you support the Constitution and form of government of the United States? ☐ Yes ☐ No

35. Do you understand the full Oath of Allegiance to the United States? ☐ Yes ☐ No

36. Are you willing to take the full Oath of Allegiance to the United States? ☐ Yes ☐ No

37. If the law requires it, are you willing to bear arms on behalf of the United States? ☐ Yes ☐ No

38. If the law requires it, are you willing to perform noncombatant services in the U.S. Armed Forces? ☐ Yes ☐ No

39. If the law requires it, are you willing to perform work of national importance under civilian direction? ☐ Yes ☐ No

Part 11. Your Signature

Write your INS "A"- number here:

A __ __ __ __ __ __ __ __ __

I certify, under penalty of perjury under the laws of the United States of America, that this application, and the evidence submitted with it, are all true and correct. I authorize the release of any information which INS needs to determine my eligibility for naturalization.

Your Signature

Date *(Month/Day/Year)*

__ __/__ __/__ __ __ __

Part 12. Signature of Person Who Prepared This Application for You *(if applicable)*

I declare under penalty of perjury that I prepared this application at the request of the above person. The answers provided are based on information of which I have personal knowledge and/or were provided to me by the above named person in response to the *exact questions* contained on this form.

Preparer's Printed Name

Preparer's Signature

Date *(Month/Day/Year)*

__ __/__ __/__ __ __ __

Preparer's Firm or Organization Name *(If applicable)*

Preparer's Daytime Phone Number

( )

Preparer's Address - Street Number and Name

City

State

ZIP Code

Do Not Complete Parts 13 and 14 Until an INS Officer Instructs You To Do So

Part 13. Signature at Interview

I swear (affirm) and certify under penalty of perjury under the laws of the United States of America that I know that the contents of this application for naturalization subscribed by me, including corrections numbered 1 through _____ and the evidence submitted by me numbered pages 1 through _____ , are true and correct to the best of my knowledge and belief.

Subscribed to and sworn to (affirmed) before me _____   _____

Officer's Printed Name or Stamp

Date *(Month/Day/Year)*

Complete Signature of Applicant

Officer's Signature

Part 14. Oath of Allegiance

If your application is approved, you will be scheduled for a public oath ceremony at which time you will be required to take the following oath of allegiance immediately prior to becoming a naturalized citizen. By signing , you acknowledge your willingness and ability to take this oath:

I hereby declare, on oath, that I absolutely and entirely renounce and abjure all allegiance and fidelity to any foreign prince, potentate, state, or sovereignty, of whom or which which I have heretofore been a subject or citizen;

that I will support and defend the Constitution and laws of the United States of America against all enemies, foreign and domestic;
that I will bear true faith and allegiance to the same;
that I will bear arms on behalf of the United States when required by the law;
that I will perform noncombatant service in the Armed Forces of the United States when required by the law;
that I will perform work of national importance under civilian direction when required by the law; and
that I take this obligation freely, without any mental reservation or purpose of evasion; so help me God.

Printed Name of Applicant

Complete Signature of Applicant

Instructions
(Please tear off this sheet before submitting request.)
(Submit in Triplicate.)

NOTE: Please type or print in block letters with a ball-point pen, using black ink. Be sure this form and the complete return address are legible. Do not leave any questions unanswered. When appropriate insert "none," "not applicable" or "N/A." (The Bureau of Citizenship and Immigration Services (CIS) is comprised of offices of the former Immigration and Naturalization Service (INS).)

What Is the Purpose of This Form?

The principal purpose of this form is to solicit information to secure a duly authenticated certification of honorable active duty service from the U.S. Government Executive Department, under which you served or are serving, to satisfy statutory requirements for naturalization as a U.S. citizen.

Submission of the information is voluntary. If your Social Security number requested on the form is not provided, no right, benefit or privilege will be denied for such failure. However, as military records are indexed by such numbers, verification of your military service may prove difficult.

If you are applying for naturalization under Sections 328 or 329 of the Immigration and Nationality Act, you should submit this form and Form G-325B, Biographic Information, with your Form N-400, Application for Naturalization, to the Bureau of Citizenship and Immigration Services (CIS).

What Is Our Authority for Collecting This Information?

Our authority for collecting the information requested on this form is contained in Sections 328 and 329 of the Immigration and Nationality Act of 1952 (8 U.S.C. 1439 and 1440).

All or part of the information solicited may as a matter of routine use be disclosed to courts exercising naturalization jurisdiction and to other Federal, state, local and foreign law enforcement and regulatory agencies, the Department of Defense, including any component thereof, Selective Service System, Department of State, Department of the Treasury, Central Intelligence Agency, Interpol and individuals and organizations that process the application for naturalization, or during the courses of investigation, to elicit further information required by the CIS to carry out its functions.

Information solicited that indicates a violation or potential violation of law, whether civil, criminal or regulatory in nature, may be referred as a routine use to the appropriate agency, whether Federal, state, local or foreign, charged with the responsibility of investigating, enforcing or prosecuting such violations.

Failure to provide any or all of the solicited information may delay the naturalization process or result in a failure to locate military records or prove qualifying military service.

Paperwork Reduction Act Notice.

An agency may not conduct or sponsor an information collection and a person is not required to respond to a collection of information unless it displays a currently valid OMB control number. This collection of information is estimated to average 10 minutes per response, including the time for reviewing instructions, searching existing data sources, gathering and maintaining the data needed, and completing and reviewing the collection of information. Send comments regarding this burden estimate or any other aspect of this collection of information, including suggestions for reducing this burden to the Bureau of Citizenship and Immigration Services, HQRFS, 425 I Street N.W., Room 4034, Washington, DC 20529; OMB No. 1615-0053. **Do not mail your completed application to this address.**

U.S. Department of Homeland Security
Bureau of Citizenship and Immigration Services

N-426, Request for Certification
of Military or Naval Service

Alien Registration Number	Date of Request

For use in connection with my application for naturalization, please complete the certification of military service on **Page 2** of this form and furnish it to the office of the Bureau of Citizenship and Immigration Services (CIS) shown in the address block below. The information shown below is furnished to help locate and identify my military records. **APPLICANT: Furnish as much information as possible. If you were issued a Report of Separation, DD Form 214, attach a copy. Fill in the blanks on this page only. Please type or print clearly in black ink. Press firmly -- all copies must be legible. Do not use pencil. (Submit in Triplicate.)**

Name Used During Active Service *(Last, first, middle)*	Social Security Number	Date of Birth	Place of Birth

For an effective records search, it is important that ALL periods of service be shown below. (Use blank sheet(s) if more space is needed.)

Active Service:

Branch of Service *(Show also last organization, if known.)*	Date Entered on Active Duty	Date Released From Active Duty	Check Which Officer	Check Which Enlisted	Service Number During This Period

Reserve or National Guard Service: ➡ If none, check ☐ None

Branch of Service	Check Which Reserve	Check Which N. Guard	Date Membership Began	Date Membership Ended	Check Which Officer	Check Which Enlisted	Service Number During This Period

Are You a Military Retiree or Fleet Reservist? ☐ No ☐ Yes

Signature *(Present Name)*	Present Address *(Number, Street, City, State and ZIP Code)*

Instructions to Certifying Officer

Persons who are serving or have served honorably under specified conditions in the armed forces of the United States, inclusive of the reserve components of the armed forces of the United States, are granted certain exemptions from the general requirements for naturalization. The law requires such service to be established by a duly authenticated copy of the records of the executive department having custody of the record of service, showing whether the service man or woman served honorably in an active-duty status, reserve-duty status, or both, and whether each separation from the service was under honorable conditions. For that purpose, the certified statement on Page 2 of this form, executed under the seal of your department, is required and should cover not only the period(s) of service shown above, but any other periods of service (active, reserve or both) rendered by the service man or woman.

Page 2 of this form should be completed, or the information called for furnished by separate letter, and the form and letter returned to the office of the Bureau of Citizenship and Immigration Services at the address in the box immediately below.

Bureau of Citizenship and Immigration Services

 Return To

Please type or print complete return address. Include ZIP code.

Certification of Military or Naval Service

☐ Name correctly shown on front of form.

☐ Name as shown in records: _____

Active Service

1. Entered Service at	2. On	3. Served To	4. Branch of Service	5. State whether serving honorably. If separated, state whether under honorable conditions. If other than honorable, give full details. Always complete Item 11.

Reserve or National Guard Service

6. Branch of Service	7. Check Which		8. Began	9. Ended	10. State whether serving honorably. State if Selected Reserve of the Ready Reserve. If separated, state whether under honorable conditions. If other than honorable, give full details. Always complete Item 11.
	Reserve	N. Guard			

11. **Statement Regarding Alienage.** *(Complete this item in ALL cases.)*

☐ Record shows this person **was not** discharged on account of alienage.

☐ Record shows this person **was** discharged on account of alienage. Details: _____

12. **Remarks.** Use for continuation of any of the above items. You should also show in the space below any **derogatory information** in your records relating to the person's character, loyalty to the United States, disciplinary actions, convictions or other matters touching on his or her fitness for citizenship.

Complete this block if subject is a "Lodge Act enlistee"-64 Stat. 316 (Army). Subsequent to enlistment under the Lodge Act on _____ ,

subject entered _____ at the port of _____
     (the United States, American Samoa, Swains Island or the Canal Zone)

pursuant to Military orders on _____ via _____

I CERTIFY that the information here given concerning the service of the person named on the face of this form is correct according to the records

of the _____
                                    (Name of department or organization)

[SEAL]   **(Official Signature)** _____

     Date _____ , _____   By _____

Alien Registration Number	Date of Request

For use in connection with my application for naturalization, please complete the certification of military service on **Page 2** of this form and furnish it to the office of the Bureau of Citizenship and Immigration Services (CIS) shown in the address block below. The information shown below is furnished to help locate and identify my military records. **APPLICANT: Furnish as much information as possible. If you were issued a Report of Separation, DD Form 214, attach a copy. Fill in the blanks on this page only. Please type or print clearly in black ink. Press firmly -- all copies must be legible. Do not use pencil. (Submit in Triplicate.)**

Name Used During Active Service *(Last, first, middle)*	Social Security Number	Date of Birth	Place of Birth

For an effective records search, it is important that ALL periods of service be shown below. (Use blank sheet(s) if more space is needed.)

Active Service:

Branch of Service *(Show also last organization, if known.)*	Date Entered on Active Duty	Date Released From Active Duty	Check Which — Officer	Check Which — Enlisted	Service Number During This Period

Reserve or National Guard Service: ➡️ If none, check ☐ None

Branch of Service	Check Which — Reserve	Check Which — N. Guard	Date Membership Began	Date Membership Ended	Check Which — Officer	Check Which — Enlisted	Service Number During This Period

Are You a Military Retiree or Fleet Reservist? ☐ No ☐ Yes

Signature *(Present Name)*	Present Address *(Number, Street, City, State and ZIP Code)*

Instructions to Certifying Officer

Persons who are serving or have served honorably under specified conditions in the armed forces of the United States, inclusive of the reserve components of the armed forces of the United States, are granted certain exemptions from the general requirements for naturalization. The law requires such service to be established by a duly authenticated copy of the records of the executive department having custody of the record of service, showing whether the service man or woman served honorably in an active-duty status, reserve-duty status, or both, and whether each separation from the service was under honorable conditions. For that purpose, the certified statement on Page 2 of this form, executed under the seal of your department, is required and should cover not only the period(s) of service shown above, but any other periods of service (active, reserve or both) rendered by the service man or woman.

Page 2 of this form should be completed, or the information called for furnished by separate letter, and the form and letter returned to the office of the Bureau of Citizenship and Immigration Services at the address in the box immediately below.

Bureau of Citizenship and Immigration Services

 Return To

Please type
or print
complete
return
address.
Include ZIP
code.

Applicant: Do Not Fill Out This Page.

Certification of Military or Naval Service

☐ Name correctly shown on front of form.

☐ Name as shown in records: _____

Active Service

1. Entered Service at	2. On	3. Served To	4. Branch of Service	5. State whether serving honorably. If separated, state whether under honorable conditions. If other than honorable, give full details. Always complete Item 11.

Reserve or National Guard Service

6. Branch of Service	7. Check Which		8. Began	9. Ended	10. State whether serving honorably. State if Selected Reserve of the Ready Reserve. If separated, state whether under honorable conditions. If other than honorable, give full details. Always complete Item 11.
	Reserve	N. Guard			

11. Statement Regarding Alienage. *(Complete this item in ALL cases.)*

☐ Record shows this person **was not** discharged on account of alienage.

☐ Record shows this person **was** discharged on account of alienage. Details: _____

12. Remarks. Use for continuation of any of the above items. You should also show in the space below any **derogatory information** in your records relating to the person's character, loyalty to the United States, disciplinary actions, convictions or other matters touching on his or her fitness for citizenship.

Complete this block if subject is a "Lodge Act enlistee"-64 Stat. 316 (Army). Subsequent to enlistment under the Lodge Act on _____ ,

subject entered _____ at the port of _____
(the United States, American Samoa, Swains Island or the Canal Zone)

pursuant to Military orders on _____ via _____

I CERTIFY that the information here given concerning the service of the person named on the face of this form is correct according to the records

of the _____
(Name of department or organization)

[SEAL]

(Official Signature) _____

Date _____ , _____   By _____

U.S. Department of Homeland Security
Bureau of Citizenship and Immigration Services

N-426, Request for Certification
of Military or Naval Service

Alien Registration Number	Date of Request

For use in connection with my application for naturalization, please complete the certification of military service on **Page 2** of this form and furnish it to the office of the Bureau of Citizenship and Immigration Services (CIS) shown in the address block below. The information shown below is furnished to help locate and identify my military records. **APPLICANT: Furnish as much information as possible. If you were issued a Report of Separation, DD Form 214, attach a copy. Fill in the blanks on this page only. Please type or print clearly in black ink. Press firmly -- all copies must be legible. Do not use pencil. (Submit in Triplicate.)**

Name Used During Active Service *(Last, first, middle)*	Social Security Number	Date of Birth	Place of Birth

For an effective records search, it is important that ALL periods of service be shown below. (Use blank sheet(s) if more space is needed.)

Active Service:

Branch of Service *(Show also last organization, if known.)*	Date Entered on Active Duty	Date Released From Active Duty	Check Which — Officer	Check Which — Enlisted	Service Number During This Period

Reserve or National Guard Service: ➡ If none, check ☐ None

Branch of Service	Check Which — Reserve	Check Which — N. Guard	Date Membership Began	Date Membership Ended	Check Which — Officer	Check Which — Enlisted	Service Number During This Period

Are You a Military Retiree or Fleet Reservist? ☐ No ☐ Yes

Signature *(Present Name)*	Present Address *(Number, Street, City, State and ZIP Code)*

Instructions to Certifying Officer

Persons who are serving or have served honorably under specified conditions in the armed forces of the United States, inclusive of the reserve components of the armed forces of the United States, are granted certain exemptions from the general requirements for naturalization. The law requires such service to be established by a duly authenticated copy of the records of the executive department having custody of the record of service, showing whether the service man or woman served honorably in an active-duty status, reserve-duty status, or both, and whether each separation from the service was under honorable conditions. For that purpose, the certified statement on Page 2 of this form, executed under the seal of your department, is required and should cover not only the period(s) of service shown above, but any other periods of service (active, reserve or both) rendered by the service man or woman.

Page 2 of this form should be completed, or the information called for furnished by separate letter, and the form and letter returned to the office of the Bureau of Citizenship and Immigration Services at the address in the box immediately below.

Bureau of Citizenship and Immigration Services

 Return To

**Please type
or print
complete
return
address.
Include ZIP
code.**

Certification of Military or Naval Service

☐ Name correctly shown on front of form.

☐ Name as shown in records: _____

Active Service

1. Entered Service at	2. On	3. Served To	4. Branch of Service	5. State whether serving honorably. If separated, state whether under honorable conditions. If other than honorable, give full details. Always complete Item 11.

Reserve or National Guard Service

6. Branch of Service	7. Check Which		8. Began	9. Ended	10. State whether serving honorably. State if Selected Reserve of the Ready Reserve. If separated, state whether under honorable conditions. If other than honorable, give full details. Always complete Item 11.
	Reserve	N. Guard			

11. **Statement Regarding Alienage.** *(Complete this item in ALL cases.)*

☐ Record shows this person **was not** discharged on account of alienage.

☐ Record shows this person **was** discharged on account of alienage. Details: _____

12. **Remarks.** Use for continuation of any of the above items. You should also show in the space below any **derogatory information** in your records relating to the person's character, loyalty to the United States, disciplinary actions, convictions or other matters touching on his or her fitness for citizenship.

Complete this block if subject is a "Lodge Act enlistee"-64 Stat. 316 (Army). Subsequent to enlistment under the Lodge Act on _____ ,

subject entered _____ at the port of _____
(the United States, American Samoa, Swains Island or the Canal Zone)

pursuant to Military orders on _____ via _____

I CERTIFY that the information here given concerning the service of the person named on the face of this form is correct according to the records

of the _____
(Name of department or organization)

[SEAL]   **(Official Signature)** _____

Date _____ , _____   By _____

INSTRUCTIONS FOR FORM N-648 MEDICAL CERTIFICATION FOR DISABILITY EXCEPTIONS

What is the purpose of this form?

The laws governing naturalization of immigrants require that applicants for naturalization demonstrate:

- knowledge of the English language (including an ability to read, write and speak words in ordinary usage in the English language); and

- knowledge and understanding of the fundamentals of the history, and of the principles and form of government, of the United States.

To implement this law, INS requires applicants to demonstrate an ability to read, write and speak basic English and to answer basic questions about the history and government of the United States (civics).

The individual asking you to complete this form is seeking a waiver of the English and/or civics requirements based on a physical or developmental disability or mental impairment. The applicant will submit this certification form to INS, which will then determine if the applicant is eligible for a waiver.

Who is authorized to complete this form?

The applicant, or applicant's authorized representative, must complete and sign Part I of the form.

A licensed medical doctor, doctor of osteopathy, or licensed clinical psychologist (hereinafter "medical professional") must complete Part II of the the form. An employee under the direct supervision of a medical professional may fill in the form based on information directly provided by the treating medical professional. However, the medical professional must sign the form.

What information is required for an applicant to be eligible for a waiver?

The medical professional completing this form must provide an accurate assessment of the applicant's impairment(s) so that the INS can determine whether to grant the waiver. The medical professional must provide:

- a clinical diagnosis and description of the applicant's impairment(s) and any applicable DSM-IV codes for each mental impairment (Part II. 2);
- an explanation of the connection between the impairment(s) and the applicant's inability to learn and/or demonstrate knowledge of English and/or civics (Part II. 3); and
- a professional certified opinion whether the applicant is unable to learn and/or demonstrate knowledge of English and/or civics (Part II. 4 and 5).

If the medical professional does not provide all the required information, INS cannot grant the waiver unless the applicant submits a revised or second form with the appropriate information.

What experience must a medical professional completing the form have?

The INS requires that the medical professional completing the form have general experience in the area of the applicant's disability, and be qualified to diagnose the applicant's disability and/or impairments.

A doctor who is a general practitioner and not a specialist may complete the form if his/her experience or other qualifications permit him/her to make a disability assessment.

What if the medical professional needs additional space to furnish the required information?

The medical professional must use the available space on the form to type or print the required information clearly in black ink. If extra space is needed to answer any item, the medical professional may attach additional sheet(s) of paper. On each additional sheet include the name and alien registration number (A#) of the applicant, the Part II item number to which the attachment refers, and the complete name of the medical professional.

The medical professional may also submit additional medical reports. On each such report include the name and alien registration number (A#) of the applicant and the complete name of the medical professional. However, a supplemental report is not acceptable as a substitute for any of the responses required in Part II of the form.

What are acceptable responses to Part II. 2(a) and 3?

Part II. 2(a) requires the medical professional to provide a clinical diagnosis and description of the applicant's impairment(s). Part II. 3 requires the medical professional to provide *detailed* information on the connection between the impairment(s) and the applicant's inability to learn and/or demonstrate knowledge of English and/or U.S. history and civics. Examples of insufficient and sufficient responses include:

Example 1:

> *Insufficient Response:*
> Part II. 2(a)- The patient is a 75-year-old female who has hypertension and heart disease. She has suffered at least 2 heart attacks, one in 1996, and in 1997. Last year, she had a cerebral vascular accident (i.e. stroke) with paralysis on the left side.
> Part II. 3- She is unable to learn English and basic U.S. history and civics. (*Note: The medical practioner failed to articulate how any of the conditions listed affect, for example, the patient's memory, ability to learn new tasks, ability to concentrate, or ability to perform basic mental activities. The medical practioner therefore failed to show that the applicant's condition has so impaired her functioning that she is unable to learn or demonstrate knowledge of English and/or U.S. history or civics.*)

Sufficient Response:
Part II. 2(a)- The patient is a 75-year-old female who has hypertension and heart disease. She has suffered at least 2 heart attacks, one in 1996 and another in 1997. Last year, she had a cerebral vascular accident (i.e., stroke) with paralysis on the left side. The patient's stroke has left her with severe and irreversible neurological damage.
Part II. 3- Because of the widespread damage to the brain tissue, the patient has suffered markedly decreased cerebral function and is incapable of remembering, articulating, or learning. (*Note: The medical professional identified the diagnosis and explained the effect the condition has on the applicant's ability to learn.*)

Example 2:

Insufficient Response:
Part II. 2(a)- The patient suffers from Down's Syndrome.
Part II. 3- He should be exempted from the English language and U.S. civics requirements. (*Note: The certifying medical professional failed to explain how the condition affects the applicant's ability to learn, and to give an ultimate opinion on whether the condition diagnosed prevents the applicant from learning or demonstrating knowledge of English and/or civics.*)

Sufficient Response:
Part II. 2(a)- The patient suffers from Down's Syndrome, which is a global impairment that affects the patient's cognition, language and motor skills.
Part II. 3- Because of the patient's global impairment, he cannot learn new skills and is not capable of reasoning. His memory is deficient, and he is only capable of performing simple daily activities. (*Note: The medical professional described the mental impairment and explained how the condition affects the applicant's ability to learn.*)

What if the applicant needs assistance in taking the English or Civics test?

In accordance with the Rehabilitation Act of 1973, the INS makes reasonable modifications and/or accommodations to allow individuals with disabilities to participate in the English and civics testing required for naturalization. Reasonable modifications and/or accommodations may include but are not limited to: sign language interpreters, extended time for testing or off-site testing.

If reasonable modifications and/or accommodations will enable an applicant to demonstrate knowledge of basic English and civics, he or she is not eligible for a waiver or those requirements, and this medical certification form should not be submitted. (An applicant who needs a reasonable accommodation to take the tests should contact his/her local INS District Office in advance of the scheduled interview.)

What are the penalties for making false statements on the form?

Both the applicant and medical professional are required to complete and sign the form under penalty of perjury. The applicant and the medical professional must declare all statements contained in response to questions on this form to be true and correct.

Title 18, United States Code, Section 1546, provides in pertinent part:

Whoever knowingly makes under oath, or as permitted under penalty of perjury under Section 1746 of Title 28, United States Code, knowingly subscribes as true, any false statement with respect to a material fact in any application, affidavit, or other document required by the immigration laws or regulations prescribed thereunder, or knowingly presents any such applicant, affidavit, or other document containing any such false statement - shall be fined in accordance with this title or imprisoned not more than ten years or both.

If either the applicant or the medical professional includes in this form any material information that the party knows to be false, the applicant and/or medical professional may be liable for criminal prosecution under the laws of the United States.

The knowing placement of false information on the application may subject the applicant and/or medical professional to criminal penalties under Title 18 of the United States Code and to civil penalties under Section 274C of the Immigration and Nationality Act, 8 U.S.C. 1324c.

Privacy Act Notice

Authority for the collection of the information requested on this form is contained in 8 U.S.C. 1182(a)(15), 1183A, 1184(a), and 1258. INS will use the information principally to support an individual's application for naturalization. Submission of the information is voluntary. However, failure to provide the necessary information may result in the denial of a request for a waiver of the English language and U.S. history and civics requirement in the applicant's naturalization application. INS may also, as a matter of routine use, disclose the information contained on this form to other federal, state, local and foreign law enforcement and regulatory agencies.

Reporting Burden

An agency may not conduct or sponsor an information collection and a person is not required to respond to a collection of information unless it displays a currently valid OMB control number. We try to create forms and instructions that are accurate and easily understood, and that impose the least possible burden on you to provide us with information. Often this is difficult because some immigration laws are very complex. Accordingly, the reporting burden for this collection of information is computed as follows: 1) learning about the form, 30 minutes; 2) completing the form, 60 minutes; and 3) assembling and filing the application, 30 minutes, and an estimated average of 120 minutes per response.

If you have any comments regarding the accuracy of this estimate, or suggestions for making this form simpler, you can write to the Immigration and Naturalization Service, HQPDI, 425 1 Street, N.W., Room 4034, Washington, DC 20536, OMB No. 1115-0071. **DO NOT MAIL YOUR COMPLETED APPLICATION TO THIS ADDRESS.**

Medical Certification for Disability Exceptions

Part I. THIS SECTION TO BE COMPLETED BY APPLICANT (please print or type information)

Last Name	First Name	Middle Name	Alien Number

Address		Social Security Number

City	State	ZIP Code

Telephone Number	Date of Birth	Gender

I, _____ , authorize _____
      (Applicant's Name)   *(Licensed medical doctor, doctor of osteopathy, or clinical psychologist)*

to release all relevant physical and mental health information related to my medical status to the INS for the purpose of applying for an exception from the English language and U.S. civics testing requirements for naturalization. I certify under penalty of perjury, pursuant to Title 28 U.S.C. Section 1746, that the information on the form and any evidence submitted with it are all true and correct. I am aware that the knowing placement of false information on the Form N-648 and related documents may also subject me to civil penalties under 8 U.S.C. 1324c.

Signature _____ **Date** _____

Part II. THIS SECTION TO BE COMPLETED BY A LICENSED MEDICAL DOCTOR, DOCTOR OF OSTEOPATHY, OR LICENSED CLINICAL PSYCHOLOGIST (see Instructions)

Purpose of this Form: The individual named above is applying to become a United States citizen. Applicants for naturalization are required to learn and/or demonstrate knowledge of the English language, including an ability to read, write, and speak words in ordinary usage in the English language, as well as knowledge and understanding of the fundamentals of the history, and of the principles and form of government of the United States. Individuals who are unable, because of a disability, to learn and/or demostrate this required knowledge may apply for a waiver. The purpose of this form is to help determine whether your patient is eligible for this waiver.

Definition of Disability: An individual is eligible for this waiver if he or she is ***unable*** to learn and/or demonstrate knowledge of English and/or U.S. history and civics because of a physical or mental impairment (or combination of impairments). These impairments must result from anatomical, physiological, or psychological abnormalities, which can be shown by medically acceptable clinical and laboratory diagnostic techniques. The impairment(s) must result in functioning so impaired as to render an individual ***unable*** to demonstrate the ***required*** knowledge.

NOTE: This ***definition of disability*** is ***different*** from the definition used by the Social Security Administration, Department of Veterans Affairs, or worker's compensation programs. If your responses do not address the applicant's disability for the purposes of naturalization, we will require the applicant to submit a revised or second form with the appropriate information.

*Provide **all** of the following required information, using common terminology that a person without medical training can understand, with no abbreviations. Type or print clearly. Illegible and incomplete forms will be returned. If you need additional space to provide your answers, attach additional pages.*

NATURE AND DURATION OF IMPAIRMENT(S)

1.   (a) Based on your examination of the applicant, the applicant's symptoms, previous medical records, clinical findings, or tests, does the applicant have any impairment(s) that affect his or her ability to learn and/or demonstrate knowledge?

    ☐ Yes   ☐ No   **Note:** If *you answer "No", applicant is ineligible for a waiver; please continue with Part II. 6.*

  (b) Has the applicant's impairment(s) lasted or do you expect it to last 12 months or longer?

    ☐ Yes   ☐ No   **Note:** If *you answer "No", applicant is ineligible for a waiver; please continue with Part II. 6.*

  (c) Is the applicant's impairment(s) the direct effect of the illegal use of drugs?

    ☐ Yes   ☐ No   **Note:** If *you answer "Yes", applicant is ineligible for a waiver; please continue with Part II. 6.*

DIAGNOSIS OF IMPAIRMENT(S)

2. (a) Provide your clinical diagnosis of the applicant's impairment(s) *and* describe the impairment(s) in terms a person without medical training can understand *(see Instructions for examples)*.

   (b) Provide the relevant DSM-IV code(s) for each mental impairment that you described above. If a DSM-IV code does not exist, write "N/A."

CONNECTION BETWEEN IMPAIRMENT(S) AND INABILITY TO LEARN/DEMONSTRATE KNOWLEDGE

The law requires that applicants for citizenship demonstrate (1) an understanding of the English language, including the *ability* to read, and speak simple words and phrases in ordinary usage; and (2) a knowledge and understanding of the fundamentals of U.S. history and civics. An applicant's *difficulty* in fulfiling the requirements is not sufficient to support a waiver. In addition, *illiteracy* in the applicant's native language is *not* sufficient, by itself, to support a finding of inability to learn and/or demonstrate knowledge.

3. Based on your examination of the applicant, provide *detailed* information on the connection between the impairment(s) and the applicant's inability to learn and/or demonstrate knowledge of English and/or U.S. history and civics *(see Instructions for examples)*.

   Note: *This description should address the severity of the effects of the impairment(s) including the specific limitations that affect the applicant's ability to learn and/or demonstrate knowledge.*

Applicant Name	Alien Registration Number
	A-

4. <u>English Requirement</u>

   (a) In your professional opinion, has the impairment(s) described above affected the applicant's functioning to such a degree that he or she **is unable** to learn and/or demonstrate an ability to speak, read, or write English?

   ☐ Yes ☐ No

   (b) If **Yes**, which of the following is the applicant unable to learn and/or demonstrate? *(Check all that apply)*

   ☐ Speaking ☐ Reading ☐ Writing

5. <u>U.S. History and Civics Requirement</u>

   In your professional opinion, has the impairment(s) described above affected the applicant's functioning to such a degree that he or she is **unable** to learn and/or demonstrate knowledge of U.S. history and civics, even in a language the applicant understands?

   ☐ Yes ☐ No

BACKGROUND INFORMATION

6. Date of your most recent examination of the applicant (mm/dd/yyyy), _____

7. Is this your first examination of the individual?

   ☐ Yes   If *Yes*, from whom does the applicant usually receive medical care (i.e., name of doctor/clinic; if the applicant does not have an ongoing source of medical care, please write"N/A")

   _____

   _____

   ☐ No   If *No*, for how long and for what conditions have you been treating the applicant? (If the conditions are the same as in Part II. 2, specify the length of time and write "Conditions -- Same as Part II. 2")

   _____

   _____

8. What is the nature of your medical practice? (e.g., family/general practice, internal medicine, psychiatry, cardiology)

   _____

Signature _____ Date _____

Type or print the following information:

Last Name	First Name	Middle Name
Business Address	City, State, ZIP Code	Telephone
License Number		Licensing State

Index

■

Little publishers have big ears.
We really listen to you.

Take 2 Minutes & Give Us Your 2 cents

Your comments make a big difference in the development and revision of Nolo books and software. Please take a few minutes and register your Nolo product—and your comments—with us. Not only will your input make a difference, you'll receive special offers available only to registered owners of Nolo products on our newest books and software. Register now by:

PHONE
1-800-728-3555

FAX
1-800-645-0895

EMAIL
cs@nolo.com

or **MAIL** us
this registration card

fold here

NOLO Registration Card

NAME _____ DATE _____

ADDRESS _____

_____

CITY _____ STATE _____ ZIP _____

PHONE _____ E-MAIL _____

WHERE DID YOU HEAR ABOUT THIS PRODUCT? _____

WHERE DID YOU PURCHASE THIS PRODUCT? _____

DID YOU CONSULT A LAWYER? (PLEASE CIRCLE ONE)   YES   NO   NOT APPLICABLE

DID YOU FIND THIS BOOK HELPFUL?   (VERY)   5   4   3   2   1   (NOT AT ALL)

COMMENTS _____

_____

_____

WAS IT EASY TO USE?   (VERY EASY)   5   4   3   2   1   (VERY DIFFICULT)

We occasionally make our mailing list available to carefully selected companies whose products may be of interest to you.

❑ If you do not wish to receive mailings from these companies, please check this box.

❑ You can quote me in future Nolo promotional materials.
Daytime phone number _____.

USCIT 2.0

"Nolo helps lay people perform legal tasks without the aid—or fees—of lawyers."

—USA TODAY

Nolo books are ..."written in plain language, free of legal mumbo jumbo, and spiced with witty personal observations."

—ASSOCIATED PRESS

"...Nolo publications...guide people simply through the how, when, where and why of law."

—WASHINGTON POST

"Increasingly, people who are not lawyers are performing tasks usually regarded as legal work... And consumers, using books like Nolo's, do routine legal work themselves."

—NEW YORK TIMES

"...All of [Nolo's] books are easy-to-understand, are updated regularly, provide pull-out forms...and are often quite moving in their sense of compassion for the struggles of the lay reader."

—SAN FRANCISCO CHRONICLE

fold here

Place
stamp here

Nolo
950 Parker Street
Berkeley, CA 94710-9867

Attn: USCIT 2.0